A HAPPY TYPE OF
SADNESS

A HAPPY TYPE OF
SADNESS

A JOURNEY THROUGH

IRISH
COUNTRY
MUSIC

KEVIN MARTIN

MERCIER PRESS
IRISH PUBLISHER - IRISH STORY

MERCIER PRESS

Cork

www.mercierpress.ie

© Kevin Martin, 2018

ISBN: 978 1 78117 582 8

10 9 8 7 6 5 4 3 2 1

A CIP record for this title is available from the British Library

Printed and bound in the EU.

For the great Gaels of Ireland
Are the men that God made mad,
For all their wars are merry,
And all their songs are sad.

From *The Ballad of the White Horse* by G. K. Chesterton

For Caitlin and Joey

CONTENTS

ACKNOWLEDGEMENTS

I wish to thank the following people for taking the time to speak and correspond with me: Keelan Arbuckle, Charlie Arkins, Steve Bloor, Johnny Brady, Denise Browne, Sarah Burke, Gerard Butler, Maria Carroll, Willie Carty, Paul Claffey, Michael Commins, Kathy Crinnion, dancers at the McWilliam Park Hotel, dancers at social-dancing classes in the Westport Woods, Roly Daniels, John Farry, Mick Flavin, Denise Fogarty, Rita Gill, Tom Gilmore, Gerry Glennon, Brendan Grace, Cliona Hagan, Dennis Heaney, John Hogan, John Marion Hutchinson, Sean Joyce, George Kaye, Dympna Kelly, Michael Kelly, Sandy Kelly, Sharon Kelly, Tom Kelly, William Kelly, James Kilbane, Uri Kohen, Niamh Lynn, Mary from Mullingar, Jim Martin, Lee Matthews, Frank McCaffrey, Susan McCann, Hubie McEvilly, Sarah McEvilly, Charlie McGettigan, Willie McHugh, Philip McLaughlin, Fiona McMahon, Henry McMahon, Karen McMahon, Shauna McStravock, Robert Mizzell, Eunice Moran, John Morrison, Louise Morrissey, Howard Myers, Tom Nallen, Máire Ní Chonláin, Hugh O'Brien, Carmel O'Donoghue, Gerald O'Donoghue, Robert Padden, Aidan Quinn, Declan Quinn, James Reddiough, Marc Roberts, Tim Rogers, Kay Ryan, Roger Ryan, Lisa Stanley, Colin Stewart, Niall Toner and Emmet Wynne. Apologies to anyone I forgot to mention; you know who you are.

Writing a book of this nature is challenging and time-consuming; it is easy to run down blind alleys and lose focus, finding it difficult to see the wood from the trees. In this regard I would particularly like to thank Wendy Logue, my editor at Mercier Press, from whom I have learned so much during the process of bringing this book to fruition. Her attention to detail and professionalism were remarkable and the finished product has benefited enormously from her commitment to the project. Thanks Wendy.

I would also like to thank Patrick O'Donoghue, commissioning editor at Mercier, for his unceasing encouragement, diplomacy skills and good cheer. The lines of communication were always open through Patrick, which is a critical factor in the completion of a project of this nature.

PREFACE

'BIG TOM' WAS THE KING

The ballrooms in this country are living proof today,
Of a man who is now a legend from Wicklow to Galway.
We love our country music, to us it's everything,
It don't matter what they tell you, Big Tom is still the King.

From 'Big Tom Is Still The King'[1]

On Friday 23 October 2015 *The Late Late Show*, Ireland's most popular television chat show, dedicated the entire night to a celebration of Irish country music for the first time. It attracted an astonishing fifty-two per cent of the national audience.[2] An average of 740,000 people tuned in for the show, while the total viewership over the course of the programme reached 1.3 million. Programme host Ryan Tubridy – a country music fan – was not surprised at the viewing figures when he discussed them on his radio show on RTÉ Radio 1 the following Monday: 'We knew that country is huge when we decided to have this special so it's no surprise to us that so many people tuned in on Friday night. It was truly one of the most enjoyable *Late Late Show*s I've ever presented.'[3] He was particularly moved by his interview with singer 'Big Tom' McBride, as were many of the viewing public. McBride looked a little frail and his voice sounded a little faded and shaky as he sang his most famous country song, 'Four Country Roads', but the audience were entranced. They could not dance because they were confined to their seats, but as the camera panned through the crowd the entire mass of people swayed and sang along together. It could have been a cult worshipping an all-powerful leader, such was the devotion on their faces. Here was an old but still physically imposing man, singing about a small village in County Galway, surrounded by a large group of worshippers gazing at him as if he was revealing the secret to everlasting existence. Faces shone and eyes glistened as the big man sang about the four country byways to his heart. There was nothing less than love in the eyes of the audience. Nothing else mattered; this was the man. They had come to worship at the feet of their king.

DJ and highly regarded country music historian and journalist Michael Commins wrote about the show in his column in the *Irish Farmers Journal*:

The Late Late Show country music special last October cemented Tom's special place as the iconic star of the country scene in Ireland. It was as if the entire show was building up to that magic moment when Tom came into the room. The standing ovations and crescendo of emotions that spread out from the RTÉ studio in Dublin was a massive endorsement of the place this man from Monaghan commands in the hearts of so many Irish people.[4]

In the world of Irish country music 'Big Tom' was the king.

INTRODUCTION

When I was a teenager my house had many American country records that my mother had brought home from visits to her sister in the United States, and I would often play Tammy Wynette, Hank Williams, Patsy Cline, Don Williams and Freddy Fender on the record player. What always amazed me about these songs was how great they were at telling a story in a few short verses. This was often a sharp counterpoint to the lyrics of much of the contemporary pop and rock music at the time, where the narrative was frequently lost in a smokescreen of sound effects and synthesizers. The foregrounding of the voice and the elemental nature of the lyrics in country songs had an appeal that a lot of contemporary fare did not have. Although I had no musical ability myself – I had to carry the flag in the school band – even I could see that in country music there was no hiding place for the singer. To get the message across you had to be able not only to sing, but also to emote.

Since then I have listened to all types of American country music and know the subject well. But while I had a wide knowledge and love of American country music, when I noticed the proliferation of home-grown country music programmes on Irish television, particularly on TG4, over the last number of years, I realised I did not know nearly as much about how country music had developed in Ireland. I decided it was time I learned more, and that interest culminated in what you are now reading.

This book is not intended to be a complete guide to Irish country music. It is a mixture of research, interviews and attendance at all sorts of happenings and events, which allowed me to take a journey through the world of Irish country music and along the way to meet and talk to some of the hard-working and talented people who have chosen to make their mark in that world. This is their story. I want to thank all the people who took the time to help me, talk to me on the phone or at various venues and guide me in the right direction when I was researching the book. To all of them, and to all the fans out there who support them, I say, 'Keep it country.'

1

JIM REEVES HAD TO GO BUT LARRY CUNNINGHAM SAVED THE NIGHT

Adios amigo. Adios my friend,
The road we have travelled has come to an end.
I ride to The Rio where my life I must spend,
Adios Amigo. Adios my friend.

From 'Adios Amigo' sung by Jim Reeves[1]

On Friday 7 June 1963 the internationally acclaimed American country music star 'Gentleman' Jim Reeves placed a white towel over his right shoulder and walked unhappily from the stage of the Orchid Ballroom in Lifford, County Donegal, shortly after he had commenced the third song of his set. The towel was a prearranged signal to his band and entourage. Reeves had had enough. He was not going to have his talents compromised by poor standards and, if his Irish fans were going to hear him, the conditions would have to be as he had requested. The American star was not going to stand there and listen to people booing him. Jim Reeves left the hall, got onto his tour bus, put his head down and told the driver to go to Derry city.

Reeves' smooth baritone voice and crooning style was distinctive in the world of country music in the 1960s. It had none of the nasal twang – the 'hillbilly' sound – which had dominated country music for so long. He simply stood close to the microphone, played his guitar and sang his melodic ballads. His was the original velvet voice of country music, closer in sound to middle-of-the-road crooners like Bing Crosby than to classic hillbilly singers like Hank Williams or Jimmie Rodgers. When he was inducted into the Country Music Hall of Fame in 1967, a bronze plaque put it simply: 'The velvet voice of Gentleman Jim Reeves was an international influence. His rich voice brought millions of new fans to country music from every corner of the world.'

In the late 1950s country music in the United States – still called hillbilly by some – had been badly shaken by the arrival of rockabilly and of rock and roll. In the minds of some industry insiders it would need to adapt if it was to keep a foothold in the commercial market. Bill Haley, Chuck Berry, Elvis Presley and their new rockabilly sounds had changed the playing field forever. Music executives worried that if country music did not change, it would be perceived as backwards and old-fashioned, with its moaning steel guitar, yodelling cowboys and country-cousin stage acts. Legendary Nashville music producer Chet Atkins heard Jim Reeves singing and made a plan. He signed the singer to RCA recording company and set about overhauling Reeves' voice and image. Reeves' earliest material had been sung with a high-pitched, nasal twang in classic hillbilly style; Atkins got him to lower his voice, added a vibraphone and bass to the music mix, and included a female choir to heighten the pop sound. It was country music with the rough edges rounded off and polished smooth – a style which became known as the 'Nashville Sound' and was to change American country music forever.

Urban music lovers warmed to Jim's crooning purr, as did those beyond the borders of the United States. Horn arrangements and full string sections replaced fiddles and steel guitars in more and more elaborate productions as the Nashville Sound developed. Reeves' mellow, romantic, smooth delivery proved a perfect marketing strategy. With the 'twang' of the steel guitar and fiddles removed, the songs appealed to both the country and pop markets. For some it was the death of real country music, but for many in the business it was manna from heaven.

Later in his life, when asked to define the Nashville Sound, Atkins famously put his hand in his pocket and rattled the change. By the time of his death in 1968 Atkins was referred to as 'The King of Music Row' and was worth a fortune.

Jim Reeves had lived an interesting life before he got to Ireland. Born James Travis Reeves in 1920 in Galloway, Texas, he had a promising career as a baseball player and had won an athletic scholarship to university to study drama, but left after six weeks. He worked in Houston shipyards and played semi-professional baseball for three years until he picked up a career-ending injury to a sciatic nerve. Determined to make his career in broadcasting, Reeves worked for a number of small radio stations in Texas. With his mellow voice and slow, drawled delivery, he proved to be a natural presenter. He had clear diction and a rhythmic style, which – combined with his naturally deep voice – would later help to make him a singing star.

In December 1952 Reeves got a job as an announcer on KWKH radio in Shreveport, Louisiana. Soon he was introducing acts on the station's famous live-music show *Louisiana Hayride*, a programme which had started broadcasting in 1948 and proved a launching pad for many music stars. One was Elvis Presley, who announced himself to the world when he sang 'That's All Right' on the show on 16 October 1954. Occasionally Reeves would sing a song, substituting for absent artists. The listeners liked what they heard and requested more.

In 1953 Jim Reeves signed with Abbott Records and released singles 'Red Eyed and Rowdy' and 'Beatin' on the Ding Dong' – novelty songs at a vast remove from his later work. 'Mexican Joe', also released in 1953, was his first song to get into the American *Billboard* music charts, and lasted twenty-six weeks in the country music top forty, including nine at number one. The song's Joe was a lovable rogue who spent his time and other people's money 'romancin', dancin', always on the go' with the 'lovely *señoritas*' down in Mexico. Despite his wicked ways, he was a popular soul and was welcomed wherever he went with the cry '*viva la* Mexican Joe'. The song was still nothing like the songs of heartache and loss for which Reeves would later become famous; it would eventually be seen as another novelty song in his repertoire – albeit a very popular one.

By the end of 1955, with an RCA recording contract, Reeves had further success with 'Bimbo' and 'Yonder Comes a Sucker'. 'Bimbo', another novelty song, was about a young boy with 'two big bright blue eyes that light up like a star' and a dog on a rope; it sounded almost like a nursery rhyme but proved to be a huge success. 'Yonder Comes a Sucker' dealt with a familiar country music theme – a lover scorned – and achieved moderate success. It was a pointer to the type of song which would soon come to dominate his work.

The song 'Four Walls', which in 1957 remained at number one for eight weeks in the American country music charts, marked a major upturn in the singer's career. Chet Atkins infamously considered it 'a girl's song' and did not rate it as a commercial prospect, but Reeves persisted in recording it. It had the sadness and heartbreak of traditional hard-core country but was delivered in his new, smoother style developed by Atkins – the definition of the Nashville Sound. The singer pines for his lover but is alone with the walls in his house. The song was simple but devastating, establishing a style for his future music and proving to be a crucial stepping stone to his worldwide success.

Jim Reeves became popular in countries where there was little previous tradition of country music; fans in Ireland, Great Britain, Europe, South Africa, Scandinavia, Ceylon (now Sri Lanka) and India all took to his slick sound. When Reeves toured South Africa he was treated like a rock star and needed police protection; such was his popularity there he recorded an album in Afrikaans – *Jy Is My Liefling* (You Are My Darling) – and starred in *Kimberley Jim*, a musical comedy set in the South African gold mines.[2]

By travelling to countries that had no familiarity with his music, Reeves created new markets; he is the still biggest-selling artist of all time in Sri Lanka. The clarity of his diction and his simple lyrics were central to his international success: speakers of English as a second language could understand the story of his songs more readily than they could follow much of the rock and pop music coming from the United States and Great Britain. The stories were straightforward, heart-wrenching and personal – country songs at their best. The worldwide reach of Reeves' music is poignantly evidenced on the many tribute websites dedicated to the American singer. A tribute by 'Leo' from India is indicative of the feelings many of the contributors express:

> I live in India in the city of Madras. Ever since I was seven years old I started listening to the greatest singer who ever lived in this world. His voice is pure as a crystal and soft as velvet. I almost live in him. My day starts with Jim and so do the beautiful starlight nights. I feel so close to him as one of his guitarists was also named Leo. In this modern evil world if there is something that will bring love and peace, it could be only the songs of Jim Reeves. Adios my friends … keep in touch. Leo J. Fernando – Madras, India.[3]

When Reeves announced a short tour of Ireland and Britain in 1963 there was huge excitement. It was cause for national pride – a reflection of an Ireland coming up in the world after the horrors of the emigration-ravaged 1950s. The year 1963 was mixed for Ireland. On the one hand, there were warnings that the country was heading for bankruptcy, and worries were frequently expressed about the future of the Catholic Church as the number of vocations continued to fall. On the other, the United States president, John F. Kennedy, visited the country to a rapturous welcome. However, despite the power brokers in Irish society viewing Kennedy's coming as a new dawn, many Irish homes still did not have running water or electricity.

Reeves and his Blue Boys toured Ireland from 30 May to 19 June, except for a short detour to Britain from 10 to 15 June. Their time in Britain was limited because the British Musicians' Union did not permit them to perform in concert as no reciprocal agreement existed for British bands to travel to the United States. Instead Reeves had a number of engagements with British radio and television stations, and made appearances at American military bases.

The Irish leg of his tour, arranged by Belfast-based promoter Phil Solomon, began well, with a press reception in the Shannon Shamrock Hotel in Limerick on 29 May at which Irish singers Maisie McDaniel and Dermot O'Brien performed. However, as Reeves' journey proceeded, problems began to develop. The now-defunct Irish music magazine *Spotlight* interviewed Reeves halfway through his tour, and his answers to journalist Peter Clarke, published on 6 June 1963, were revealing:

In reply to my first query as to whether he was enjoying his tour he said simply and politely 'Yes'. Too simply and politely, I thought, so I decided to prompt him further and I asked him if there had been any hitches, anything he didn't like about the tour. 'Well,' he said, 'the pianos in many of the ballrooms I've sung in have been in a terrible condition. In some places they had to borrow the instrument from a private house. My act depends on a piano as the Blue Boys are only a quartet, and I cannot put on a really good show without one. The audience here are the best I've ever come across but the pianos are the worst.'[4]

It was not just the pianos that bothered the American and his entourage. The venues were often draughty, breeze-block ballrooms with basic facilities both for the public and backstage, and there were too many engagements for the band's liking. Sometimes Reeves had to play twice a night in different venues separated by poor roads, the condition of which shocked the Americans. The shows were usually timed for 10.30 p.m. and 12.30 a.m., leaving little time to get between venues and consistently impatient audiences.

Having played a show in the Atlantic Ballroom in Tramore, County Waterford, the band had to make a journey to Kiltimagh in County Mayo for the following night's performance – more than 320 kilometres across the Irish midlands, where many of the roads were still little more than potholed lanes. It is unclear exactly what happened on the evening of 6 June 1963, but one thing is certain: Reeves never made it onto the stage of the Diamond Ballroom in Kiltimagh. Leo Diamond junior, son of the owner, later recounted his father's version of events:

> He threw a tantrum when he found out he was down to perform at another show 40 miles away in Sligo. He came in the back door of the hall and didn't stay long. He refused to do the two shows.[5]

Other reports mention the quality of the piano. Whatever the truth, the punters left disappointed. Walt Disney had been to Kiltimagh at the invitation of a local businessman a few years previously, but it is the non-appearance of Reeves on the stage of the local dance hall, rather than the visit of Disney, that has remained in the folk memory of the people.

Having lasted all of six songs in the Majestic Ballroom in Mallow, County Cork, in an earlier show, Reeves addressed the audience:

> My goodness I've been in Ireland for the past week but never have I seen so many faces under one roof. Unfortunately my performance tonight will not be on a par with other performances. You might well ask 'Why?' It's because of the goddamn piano over there. Totally out of tune.[6]

The punters were unimpressed; some booed while a few at the front even threw orange and apple skins. Reeves quickly left the hall and retreated to his waiting bus. Hall owner Jack O'Rourke spoke to Vincent Power about the night Reeves came to town:

> His performance was a disaster. It would have been a wonderful occasion if the guy had just cooperated. I don't want to be ungracious to Jim Reeves, now that the poor man is dead, but he was the most uncooperative performer I've ever met. I think it had something to do with the fact that he was the top artist in the world at the time. He was such a superstar in his own mind that he literally did what he liked. I saw the other side of Gentleman Jim – the nasty side.[7]

The reality is that Reeves *was* a superstar – it was not just a figment of his imagination – and he was used to facilities and arrangements vastly better than those available in Ireland at the time, particularly at home in the United States.

Marie Barnes (now Wynne; she later married Emmet Wynne of the Airchords) was the lead vocalist with The Diamonds showband, who supported Jim Reeves when he played in the Crystal Ballroom in South Anne Street, Dublin, on his Irish tour. In a telephone interview she spoke about the night:

> I remember him walking through the audience with a big black cape with a red collar. He looked a bit like Batman. My impression was that he didn't have much time for people. He seemed very sharp, even with his own band. I didn't think much of the way he spoke to them. He checked the piano and clicked his fingers and that was it. He got on the stage, did his thing and got off again. His show was about an hour or so. He was a wonderful singer, with great emotion in his songs. I do wish I'd had a picture taken with him but I was very young then and we were in awe of him.[8]

The tour was not all negative. Local newspapers of the time contain glowing reviews of shows where Reeves' standards were met. Reeves was ecstatically received in the Mayfair Ballroom in Kilkenny, the Las Vegas Ballroom in Sligo and the Pavesi Ballroom in Donegal town, amongst others. When he sang 'Danny Boy' in recognition of his Irish ancestry, the crowds were thrilled that this American superstar of country music actually knew an Irish song.

Reeves found more appropriate facilities in Northern Ireland, where the economy was more advanced and the political turmoil of subsequent years had not yet impinged on civil life. On 7 and 8 June he performed at St Columb's Hall in Derry city, which was then managed by a young priest called Edward Daly, later to become head of the Catholic Church in Ireland. Daly spoke to Joe Cushnan of the *Belfast Telegraph* about the performances:

> Both nights were sell-outs and Jim was relieved that he was finally playing in a proper theatre with decent dressing rooms. His style of singing suited theatres more than dance halls … Jim played for about an hour each night giving very good, relaxed performances. I have nothing but positive reactions to the Derry leg of his tour and to the man himself.[9]

Albert Reynolds, who later became taoiseach (prime minister) of Ireland, was involved in the music business and had booked Reeves to perform in Mullingar and Portlaoise on 4 June. However, the shows were cancelled as Pope John XXIII died the day before and Catholic Ireland was plunged into compulsory mourning. Reynolds went to see Reeves in his Dublin hotel to tell him he would still be paid, but the singer would not take the money because, he said, while he was not a Catholic, he still respected the pope. Reynolds, used to the murky waters and wheeling-and-dealing of the live-music industry, was surprised but delighted that he would not make a loss for the night.[10]

After his return to the United States, Reeves had intended to record an album of Irish songs but, sadly, fate intervened. A little over a year later he was killed in an aeroplane crash, along with his manager Dean Manuel, when their single-engine plane met a violent thunderstorm over Brentwood, Tennessee, on a flight from Batesville, Arkansas, to Nashville. Reeves had learned to fly only a year earlier and made a crucial error by turning directly into the rainstorm. He was forty years old and his death caused reverberations and mourning around the world.

When Reeves was inducted into the Country Music Hall of Fame the introduction was simple:

> His rich voice brought millions of new fans to country music from every corner of the world. Although the crash of his private airplane in 1964 took his life … posterity will keep his name alive … because they will remember him as one of country music's most important performers.

Jim Reeves' continued popularity after his death was enormous. The British charts contained nine of his songs in the top twenty in the week following the crash. He had left behind over eighty unreleased singles, which were gradually put on the market along with older material – between 1970 and 1984 he continually had a hit in the charts. In the United States thirty-three of Reeves' singles charted after he died, including thirteen top ten and five number one hits. In 1982 technology allowed Reeves and Patsy Cline to reach number five with the duet 'Have You Ever Been Lonely'. Of Reeves' thirty-three hit albums, only three entered the charts during his lifetime. In 2009 a re-released album of his greatest hits reached the top ten in Great Britain.

In 1998 Jim Reeves was inducted into the Texas Country Music Hall of Fame in Carthage. The inscription on the memorial statue erected describes Reeves' musical vision: 'If I, a lowly singer, dry one tear or soothe one humble human heart in pain, then my homely verse to God is dear and not one stanza has been sung in vain.' It was a humble and dignified epitaph for a singer who, in his short life, achieved worldwide popularity.

***

On the night Jim Reeves left the stage of the Orchid Ballroom in Lifford in disgust in 1963, Larry Cunningham and his band the Mighty Avons from Granard, County Longford, were playing support.

Cunningham had taken his band in the direction of country music and was familiar with Reeves' catalogue; some said he was dependent on it. The story goes that, amid the confusion, Larry stepped forward and spent the remainder of the night singing covers of Reeves' songs. The audience were happy – he could hit the deep notes equally as well as Reeves – and his career continued on an upward curve. Cunningham recalled the night for Vincent Power:

> We were privileged to be doing relief for him [Reeves] in Lifford. He only sang a medley of five or six songs but the sound he got, with poor amplification and not the best of acoustics in the hall, was as good as you'd hear on a stereo today. There was uproar after he finished. They'd have burned the place down only we went out and I tore into a few of his songs and settled the crowd. He didn't give them value for money because he didn't stay on long enough. He went on to Donegal town [*sic*] the same night and did a powerful show.[11]

Reeves later claimed that the piano in Lifford had had broken strings, had spiders crawling out from underneath it and was out of tune.

The story circulated in the Irish media suggested that Larry Cunningham averted disaster by playing the music of Jim Reeves after the American left the stage in annoyance, a view later disputed by Larry Jordan, author of *Jim Reeves: His Untold Story*:

I've been getting emails from people in the UK and Ireland alerting me to the fact that a man named Larry Cunningham, an Irish singer, recently passed away. Mr. Cunningham was much admired, and my condolences go out to his family. But I have noticed that in the press coverage of his passing this gentleman is given credit for having supposedly 'rescued the situation by singing a medley' of Jim's hits, after Reeves cut short his performance at the Orchid Ballroom in Lifford, Co. Donegal, in June 1963. This notion has been repeated many times over the years and has taken on the mantle of truth.[12]

The reality, according to Jordan, was different:

Mr. Cunningham warmed up the audience by singing Jim's songs before Reeves himself appeared! When Jim took the stage, and started singing some of his hits, the audience became unruly because they had already heard Cunningham do them. This, combined with an out-of-tune piano, compelled Reeves to cut his show short.[13]

Jordan quoted 'one of the audience members', who said the decision to do a warm-up using Reeves' hits just prior to Reeves' own appearance was 'a gross professional misjudgement' which was bound to upset both audience and artist. In the press coverage that followed the debacle in Lifford, Cunningham was credited as having 'saved the day' after Reeves walked off stage, and the out-of-tune piano had mistakenly gone into popular folklore as the sole reason for his quitting the show, according to Jordan. He wished to set the record straight:

Jim was very much the victim of an unscrupulous promoter, logistical difficulties that were not his fault, the failure by ballroom owners to supply pianos despite their contractual commitments to do so, and some local press coverage that sought to shift the blame to Reeves instead of where it belonged. Whatever Larry Cunningham did to defuse a tense situation after Jim left the stage, it also should be noted that he created a problem for Reeves prior to the star's appearance. The fact that this has been lost through history just shows you that once untruths take root, they grow and flourish. This is one of them.[14]

Cunningham knew the piano was poor before Reeves and his band took to the stage. When the Avons were rehearsing earlier in the day they did not require the piano and when they went to move it the back fell off. Leo Jackson, one of the Blue Boys, mentioned the ill-fated piano to Michael Streissguth, author of *Like a Moth to a Flame: the Jim Reeves Story*: 'Half the keys were missing. The white keys were black because the ivory had gone from them. The strings were broken and wrapped around other strings.'[15] He later discussed the point with Paschal Mooney on RTÉ Radio:

We were a small group with only four pieces. In Jim's contract with the Solomon guy, the promoter, it was agreed that a piano would be there, tuned to A. Jim asked Dean Manuel to check the piano and while Dean could get music out of almost anything he could get nothing out of that piano. It was an old upright piano with the back falling off it.[16]

Larry Cunningham had mixed feelings about the night, as he told Tom Gilmore, author of *Larry Cunningham: A Showband Legend*:

What hurt me more afterwards was that he played for an hour and a half at another venue during the tour. He then stood on the running board of his car for ages afterwards signing autographs for the fans. But in my opinion he did not even recognise us as a support band.[17]

Cunningham claimed he had never thought of making a record up to that point in his career. However, shortly after Jim Reeves died, Eddie

Masterson, a Sligo solicitor, gave the singer a written tribute to the music of Reeves, which he had scribbled on the back of a cigarette pack. Masterson, a colourful character known as 'the showband solicitor', famously lived in a room in Barry's Hotel in Dublin for seventeen years. Cunningham put the words to slow-waltz music and added some of the most famous choruses and melodies from Reeves' songs. His 'Tribute to Jim Reeves' was the first Irish single to break into the British charts, and it brought Cunningham an appearance on the BBC music show *Top of the Pops* in 1964 – its first year on television. It was a remarkably unlikely hit from a very unlikely source, but the song struck a chord with both British and Irish audiences and received extensive radio play; listeners were enthralled by the deep tones in Cunningham's American-accented voice, remarkably similar to that of the great Jim Reeves.

Six years later Cunningham travelled to Nashville to make a tribute album to his idol; it was called *Larry Cunningham Remembers Jim Reeves* and on it the Irish singer had the privilege of working with members of Elvis Presley's backing band. When speaking about his work with the Reeves catalogue, Cunningham pointed out that he did not consider himself a singer of the same calibre as the American: 'There is no night I go on-stage without doing a small tribute featuring some Jim Reeves' songs that he recorded because no one else can ever sing them the way that he did. He was the original and the best.'[18]

In 2006 Cunningham spoke about his appearance on the BBC:

> I wasn't intimidated by *Top of The Pops*, because I didn't know any better. It was all happening so fast. Before *Top of The Pops* meself and the band were only playing in four counties, Longford, Leitrim, Cavan and Monaghan, and we couldn't get a booking outside of them. After *Top of The Pops* we got bookings all over Ireland.[19]

The song 'Tribute to Jim Reeves' cemented Larry Cunningham's place as the first great success of Irish country music; it even had the distinction of being translated into Dutch. Some 40,000 copies of the single were sold in Britain in the first two weeks, and in early 1965 Cunningham was awarded a silver disc for worldwide sales of 250,000 copies. Cunningham's repertoire – a mixture of Jim Reeves covers, traditional country songs and Irish traditional songs – was the musical stew that was to form the template for the rest of his career and the basis of Irish country music.

***

Larry Cunningham, one of seven siblings, had grown up in Cloneen near Granard, on a farm run by his parents, Michael and Julia. Like so many Irish country performers, he was on the stage from a young age and learned many of his tunes by listening to traditional musicians such as Vincent Lowe and Jackie Hearst on Raidió Éireann, the national broadcaster. By the age of twelve he could play the fiddle and tin whistle and was a regular at the local town hall. Cunningham recounted his first introduction to show business to Tom Gilmore. A few months after the local football team won the county Gaelic football championship, Pat Murphy, one of the teachers in Cunningham's Cloneen primary school, wrote a song in the team's honour and Larry was prevailed upon to sing it at a celebration in the town hall. Cunningham remembered the table with the cup on top as being taller than himself.[20]

Before settling down in Ireland, Cunningham worked as a carpenter in Derby in England, where he played the fiddle with a céilí band several nights a week:

We got union wages at that time, which was three pounds ten shillings Sterling per night, three nights a week. That was more than any bank manager was earning per week at home and I was getting it for three nights' work.[21]

Over the years Cunningham had developed an interest in 'cowboy songs', a term once frequently used in Ireland to describe country and western music. He had first encountered the music when he saw McCairtains' Road Show in a local hall and, eager to learn similar songs, wrote to his sister in Australia to see if she could come up with anything. For the price of a half-crown he received an album with 'every Hank in the business on it' – songs by American stars Hank Williams, Hank Locklin and Hank Thompson.[22] Cunningham committed two Hank Locklin songs to memory – 'Geisha Girl' and 'Fraulein' – which were later to feature in his stage repertoire.

Having returned to Ireland, Cunningham played part-time in the Grafton Showband before joining the Mighty Avons in 1961. Peter Smith, one of three brothers in the founding line-up of the Avons, spoke to *The Anglo-Celt* newspaper about the origins of the band:

> We needed a good country singer at the time. We had been doing all sorts of Rock and Roll and Pop. It was going well for us, then Larry joined and he had a great voice and was a great country singer.[23]

Cunningham was the star of the Mighty Avons until his departure in 1969 for 'health and business reasons'.

The highlights of Cunningham's early shows were his renditions of the Reeves catalogue, but as his career advanced he brought more country songs with Irish themes, images and instrumentation into his performances. It was this mixture of the themes and sounds of American country and western music and Irish traditional céilí and ballad music which formed the basis of the unique mixture that became 'country and Irish' music and made Larry Cunningham and his band one of the first big stars of the genre.

In 1965 Cunningham had a huge hit with 'Lovely Leitrim', a song he had learned from his mother and with which he was to become synonymous for the rest of his life, despite his Longford birth. A story goes that Liam

Devally, the presenter of a popular show on RTÉ Radio 1, played 'Lovely Leitrim' – originally the B-side of single 'There's That Smile Again' – for a patient. At that time only singles under two minutes and fifty seconds in length were played; this required Larry to cut out two verses of the song. That one outing of the single generated huge sales, and Cunningham never looked back.

'Lovely Leitrim' is a classic example of a type of song which has remained central to Irish country music: a dream of the singer's native Ireland, a description of the beautiful places there, and a wish to return home because there is nowhere else as desirable. In 'Lovely Leitrim' the narrator travelled to the east and to the west and to islands all over the world, but nothing compared with his native Ireland. It stayed at number one in the Irish charts for four weeks. 'Up to then,' Cunningham famously observed, the crowd would 'throw pennies at you if you were a band playing a ballad. But "Lovely Leitrim" changed all that.'[24]

The song was written by Phil Fitzpatrick from Aughavas, County Leitrim, who later emigrated to the United States, where he became a policeman in New York. He was tragically shot dead in the line of duty in 1947, never getting to hear his own composition sung by the man who made it famous. Cunningham once performed it five times in a row at a concert to a teary-eyed emigrant audience in New York, such was the song's popularity among exiled Irish communities.

The demand for country ballads pronouncing love of home and place was huge, and Cunningham duly obliged: 'Among the Wicklow Hills' (1966) was particularly successful, reaching number two in the Irish charts. The theme was familiar: the story of an emigrant and his tortured connections to his native country. His mother wishes he could come home, and there is also a girl waiting for him. All his mother can do is pray for her son to come back to the hills, find the girl and once again run free. The emigrants who listened to the song could identify. They might wish to return to their home place, but the reality for most was there was nothing to go home to. The state did not have the means to support them, so until things got better they had to stay where they were. Although not everyone wanted to return to Ireland, most emigrants could empathise with Cunningham and his band's songs of loneliness and heartbreak.

Cunningham had further hits with 'I Guess I'm Crazy' (1965), 'Snow-flake' (1966), 'Fool's Paradise' (1967), 'Three Steps to the Phone' (1967) and 'The Old Bog Road' (1973). The last of these was originally a poem by Irish nationalist Teresa Brayton set to music by Madeleine King O'Farrelly from Rochfortbridge, County Westmeath, and once again appealed to the heartstrings of the lonely emigrant. This time the narrator is working in New York but longs to be back in a field of Irish wheat, swinging a scythe. His mother died the previous spring, but he could not get home. In the end he realises that he must live with the grief, it being the 'bitter load' of the emigrant. All he can do is wish his country and the bog road the best.

In March 1968 Cunningham released 'The Emigrant JFK', a tribute to John Fitzgerald Kennedy, the assassinated president of the United States of America. It was a perfect subject for the Irish country music market. Kennedy's ancestors were from Wexford and he was revered by many in Ireland: he was the first Irish Catholic to become leader of the free world and his visit to the land of his forebears had attracted global interest. Such songs about emigration and emigrants were sung from the stages of halls all over Ireland. Although neither the artists nor the audiences were away from home, the simple tales of exile had a deep resonance with a nation long used to mass emigration, and Irish people did not have to be emigrants themselves to relate to these tragic stories. There was always a family member, neighbour, friend or acquaintance who had travelled the lonely road of an unwanted emigration. It had always been a cancer eating Irish society and was a subject guaranteed to evoke an emotional response in the Irish mind. Larry Cunningham was happy to satisfy the market. The stories of the songs sung by Cunningham and his band appealed to the people, but so too did the glamour:

In a drab country, where men wore dark suits and belted-up overcoats, Larry arrived in his Mercedes-Benz, put on his red jacket and offered the promise of connection to a different reality, an exotic world of truck stop diners, jukeboxes and two-lane blacktop, somehow magically transported to the parish halls of Roscommon, Cavan and Westmeath. For an hour or two, there were no creamery cheques to worry about, no disputes with the family about who was getting the farm, and although Larry might be taking Nuala for a ride in his Mercedes after the show, you were taking Bridie home in the Austin A40 … Maybe for that brief moment, you were looking through the windscreen of a '58 Dodge pickup, and it was time to go huntin' coyotes with your gal.[25]

Cunningham went on to perform with American country singers Loretta Lynn, Hank Williams Junior and Johnny Cash; to play at New York's Carnegie Hall (the first Irish person to do so); and to perform for Princess Grace of Monaco, who was of Irish extraction. He holds the record for the largest crowd (over 6,850) at the (now closed) Galtymore Ballroom in Cricklewood, London, on St Patrick's night 1966. In 2008 he spoke to *Irish Times* journalist Ronan McGreevy about his memories of that night:

I remember being above in a small little band room and I looked out the door. As far up Cricklewood Broadway as I could see, there was four in a row for the guts of two miles trying to get in. I looked out and I remember the fear that went through me because I was a builder and not a singer and I was only doing it for a laugh. The bouncers were trying to shove the crowds out of the way to get us on stage. I was brought down with one bouncer in front and another behind as if you were leading a cow to a bull.[26]

In 1969 Cunningham formed the Country Blueboys, and in October 1971 appeared at the highly regarded Country Music Convention Center in Nashville. Pat Campbell of the BBC later contributed sleeve notes to

Cunningham's album *Songs Fresh from Nashville* and wrote of the response the Irish artist got on his appearance there: 'How they acclaimed him, a standing cheering ovation, which gave my Irish heart a lift it hadn't had in years.'[27]

While in Nashville, Cunningham recorded the single 'Good Old Country Music', which gained some radio play in the United States. Larry's manager at the time, Mick Clerkin, spoke to Tom Gilmore about the experience:

> Many radio stations in the US felt that the song had a very good chance of being a hit there for Larry. It was a good up-tempo type of song which got a good response from the listeners there. People would phone in when we were on the various radio programmes and there was a buzz about it. I think that if Larry was in a position to live there it could have worked for him.[28]

The production values were excellent, with backing vocals by members of The Jordanaires, but Larry Cunningham was not interested in moving to the United States:

> I wouldn't leave Ireland at that time for all the tea in China so unfortunately that is as far as success in the US went ... I can't really say that I know well, but I imagine that if I moved out there it could have happened.[29]

Following his marriage to Beatrice Nannery in 1972, Cunningham scaled back his touring but appeared in occasional concerts and made a couple of recordings. He had a top-ten hit in Ireland that year with 'Slaney Valley', another song about the love of an idyllic home place.

In 1974 'Lovely Leitrim' was re-released, but only made it to number nineteen in the charts. In 1975 'My Kathleen' spent fourteen weeks in the Irish charts, reaching number three. In 1976 Cunningham had a hit with Margo when they performed a duet called 'Yes Mr Peters', a song popularised by Loretta Lynn and Conway Twitty in the United States. Larry had his final domestic hits with 'The Story of My Life' and 'Galway and You', both in 1983, and 'Walk on By' in 1984, which, fittingly, was an old Jim Reeves song.

Cunningham appeared at the highly regarded International Festival of Country Music at Wembley on numerous occasions from its inception in 1969, right up to 1988, when he sang a sublime version of the Hoyt Axton song 'Water for My Horses'. Larry's appearances at Wembley were a testament to his tenacity and endurance. On his first appearance, Bob Powell, editor of the influential British magazine *Country Music People*, had not been kind in a review of his performance: 'Larry Cunningham and the seven piece Mighty Avons are one of Ireland's most popular showbands. But in spite of the fact that they feature country songs in their act they are a showband, and seemed out of place at Wembley.'[30] Following Cunningham's performance in 1971, Powell revised his opinion: 'Two years ago, Larry Cunningham impressed me not at all, but this year he was much, much better.'[31]

In later life Cunningham became a town councillor, ran a supermarket and dry cleaner's, and kept up his carpentry skills. Like many of his fellow country music artists, he had an immense pride in his local place and was thrilled to be elected Longford Person of the Year in 2004.

On 28 September 2012 the 'Father of Country and Irish Music' passed away. The RTÉ journalist Derek Davis was asked to speak about Cunningham on a tribute show organised by presenter and performer Frankie Kilbride of Shannonside Northern Sound radio; as a singer himself, Davis was eloquent in his response:

He effectively invented country and Irish ... people overlooked the fact that Larry had a timbre and range in his voice that could be very classy indeed. Larry had a quality in his voice and a breadth of tone that was very

appealing and he could handle it … you see he was associated with that Jim
Reeves baritone and he was very good at it but there was a lovely quality in
it … he could put great tenderness and emotion into it.[32]

Kilbride asked Davis about meeting Cunningham. Davis responded:

Larry was never the type of man to talk down to you … Larry would talk
to any man … he had the gift of not forgetting who his friends were, not
forgetting who his neighbours were … Larry was a decent man … he never
got the big star syndrome.[33]

Davis had a further interesting take on Cunningham's voice: 'It was the
voice of a real man. It wasn't the whining bleat of a pubescent schoolboy
… which has its place in popular music. This was the voice of a real man …
and a real man who could read a crowd.'[34]

Larry Cunningham did much to establish a music with its own unique
themes, rhythms and sound, which would come to establish itself in the
centre of Irish culture. Father Brian D'Arcy, long-time friend of the Irish
show-business community, paid an eloquent tribute to the singer:

Larry was not a celebrity, he was a star and there is a difference. A star is a
real human being who wins respect, a celebrity is a lot less than that. You
will not be forgotten as we will always dance to your music and sing your
songs and tell your stories.[35]

This was in keeping with the 'star comment' Cunningham provided to
Brian Carthy in his book *The A–Z of Country and Irish Stars* in 1991: 'To be
successful you must be yourself, don't pretend to be something you're not.
Respect those who support and believe in what you do. After all it takes
people like them to make people like me.'[36]

2

'THE CIRCLE IS UNBROKEN': A VERY SHORT HISTORY OF AMERICAN COUNTRY MUSIC

Country music long ago ceased to be simply an American cultural expression. It is now a phenomenon with a worldwide appeal.

Bill C. Malone, *Country Music, U.S.A.*[1]

Jim Reeves was one of the early acts who became international ambassadors for what is often seen as the quintessential American music form. Country music started in the United States as a mix of different sounds, genres and influences; it is a complex musical jigsaw to which the Irish added a significant part. To understand Irish country music it is, therefore, important first to understand the beginnings of American country music.

Deceased singer and country music historian George Hamilton IV – widely known as the 'International Ambassador of Country Music' for his contribution to the globalisation of the genre (he was the first country music artist to play in the Soviet Union) – said country music spent its childhood in the British Isles, its youth in the Appalachian Mountains in the United States and its adult years in Nashville, Tennessee. It was during its youth in the Appalachians that the Irish, particularly those from Ulster, would play an important part in the development of this style of music.

In the seventeenth and eighteenth centuries thousands of Ulster Scottish emigrants – often referred to as Scots Irish or Scotch Irish in the United States – made their home in rural America; by 1790 three million called the country home. They were mainly Presbyterian Scots who had previously settled in Ulster as part of Britain's plan for a Protestant plantation in Ireland from the early seventeenth century on. The Ulster Scots, having found poor agricultural returns and discrimination in the north of Ireland, settled largely in the poorer south-eastern areas of the United States, predominantly in Appalachia, the states surrounding and containing the Appalachian Mountains. Here there was nobody to discriminate against them and they could buy their own land at a reasonable price; no longer would they have to pay extortionate rents to condescending landlords.

It was a hard-drinking and hard-living culture, and, among other Appalachian residents, the Ulster Scots acquired a reputation for their hot-tempered and intemperate ways. An old saying suggested the different priorities of the immigrant groups in the Appalachians: on first arriving in the region the English would build a church, the Germans a barn and the Ulster Scots a whiskey still. With them, the Ulster Scots brought their beliefs, values, musical instruments, songs and dances. Over time, British and Irish folk ballads, instrumental dance tunes, blues music of African-Americans from the south, southern religious music and popular American music intermingled to form unique new sounds. This musical stew, variously referred to as 'hillbilly', 'old-time' or 'mountain' music, formed the bedrock of country music. The Ulster Scottish contribution was only one of many influences, but its sounds and themes have trickled down through the years and can still be heard in country music today.

Although the origin of the word 'hillbilly' is disputed, the Ulster Scots have a good claim to it. Protestant folk songs celebrated the victory of

William of Orange over the Catholic forces led by James II in 1690 at the Battle of the Boyne. William was widely referred to as King Billy and continued to be a hero in the culture of the Ulster Scots. Given that these settlers overwhelmingly lived in the hills, the argument that this is the origin of 'hillbilly' sounds strong, although other possibilities have been suggested. In Ulster Scots dialect the word 'billie' has long been used to mean a friend or mate. They also considered themselves 'hill folk'. Taken together – hill dwellers who are friends with each other – this sounds plausible as another potential explanation for the origin of the term. Wherever 'hillbilly' came from, it stuck, although these days it is more often than not used as a derogatory term to suggest backwardness.

The fiddle was arguably the biggest contribution the Ulster Scots made to the music of North America. This portable instrument provided the soundtrack for community and family dancing, and fiddle-playing competitions were popular. As the various influences mixed, the sounds became more varied. Fiddles, guitars, banjos and vocalists formed groups – commonly referred to as string bands – that played music in houses for the entertainment of family and friends. Songs, many of them from the home countries, were adapted and became part of the repertoire. Traditional Irish songs and tunes often evolved into 'hillbilly' songs, with many having English words set to Irish and Scottish fiddle tunes. 'Johnny I Hardly Knew You' became the more upbeat 'When Johnny Comes Marching Home', while 'The Bard of Armagh' (sometimes called 'The Unfortunate Rake') became 'Streets of Laredo'. The melody of 'Spailpin Fanach' (The Rambling Labourer) was reset to form the famous 'The Girl I Left Behind'. (It was also set to the lyrics of the famous Dublin ballad 'Waxie's Dargle'.)

Numerous songs and fiddle tunes played in Appalachia mentioned Ireland in the title or lyrics: 'The Irish Christening', 'Irish Clog', 'The Irish Frolic', 'The Irish Police', 'Irish Washerwoman', 'The Irishman and the Barber', 'Patty on the Turnpike' and 'Molly Put the Kettle On' were all popular fiddle tunes in the middle of the eighteenth century. Even 'Cotton

Eye Joe' – the 'country music anthem of Texas' and soundtrack to line dancing the world over – is likely to have originated from an old Irish traditional reel 'The Mountain Top'.

Early songs were unaccompanied and commonly sung in a high-pitched, nasal voice sometimes referred to as 'womanish'. When this is added to the tendency to tense the throat, the similarities with traditional Scottish and Irish singing are readily apparent. Lyrics were set to simple melodies with basic instrumentation and were often accompanied by a 'drone' sound – a note or chord which sounds continuously throughout most of a song, providing a trance-like accompaniment for the melody; the fiddle, bagpipes and slide guitar are all capable of producing it. Irish music also brought improvisation to the fore. It was a soundtrack to dancing, and the dance came first; if this meant prolonging the tune, the fiddler obliged.

The living standards in Appalachia were poor, and livelihoods were hard-earned from poor land, forestry and, later, open-cast mining for coal. The themes of poverty, sadness, heartbreak and death were frequent in the songs and music, and they accurately reflected the lives lived by the performers. Songs about the history of repression suffered by the Ulster Scots and about efforts to take on the establishment were common. Much of the lyrical content was decidedly downbeat, but it could hardly be otherwise.

The wrath of God, the importance of living a morally upright life and adherence to the words of the Bible were all consistent themes in early country music. Ideas were often set in opposition: hard work and hard drinking, the desire for a stable family set against the quest for freedom from responsibility and the right to roam. A man – invariably it was a man – might leave his job at the end of the day and go happily home to his family and play his fiddle on the porch. Alternatively he might start drinking excessively, get into the inevitable fight and end up with a mean woman. The themes were timeless and primal: birth, death, longing, loss, salvation and joy. They were not abstract; nor were they based on fashionable ideas or images but on sound, heart and spirit. They were real stories for real people.

In many ways the songs were the soap operas of their time – melodrama with 'twang' – but above all else they told stories.

'Barbara Allen', one of the most famous of all Appalachian folk ballads, originated in Scotland and is a poignant example of the heartbreak and loneliness common in the lyrical content of much of the music. It tells of a woman who rejects her lover because he has 'slighted' her and hurt her feelings. The song does not give many details about the background incident, but Barbara's lover dies of a broken heart from her rejection, and it is only after his death that she realises her mistake. This realisation results in her death, also of a broken heart. Their tragic love lives on in the symbolic intertwining of the rose and briar growing from their graves: 'They grew and grew to the steeple top/Till they could grow no higher/And there they twined in a true love's knot/Red rose around green briar.' It is bleak and elemental – an appropriate reflection of the lives of the people.

Songs were direct and often shocking in their raw description of human actions and emotions. In 'The Banks of the Ohio' the narrator invites his beloved to take a walk by the river, where he proposes marriage to her but she refuses. He does not take this kindly:

I plunged a knife into her breast
And told her she was going to rest
She cried, 'Oh Willy, don't murder me
I'm not prepared for eternity.'

I took her by her golden curls
And drug her down to the river side
And there I threw her in to drown
And I watched her as she floated down

And going home 'tween twelve and one
I cried, 'Oh Lord, what have I done?'

I've killed the only girl I love
Because she would not marry me.

The setting for performance in Appalachia was predominantly the home. American country music expert Bill C. Malone describes a typical house-dance in his important book *Country Music, U.S.A.*:

> Once the word was given out that a dance was to be held in some farmer's house, a room or two was stripped of furniture and a fiddler was hired to keep the dancers moving. Often a fiddler worked alone for hours … Most fiddlers had to be content at playing part-time at house parties or community social functions, and a fiddler was generally nothing more than a farmer or a laborer who made music when his neighbors called upon his services.[2]

'Hillbilly' music was not commercially recorded until the 1920s. Recording technology had been around since the late 1800s but was largely used to release classical and jazz music. 'Fiddlin' John Carson, a state fiddling champion and popular radio performer, is frequently credited with the first commercially successful, professionally recorded country tunes. Appropriately, the Georgia native learned to play on a fiddle brought by his grandfather from Ireland. His recording of the famous 'The Little Old Log Cabin in the Lane' and 'The Old Hen Cackled and the Rooster's Going to Crow' by OKeh Recording Company in 1923 began the move to commercialism. Commercial recording allowed 'hillbilly' musicians like Carson to make a living from music for the first time, and gradually more artists emerged from the rural areas of the south-eastern states to make the genre recognisable across the United States. The music was marketed under an array of names, including 'old-time music', 'old, familiar tunes', 'old-fashioned songs from Dixie', 'mountain music' and 'hill-country tunes', but the word 'hillbilly' was not officially used until 1925, when Al Hopkins and the Hillbillies took to the stage.

Some performers sang to their own fiddle accompaniment, others to the banjo or guitar. Stringed instruments were predominant, but close listening to early recordings demonstrates the remarkable variety of accompaniment used. It included kazoos, whistles, French harps, Jew's harps, zithers, organs, pianos, mandolins, autoharps, Hawaiian steel guitars, ukuleles, accordions, tenor guitars, cellos, trumpets and clarinets.

With the invention of the lightweight carbon microphone in 1926, recording facilities could be easily transported. Ralph Peer saw the opportunity to record the music of poor, white southerners – this had not previously been committed to vinyl. Peer hit recording gold – the birth of commercial country music. His 1927 recordings made in Bristol, on the Virginia–Texas border, came to be seen as a foundation stone of country music. Both Jimmie Rodgers, the first superstar of the music, and The Carter Family – 'The First Family of Country Music' – recorded in the same session.

In the same year Carl Sandburg published *The American Songbag*, dedicated, he wrote, to 'those unknown singers – who made songs – out of love, fun, grief – and to those many other singers – who kept those songs as living things of the heart and mind'.[3] He described what he believed lay at the core of the songs: 'there are persons born and reared in this country who culturally have not yet come over from Europe', and goes on to reference the 'medieval European ballads brought to the Appalachian Mountains' as a key source.[4] In the book he includes the words, music and histories of almost 300 songs, as well as copies of old sketches and woodcuts. One section of the book, entitled 'The Ould Sod', contains songs brought over from Ireland, which had remained unchanged by the journey.

James Charles 'Jimmie' Rodgers was famous for his rhythmic yodelling and was variously known as 'The Singing Brakeman', 'The Blue Yodeller' and 'The Father of Country Music'. He was the first to bring the different elements of hillbilly music together, and was both an excellent interpreter of others' songs and a writer of his own. Rodgers, formerly a railroad employee, brought the glamour of the travelling man to the music and, based on the subject matter of his songs, it seemed he had been everywhere and lived a full life. Like his personality, his music suggested a free and open spirit, a willingness to experiment and an ability to accommodate various styles. He was particularly attracted to the western United States and was among the first country artists to wear a cowboy hat. Among Rodgers' best-known numbers are the current standards 'T for Texas', 'In the Jailhouse Now' and 'My Rough and Rowdy Ways'. In 1961 Rodgers became one of the first inductees into the Country Music Hall of Fame, and in 1986 he was inducted into the Rock and Roll Hall of Fame.

The Carter Family – Alvin Pleasant (A.P.) Delaney Carter, his wife, Sara Carter (née Dougherty), and his sister-in-law, Maybelle Addington Carter – were true pioneers in American country music. A.P. collected songs from all over the rural south-west, and the band's music and interpretations of this material had a profound and lasting effect on the genre. Cecil Sharp had made an attempt to collect the songs of the emigrants from the British Isles in his 1917 book *English Folksongs from the Southern Appalachians*, but fruit-tree salesman A.P. roamed more widely and collected more material. The Carters were the first vocal group to become country stars, and their recordings of 'Will the Circle Be Unbroken', 'Keep on the Sunny Side' and 'Wildwood Flower' made them country standards. They were the opposite of Jimmie Rodgers in many respects. Their music frequently emphasised the values of home and stability, laced with images of the fireside, family, religion and the beauty of nature.

The Carter Family's sound was unique. Maybelle played both the lead and rhythm on the guitar, using a much-copied 'brush technique' – the thumb picked the melody on the bass strings, with the fingers providing rhythm by downward stroking of the treble chords. A.P. contributed his sometimes-off-key lead vocals. Sara pitched in with her autoharp and usually led the vocals, sometimes singing solo. Maybelle's daughter June later married Johnny Cash, continuing the country music dynasty. The

Carter Family were duly elected to the Country Music Hall of Fame in 1970, and their haunting sound is still emulated the world over.

The coming of radio to the United States changed things in the world of music forever. Stations began to broadcast live 'barn dances' featuring rural musicians and vocalists. WLS radio station from Chicago was the first to achieve fame with its version of a programme based on country music. Owned by Sears, Roebuck and Company, the 'World's Largest Store' (hence WLS), the *National Barn Dance* programme became hugely popular, and was quickly syndicated to other radio stations across the nation. However, it was an announcer lured away from WLS who started the most influential country music radio programme of all and created the engine which would drive country music to even greater heights. WSM radio, owned by National Life and Accident Insurance – the motto of which was We Shield Millions (hence WSM) – brought George Hay to the station from WLS. His WSM barn dance followed the National Broadcasting Company Network's *Music Appreciation Hour*, a selection of classical music presented by Walter Damrosch. Following a show one night, Damrosch remarked, 'There is no place in the classics for realism.'[5] George Hay had a suitable answer for the learned Dr Damrosch:

Friends, the program which just came to a close was devoted to the classics. Doctor Damrosch told us that there is no place in the classics for realism. However, from here on out for the next three hours, we will present nothing but realism. It will be down to earth for the 'earthy'. For the past hour, we have been listening to music taken largely from Grand Opera. From now on, we will present the 'Grand Ole Opry'.[6]

Country music was for the common man and woman; not for them the sounds of opera and the classics – the music of the cultural elite.

The opening of the programme, first broadcast on 28 November 1925, was not a particularly grand spectacle. Hay simply put old-time mountain fiddler Uncle Jimmy Thompson in front of a microphone and had him play for an hour. The story goes that Thompson was not happy to have to finish after such a short time: 'Shucks, a man doesn't get warmed up in an hour. I just won an eight-day fiddlin' contest down in Texas.'[7] For many years, Hay – who referred to himself as the 'Grand Old Judge' – began the show by blowing on a steamboat whistle and calling loudly, 'Let her go boys.' Fiddlers, singers and clog dancers dominated the early years of the show, but it later expanded to include string-band music and comedy sketches. Hay dictated the content and design of the show, which was broadcast in front of a live audience, and insisted on maintaining a 'down home on the farm' atmosphere, with singers wearing check shirts and overalls, and stage sets including hay bales and wagon wheels.

The *Grand Ole Opry* is now one of the longest-running shows in the history of radio in the United States. It is, according to its publicity, 'The Show that Made Country Music Famous' and holds such significance in Nashville that its name is included on the city and county boundary-line signs on all major roadways. After starting in the radio studio, the *Opry* moved to the Ryman Auditorium – the so-called 'Mother Church of Country Music' – in 1943, before moving to the Grand Ole Opry House in 1974, although it still returns to the Ryman for three months each winter.

The rapid success of country music was astounding; more than 50,000 records were released before the Second World War, although the advent of radio had a negative effect on sales. Early radio shows almost never featured records – many of the early '78'-size discs were stamped with the warning 'not licensed for radio broadcast' – and the vast majority hired string bands to play the music live. Music which had once been confined to rural areas of the southern United States was now heard in big cities and was even played in New York's Carnegie Hall, the centre of high musical culture. Nashville – the main record-producing centre of country music – released half of all American recordings between the two world wars. More than 2,000 radio stations programmed some country music; many played nothing else.

The clothes of the 'wild west' – Stetson hats, rhinestones, cowboy boots and so on – were a later addition to country music and they came from the other type of music that is now an integral part of the country genre – western music.

***

Western music evolved separately from 'hillbilly' but in similar circumstances. They were natural companions – glorifying the open country, the pioneering spirit and the beauty of nature. The image of the cowboy was impossible to resist for many. He was wholesome and unthreatening, a symbol of individuality and freedom – twin foundation stones of American life. The cowboy lived the dream and had a code of honour which commanded respect from all. In reality he was rapidly disappearing, kept alive largely by cinema and stage shows; the era of real-life gunslingers was virtually over by the start of the twentieth century.

Cowboys may have sung to themselves while tending their animals or around the campfire at night, but it would be the early twentieth century before western music became recognised as a distinct type. *Songs of the Cowboys* by Nathan Howard 'Jack' Thorpe and *Cowboy Songs, and Other Frontier Ballads* by John Lomax brought together collections of cowboy songs for the first time. There were some genuine singing cowboys – such as Carl T. Sprague, Harry McClintock and Jules Verne Allen – but Hollywood quickly took over, and manufactured singing cowboys – for example Gene Autry and Roy Rogers – and their movie creations would come to be the image of the musical 'wild west'.

Orvon 'Gene' Autry – born in Tioga, Texas, in 1907 – had no connections with the world of cowboys. However, his appearances in 'horse operas' – a term made popular by silent-era western-film star William S. Hart to describe musical westerns of the 1930s – made him the perfect example of the lean, clean-cut cowboy dressed in western shirt and wing tips. Autry had a singing career before he became a movie cowboy and was best known for his ability to copy the yodelling of Jimmie Rodgers. His first movie, the 1934 film *In Old Santa Fe,* was an immediate hit. Autry did not have the nasal and parched voice one might expect of a cowboy, and – like Jim Reeves after him – he was closer to Bing Crosby in sound than to any traditional hillbilly singer; this vocal style was to become characteristic of westerns. Few of his songs dealt with the many painful realities of cowboy existence; they were instead fantasies in keeping with the fantastic world they represented. Times were desperate in the United States, and westerns and singing cowboys could help people forget the effects of the Depression for a little while.

Autry lived a clean life, further endearing him to the viewing public. He did not drink, smoke or become involved with his female co-stars. He was also a patriot, signing up to fight in the Second World War. But by the time Autry returned from the battlefields, Roy Rogers had become the new star of westerns featuring singing cowboys. When Autry finally decided to hang up his stirrups after the release of *Last of the Pony Riders* in 1953, he had acted in more than ninety films. His success had turned cowboy culture into an industry, and western dress became the uniform of country and western singers the world over. Subsequently he had a successful career in television and business, and died a very wealthy man.

Roy Rogers – born Leonard Franklin Slye in Cincinnati in 1911 – had first played backing to Autry on the song 'Tumbling Tumbleweeds' from the movie of the same name. In 1933 he formed Sons of the Pioneers, and following the release of the movie *Under Western Stars* gained immediate popularity, going on to star in more than eighty movies. Although Rogers was regarded as a better actor than Autry, he did not have as successful a music career outside the movie industry. He did, however, set a country-and-western-music first by signing a deal which allowed him to retain full rights to his name, voice and image. He eventually became a wealthy man from endorsements and merchandising. Like Autry, he made a successful transition to television, and his *Roy Rogers Show* ran for six hugely lucrative years: with the help of his third wife Dale Evans, Trigger the horse and Bullet the wonder dog, Rogers solved the problems of the world while also incorporating religion into his performances. The death of his second wife and one of his children brought spirituality to Rogers' life. Each week he would read out his 'Cowboy Prayer' at the start of his television show for his Roy Rogers Riders Club: 'Dear Lord, when trails are steep and passes high, help me to ride it straight the whole way through.'

Rogers was a happy cowboy who never wanted to finish performing: 'When my time comes just skin me and put me right up there on Trigger as if nothing had ever changed.' In the end he was not preserved, but Trigger was and could be viewed at the Roy Rogers Museum in Victorville, California. Later the museum was moved from Victorville, and following the death of Rogers it was closed – all its displays were sold at auction.

The country-music-singing cowboy was not confined to the American studio and screen. Canadian Hank Snow ('The Yodelling Ranger') and Antipodean Tex Morton ('The Boundary Rider') both sang as they roamed their respective prairies. Morton, who was known as 'The Father of Australian Country Music' – despite being originally from Nelson, New Zealand – also worked in a circus and acted in vaudeville.

Initially, hillbilly and cowboy music were frequently played together on radio stations. Then the cowboy-hat-wearing Jimmie Rodgers brought both together, and 'hillbilly and western' soon became a common term for the music. Ernest Tubb, one of the most influential figures in the development of the Nashville country music industry, wore cowboy hats and boots for his debut on the *Grand Ole Opry*, despite never singing any western music. Bands assumed western names – the great Hank Williams calling his the 'Drifting Cowboys' – and, with the declining popularity of the term 'hillbilly', the music came to be called 'country and western'; over time 'western' was dropped, but the clothes and accessories stayed.

***

Like most other types of music, country has subgenres and, of those, bluegrass is the best known. Its venerable sound owes much to the old-time music of Appalachia as well as to elements of gospel and blues. While the music has deep roots, the term 'bluegrass' only gained currency in the 1940s with the arrival on the scene of Bill Monroe – known as the 'Father of Bluegrass' – and his reinterpretations and additions to long-embedded sounds.

Monroe's band, the Blue Grass Boys, took their name from the colour of *Poa pratensis*, commonly known as Kentucky bluegrass or smooth meadow grass. Monroe based his music on the old-time fiddle bands and singers of the late nineteenth and early twentieth centuries, playing and singing their melodies in a new way. Bluegrass is characterised by the use of unelectrified string instruments – most commonly the fiddle, five-string banjo, acoustic bass, guitar, mandolin, Dobro guitar (also called a resonator guitar) and harmonica. It has no percussion and is often referred to, in the famous words of Monroe, as the 'high lonesome sound'. He further explained his conception of the music:

> It's Scottish bagpipes and old time fiddlin' … It's blues and jazz and it has a high lonesome sound. It's plain music that tells a good story. It's played from my heart to your heart and it will touch you. Bluegrass is music that matters.[8]

Commonly, one or more instruments take a turn playing the melody, with the others providing accompaniment – a structure referred to as breakdowns – characterised by fast tempos and complex chord changes. It was the addition of the Earl Scruggs driving-banjo sound to Monroe's high-lonesome singing voice and chopping mandolin that came to define bluegrass. Scruggs played with Monroe for only two and a half years before leaving with Lester Flatt, but he changed the sound of the band with his five-string banjo technique.

While bluegrass has its adherents, another subgenre, known as honky-tonk music, defines country music for many. The precise origin of the term 'honky-tonk' is disputed, but the type of drinking establishment and music it came to describe is well known in the United States. Nick Tosches found the first reference to such a venue in a newspaper circulated in the east Texas–Louisiana–Oklahoma area. In the 24 February 1894 edition of *The Daily Ardmoreite* published in Ardmore, Texas – a distinctively Irish-sounding name – a report read: 'The honk-a-tonk last night was well attended by ball heads, bachelors and leading citizens.'[9] (Sadly, the article does not explain who the 'ball heads' are!) These often tough venues, which proliferated in the southern and south-western states in the 1940s – particularly in the east Texas oil-boom towns – were a fertile environment for the development of the country genre. In the roughest, the bands performed behind chicken wire for their own protection, and some of the more dubious venues provided prostitutes. 'Honky-tonk' ultimately came to describe hillbilly or country music played with a full rhythm section, with steel guitars and fiddles prominent in the mix. Vocalists tended towards the rough and nasal – in the Hank Williams mode – but later developed a clearer and sharper sound, exemplified by singers like George Jones, widely regarded as one of the greatest-ever country music vocalists. The often rowdy nature of the establishments meant loud amplification was necessary.

The lyrics of honky-tonk country songs focused on the difficulties of the everyday lives of people – lost love, adultery, loneliness, alcoholism and poverty. These were the same concerns as those of the earlier Ulster Scot settlers; as Bill C. Malone noted: 'Protestant culture still gripped the minds of the honky-tonk musicians, colouring the lyrics of even their drinking and cheating songs.'[10]

By the end of the 1940s many mountain dwellers had moved to urban settlements, but, as Malone observed, the subject matter of their music remained the same: 'the problems and changing social status of the ex-rural dweller … family fragility, the insecurities of love, marriage dissolution, drinking and having a good time'.[11] The 1950s represented the golden age of honky-tonk: Webb Pierce, Hank Locklin, Lefty Frizzell and Faron Young were to the fore, along with Jones and Hank Williams.

No account of country music, however brief, is complete without mentioning the role of Hank Williams Senior. Hiram 'Hank' Williams, born on 17 September 1923 in Mount Olive, Alabama, was the third child of Lon and Lillie Williams, and grew up in a dirt-poor household. His father worked as a logger before entering the Veterans Administration Hospital when Hank was six; they rarely saw each other over the next decade. Hank spent his early years in a south Alabama log cabin; later his mother moved the family to Montgomery, where she ran rooming houses – one of several changes of residence during his early days. He suffered from a spinal complaint which caused him considerable pain; it led to his trademark hunched posture and later reliance on prescription painkillers. He could not write or read music but was a quick learner by ear, and while living in Georgiana he found a willing tutor, Rufus Payne, a street singer of African-American blues, who taught him how to sing and play the guitar. Williams' mother was a church organist, and her hymns and southern gospel songs further widened his musical knowledge.

Hank Williams made his radio debut at the age of thirteen and formed the Drifting Cowboys within a year. His career, despite his alcoholism and drug addiction, was extraordinarily successful. The singer's deeply troubled marriage to Audrey Mae Sheppard provided inspiration for many of his greatest songs, including 'Long Gone Lonesome Blues', 'Lost Highway' and 'I'm So Lonesome I Could Cry' (all 1949), 'I'll Never Get Out of this World Alive' (1952) and 'Your Cheatin' Heart' (released in 1953 after his death).

Williams' howl was the loneliest one in the wilderness of broken hearts – the most lost of those who travelled the 'lost highway' of which he so famously sang. It was, as he said, all about sincerity:

It can be explained in one word, sincerity. When a hillbilly sings a crazy song, he feels crazy. When he sings 'I Laid my Mother Away' he sees her laying right there in the coffin. He sings more sincere than most other entertainers, because the hillbilly was raised rougher than most entertainers. You got to know a lot about hard work. The people who has been raised something like the way the hillbilly has knows what he is singing about and appreciates it.[12]

Hank Williams' death from an overdose of alcohol and morphine in the back of a Cadillac was a fittingly tragic ending for the saddest of all sad-song singers. Fired from the *Grand Ole Opry* for his unreliability, he was reduced to playing in scattered honky-tonk bars and clubs. Williams had become an embarrassment to Nashville and it dispensed with his services. He would no longer leave the audience of the *Opry* with his famous closing line: 'Friends … if the good Lord's a-willing and the creeks don't rise, we'll see you 'fore long.'

With the advent of the 'Nashville Sound', the great honky-tonk artists were gradually sidelined and they largely disappeared from radio playlists. Chet Atkins and Owen Bradley were the chief architects of this change in direction, characterised by lush string arrangements and the elimination of the fiddle and moaning steel guitar, with Jim Reeves, Eddy Arnold and Brenda Lee the most prominent artists in the field. Not everyone was impressed. The author Brian Hinton hates it: 'It was extremely palatable to mass audiences, but was essentially background music and essentially crap … as bland as white bread … supper club music.'[13]

For lovers of honky-tonk and hillbilly music it was to get worse. The 1970s was the era of 'countrypolitan', a further move towards middle-of-the-road music with more orchestration, keyboards, stringed instruments and elaborate choirs. The work of Dolly Parton, Glen Campbell and Ronnie Milsap at that time was typical of this 'crossover' music.

Bill C. Malone notes that country music is not any one type of sound:

It is a vigorous hybrid form of music constantly changing and growing in complexity just as the society in which it thrives also matures and evolves. It is a music which is as old as the South.[14]

Many purists argue that country music has been on a constant downward trajectory, and much of what is now marketed as such bears little relation to the genuine article. Some of the songs are little different from what is on offer in the mainstream popular and rock music charts, according to these critics of contemporary American country music.

At his 2014 press conference to announce his ill-fated upcoming tour of Ireland, country music superstar Garth Brooks was asked if he would 'save country music'. This was, he said, something he could not do single-handedly. He spoke of 'an unwritten rule' in Nashville, which he termed the 'Easter-egg effect'. When an artist found success with a particular way of interpreting a song, other artists flocked to do the same thing like children at an Easter-egg hunt, he explained.[15] Brooks, arguably, started the biggest Easter-egg hunt in the history of country music. That, however, is not yet our focus; that is in the United States, where arguments over the nature of 'real' country music rage on, while Daniel O'Donnell and his friends play on regardless on the other side of the Atlantic Ocean. It is time to turn to the world of Irish country music.

3

'BRINGING IT ALL BACK HOME': COUNTRY COMES TO IRELAND

Live country music is arguably the most popular form of public entertainment in rural Ireland today. Hotels host dance nights attended by hundreds in what has become a multi-million-euro industry, while the numbers of performers, concerts and media outlets have risen significantly. Local and regional newspapers advertise huge numbers of dances and concerts. Local radio stations fill much of their schedules with Irish country songs, while the number of Internet radio stations and cable-television programmes broadcasting country music has dramatically increased in recent years. Many pubs in rural Ireland feature live country music on their entertainment schedule more often than any other genre.

Yet up until the 1950s live country music was not one of the available entertainment options in Ireland. There was music and there was dancing – homes and crossroads had been the scenes of dancing in Ireland for centuries – but there was no country-music-led dancing.

From the late nineteenth century, céilí bands were encouraged as an expression of national identity by the Gaelic League – a social and cultural organisation established in 1893 by Douglas Hyde (who would later become president of Ireland) to promote Irish language and culture. The Irish word céilí simply means 'a gathering of people for dance'. The first official céilí dance organised by the League was held in London on 30 October 1897, in Bloomsbury Hall beside the British Museum. The London branch of the organisation, set up in October of the previous year, aimed to create an attractive social environment where the sexes could mingle and practise their Irish-language skills. These dances quickly became popular and spread to Ireland, where dancing masters moved around the country teaching dance formations. Céilí dances ranged in difficulty from the simple 'Siege of Ennis' and 'Walls of Limerick' to the complicated 'Sixteen-Hand Reel' and 'High-Cauled Cap'. They could be performed by hundreds of people at a time; different dances catered for different numbers of people.

In Ireland, céilí bands playing traditional music became particularly popular and common from the 1920s onwards. Crucially, in the new twentieth-century Irish state, founded after the War of Independence with Britain, the Catholic Church was the greatest power and largely controlled the type of music played in public. Céilí bands were promoted by the Catholic clergy as a wholesome form of entertainment in opposition to any of the new-fangled types of dancing existing in other countries. The Catholic Church campaigned against informal house dances and crossroads dances, seeing them as opportunities for immorality, but was happy to hold céilí dances under its own watchful eyes. In his Pastoral Letter of 1924, Cardinal Logue outlined the Church's position: 'It is no small commendation of Irish dances that they cannot be danced for long hours ... They may not be the fashion in London and Paris. They should be the fashion in Ireland. Irish dances do not make degenerates.'[1]

This conservative approach was in tune with the new state. The Carrigan Report of 1931, which dealt with the legislation pertaining to child prostitution, outlined the danger the authorities perceived in social dancing:

The testimony of all witnesses, clerical, lay and official, is striking in its unanimity that degeneration in the standard of social conduct has taken place in recent years ... This is due largely to the introduction of new phases of popular amusement, which being carried out in the Saorstat in the absence of supervision, and of the restrictions found necessary and enforced by law in other countries, are the occasions of many abuses baneful in their effect upon the community generally and are the cause of the ruin of hundreds of young girls ... The 'commercialised' dance halls, picture houses of sorts, and the opportunities afforded by the misuse of motor cars for luring girls, are the chief causes alleged for the present looseness of morals.[2]

In 1934 the Gaelic League launched an 'Anti-Jazz Campaign' with a strong statement: 'It is this music and verse that the Gaelic League is determined to crush ... its references are to things foreign to Irishmen.'[3] A letter from Cardinal McRory, Archbishop of Armagh, backing such a campaign organised in Leitrim, was read out at all Catholic masses:

I heartily wish success to the Co. Leitrim executive of the Gaelic League in its campaign against all-night jazz dancing. I know nothing about jazz dancing except that I understand that they are suggestive and demoralising: but jazz apart, all-night dances are objectionable on many grounds and in country districts and small towns are a fruitful source of scandal and ruin ... To how many poor innocent young girls have they not been an occasion of irreparable disgrace and lifelong sorrow?[4]

The secretary of the Gaelic League also attacked the broadcasting of jazz on the national broadcaster, Radio Éireann (then known as 2RN): 'Our Minister of Finance has a soul buried in jazz and is selling the musical soul of the nation ... He is jazzing every night of the week.'[5] A number of county councils adopted resolutions condemning jazz and all-night dancing, and district justices referred to the dangers of 'nigger music' and the 'orgy' of unrestricted all-night dances. In January 1934 a large demonstration took place in Mohill, County Leitrim, where an estimated 3,000 people marched with five traditional bands and banners with slogans including 'Down with Jazz' and 'Out with Paganism'.[6] The Catholic Church particularly highlighted the lack of toilets at outdoor dance events as unacceptable and immoral.

After sustained pressure on the government by the Church and religiously motivated politicians, the Public Dance Halls Act of 1935 put the running of all such functions into the hands of the clergy and their parochial halls. But according to Junior Crehan – a legendary fiddle player and folklorist from Mullagh, County Clare – the clerics and political authorities were more interested in the money than personal hygiene: 'You had to pay three pence tax to the shilling going into the hall … They didn't care if you made your water down the chimney as long as they collected the money.'[7]

All the instruments in a céilí band played the melody together. Instruments used included accordion, concertina, harmonica, uilleann pipes, banjo, fiddle, mandolin, flute, tin whistle, drums and piano. The music was a simplified, scaled-down version of the traditional form, and the emphasis was on rhythm with little experimentation or improvisation. Purists of traditional Irish music often hated them. Renowned composer Seán Ó Riada was particularly critical: 'The most important principles of traditional music – the whole idea of variation, the whole idea of the personal utterance – are abandoned. Instead everyone takes hold of a tune and belts away at it with as much relation to music as the buzzing of a bluebottle in an upturned jam jar.'[8]

Some of the most popular – such as the Vincent Lowe Trio, the Tulla and Kilfenora Céilí Bands from County Clare, the Kiltormer Céilí Band from outside Ballinasloe, County Galway, and the Gallowglass Céilí Band from Naas, County Kildare – toured the country, playing in the parochial halls and often, where no suitable halls were available, in marquees specially erected for music and dancing. In the summer, bands played in local carnivals, a dominant feature in the social life of rural Ireland for decades afterwards.

With the dominance of traditional music, the Anti-Jazz movement and the control of the Catholic Church over the social lives of the Free State's citizens, it is perhaps surprising that country music was able to make any inroads into the Irish musical scene. Those Irish who had access to cinema screens in the 1930s may have been aware of this style of music from the soundtracks of western movies, but this medium would have had a limited audience and was not a significant factor in the spread of country music in Ireland.

It was the coming of war in 1939 that really brought this style of music to the attention of the Irish. The American military forces based in Europe during and after the Second World War were central to exposing a wider audience to country music. The American Forces Network (AFN) radio, although aimed at the American troops during the occupation of Europe, could be picked up by anyone within range of the signal and was a key factor in spreading the popularity of country music – as well as other American genres – across Europe. On the island of Ireland, those in Northern Ireland and the border counties had the best reception because of the military bases located there. The largest American presence was at Langford Lodge on the eastern shores of Lough Neagh – the area which would become the heartland of Irish country music and from which many Ulster Scots had set off on their journey to America. Even the landscape of this part of Northern Ireland is similar to the rolling hills of the American south-east, where the vast majority of those immigrants eventually made their new home, as journalist Michael Commins astutely observed.[9]

AFN radio started broadcasting from London in July 1943; from the beginning, one of the most popular shows was an edited version of the *Grand Ole Opry*. Sound engineers of the famous American country and western radio programme removed advertisements, recorded the remainder on vinyl and distributed it to AFN radio stations around the world. For many, this was their first exposure to American country music and it was spoken about reverently by many of those interviewed for this book. Niall

Toner – eminent country and bluegrass musician and presenter of *Roots Freeway* on RTÉ Radio 1 – frequently mentions the AFN programme as the spark which lit the fire of his lifelong love of country music. Famously, Van Morrison, the Belfast-born singer-songwriter even wrote a song where he talks about trying to tune his radio to AFN radio ('In the Days Before Rock 'n' Roll').

Such was the quality of these recordings that some were later released as albums, including selections of Hank Williams' performances from the Opry stage. Henry McMahon, influential country music songwriter and long-time member of Big Tom and The Mainliners, spoke about AFN radio in a telephone interview: 'I remember it well. You could hear it at three in the morning or three at night for some reason. We would be waiting for it to come on in the middle of the night.'[10] McMahon recalled a fascinating story about the radio station:

> A few years ago Tommy Cash, Johnny Cash's brother, was on a tour of Ireland and did an interview with Paul Claffey on Midwest Radio. It turned out that he had been a DJ on AFN when he was in the military. Tommy Cash told Claffey they couldn't think of anything else to do with him so they put him on the radio. His programme was called the *Stickbuddy Jamboree* for some reason.[11]

Country music was, and always has been, much sought-after by members of the United States military. *Billboard* magazine carried a report in its 25 September 1961 issue stating the AFN had decided to increase the broadcasting of country and western music by thirty-five per cent on the basis of the results of a survey carried out among troops based in Europe. The article quoted an 'army disk buyer':

> It is more than merely music with the troops. Country and western strikes the troops as part of the American heritage, and the troops prefer it to the

sophisticated, schmalzy [*sic*] music that may appeal to the cocktail hour crowd, but which leaves the GI cold.[12]

American military personnel had been 'peppering' radio authorities demanding 'more real American music – country and western'. The disk buyer was dismissive of 'those musical sophisticates' who wanted to ban the music from radio airwaves because they considered it 'hick' and 'hillbilly', furthering the notion that Americans are 'cultural barbarians'. The army source said the authorities were aware that thirty million Europeans 'eavesdrop' on AFN, but, despite the 'sophisticate minority' in the military who wanted the radio only to broadcast 'Bach, Brahms and Beethoven with a slight leavening perhaps of avante-garde jazz', the authorities would respond to the wishes of the majority and increase the amount of country music on air.[13] These days AFN 360 Country broadcasts music twenty-four hours a day to American troops around the world.

A European broadcaster had a similar influence on Irish audiences. Big Tom McBride and other Irish country artists have frequently spoken in interviews about the influence hearing country music on Radio Luxembourg had on their musical direction. This station was hugely popular in Great Britain before the advent of pirate and modern commercial radio, and for a long time it owned the most powerful radio transmitter in the world. Radio Luxembourg had a big listenership in Ireland too. In 1955 the Statistical and Social Inquiry Society of Ireland published a paper from the Central Statistics Office (CSO) on *Radio Éireann Listenership Research Inquiries 1953–1955*, the first project of its kind in Ireland. By modern standards the research methods were weak, but the results are notable. In 1953 some fifty-two per cent of all listeners between the ages of fourteen and twenty-four had listened to Radio Luxembourg the previous day, twenty per cent had tuned in to AFN at some stage of the day, eighty-two per cent had heard Radio Éireann and twenty per cent had spent some time listening to the British Home

Service. Older age groups listened more to the state broadcaster and less to the offshore stations.[14]

It was to Radio Luxembourg that many of the first generation of Irish country music performers tuned in. According to Michael Commins, the national broadcaster largely ignored country music. (It also gave limited air time to traditional Irish music.) This was, he said, a form of 'musical apartheid'.[15] It did not suit the tastes of those producers and presenters of the station attempting to portray a modern Ireland, who preferred to treat the nation to middle-of-the-road performers like Perry Como and Bing Crosby, along with classical music favourites. 'Cowboy' music, as it was sometimes disparagingly referred to according to Commins, was far removed from their minds and schedules, and represented a backward version of the country in their estimation. Subsequently pirate radio stations such as Radio Caroline and North Sea Radio broadcast American country music as part of their schedules.

For those who liked what they heard, it could be difficult to acquire recordings of this new kind of music. Up until the 1970s in Ireland, the distribution system for imported recorded music was poor and LPs (long-playing records) available locally were expensive. However, recordings could be sent or brought home from the United States by relatives who had emigrated there and by merchant seamen, amongst others, and such imports were valued commodities.

Once the music became popular, of course, Irish acts started to tap into this new market and develop their own style of country music, now re-ferred to as 'country and Irish' or 'country 'n' Irish'. While the sound of traditional Irish country music is not far removed from American country music – typically it has the same 'twang' and the same themes of heartache, home, family and life gone wrong – mixed in are a more insistent drum-beat, a bit of accordion and some traditional Irish melodies and places. The accordion, particularly the piano version, allows for the inclusion of introductory sections, harmonies and improvised solo passages. Many of these acts were part of a phenomenon that started in the 1950s and spread across the island, providing what would become a hugely popular form of entertainment, particularly for the younger members of the population, and allowing the dissemination of all styles of music throughout the island – the showband.

From the end of the Second World War to the late 1950s, orchestral-type 'big bands' provided a sedate soundtrack to the social life of Irish people. These entertainers sat behind music stands and played a wide selection of material from Irish folk to standard dance numbers. Journalist Sam Smyth provides a vivid, if a little cynical, description:

> Musicians sat like ciphers on an assembly line syncopating strict tempo accompaniment to ballroom dancers, who conducted their serious business at arm's length wearing fixed smiles … the band sat behind music stands wearing evening dress and world-weary expressions; those musicians who could afford them, kept looking at their watches.[16]

This was a sedate scene, with women on one side of the hall waiting for the men on the other side to cross 'no-man's-land' and ask for a dance. It was an environment brilliantly described in William Trevor's short story 'The Ballroom of Romance' and portrayed in the subsequent film of the same name directed by Pat O'Connor, who described his work as a 'depiction of a primitive mating ritual with low expectations on both sides as men lingered along one half of the wall and girls on the other … a shorthand for "the kind of dismal dump this country used to be"'.[17]

It was not just the country dance halls that were thus limited. Journalist Eanna Brophy described the bleak nature of the bigger ballrooms in the city:

> The ballrooms were Spartan places, built with blocks with not much effort made to disguise them. They may have had their romantic sounding names in neon at the front but inside they had all the charms of the cattle marts

which were built about the same time (and, of course, women always complained that the similarity did not end with the building, but the rituals of the dance floor were not too different from those of the sales ring). The toilets were primitive, the seating sparse and the tables Formica. The band's 'dressing rooms' were legendary for their awkwardness; you were lucky if there was a nail in the wall to hang up your suit.[18]

Despite this, the big bands paved the way for the showbands, which would introduce a newer, more modern sound to the dance-goers. The showbands were dance bands which covered music ranging across all the genres. While pop and rock and roll were the most popular songs, some bands also featured an element of country and western.

By common agreement, the Clipper Carlton from Strabane, County Tyrone, were the first 'showband' in Ireland. In getting up off their chairs and incorporating dance steps into their acts, they started a musical revolution; by 1955 the Clippers were wearing shiny suits and copying the music of Bill Haley, Elvis Presley and Nat King Cole, amongst many others. Their shows even included comedy routines and a section called 'Jukebox Saturday Night', during which members of the band dressed up to impersonate stars of the day. For the first time, stage musicians were starting to look as if they were having fun, in keeping with the changing nature of Irish society.

The arrival of showbands was a shock to 'Dancealot', the entertainment correspondent with the *Irish Pictorial*:

It seems to have been my unhappy lot recently in the course of duty to suffer from several Showbands, who if they intended making a SHOW of themselves could not have been more successful. I'm not opposed to showbands generally ... but lately I've been unlucky. I heard three or four bands in a row and could find nothing good to say about any of them! The bands in question reached an all time low musically, the sounds they made being appalling ... Which goes to show that you can get a percussionist who can belt the skins and cymbals hard and loud enough to provide a jive beat, gather together indifferent musicians who fancy themselves as singers who can busk on musical instruments and you're in the Showband business![19]

Despite Dancealot's reservations, the showband scene thrived. The cities and countryside began to reverberate with new sounds coming from halls such as the Adelphi, Ritz, Embassy and Dreamland. At the height of the boom there were more than 600 showbands working in Ireland, many of which earned a decent living.

Country songs were particularly popular in the rural areas, and some showbands carried specialist country singers for these performances. Brendan Bowyer and the Royal Showband had Tom Dunphy sing their few country songs, while Ben Dolan of the Drifters showband (led by his charismatic brother Joe) from Mullingar, County Westmeath, only knew three country songs, but the audience loved them, according to Michael Commins.[20] In late 1961 Dunphy recorded 'Come Down From the Mountain, Katie Daly' – arguably the first country hit for a showband – and would have further country music success with 'If I Didn't Have a Dime'. Some might not agree with this identification of Dunphy as the first showband singer to record a country song. Tom Gilmore makes an interesting case for a recording of a cover version of the Bobby Bare song 'Detroit City (I Wanna Go Home)' by the Johnny Flynn Showband from Tuam, County Galway.[21] Unfortunately the recording was made and pressed in the United States and could not be released in Ireland because of the different size of the hole in the middle of the record – or so the story goes.

In his chapter in *The Blackwell Guide to Recorded Country Music*, Gilmore traces the country music thread which ran through the showband scene. *Presenting the Capitol Showband*, released in 1962, was the first LP released by an Irish showband; although it contained mostly Irish ballads set to a typical showband beat, the old country classic 'Silver Threads and Golden Needles' became one of the most popular songs on the album. There were other country songs among the standard interpretations of the pop repertoire. Eileen Reid and the Cadets had a number four hit with the country song 'I Gave My Wedding Dress Away' in October 1964, while in the same year The Pacific Showband, with lead singer Sean Fagan, had a hit with a cover of the Jim Reeves classic 'Distant Drums'. Even the strongly pop-oriented Dixies from Cork recorded the country-oriented songs 'He's Got You' and 'Ebony Eyes' in 1966.

The popularity of the showbands and the increasing number of venues that were made available to these acts also allowed bands that were straightforward Irish country music acts to thrive at the same time in the same venues. Larry Cunningham and Tom McBride, amongst others, coincided with the showband scene, but for them the designation of Irish country music band would be more appropriate. That both artists – as well as other country acts – enjoyed enduring popularity after the vast majority of the showbands had gone by the wayside is indicative of the love Irish audiences have had for country music and the loyalty of the artists' fanbase, a characteristic of country music the world over.

By the late 1960s the era of the showband was coming to an end. New acts such as the Dubliners, Planxty, the Wolfe Tones and Johnny McEvoy, invigorated by the fiftieth anniversary of the 1916 Rising, focused on the more traditional music and there was a rise in the popularity of songs celebrating the glory of the nation. Pubs throbbed to the sound of raucous republican ballads as dance halls started to crumble around the country. Pubs upgraded their facilities to accommodate music, adding on lounges for the additional comfort of their female clientele. Unlike the dance halls, lounge bars and hotels were able to apply for legal exemptions allowing alcohol to be served late into the night. In a modernising society, people were no longer going to put up with the abysmal standards of the old dance halls.

Opportunities for bands plying their trade on the live-music circuit tightened up, and it was substantially cheaper for pubs and hotels to pay for someone to play records, or hire a duo or one-man operation, than to pay large bands. Larry Cunningham reckoned the ballroom owners should have moved faster to make their venues more comfortable for the punters. He told Tom Gilmore he believed that if they had, the ballrooms could have competed against the discos and the singing pubs: 'If they had got bar and restaurant licences the scene could have lasted another 10 years.'[22]

The advent of disco music proved a fatal blow for many live-music outfits. In a telephone interview, singer Susan McCann recalled the time she noticed the changes:

I'd be coming back from a gig somewhere and we'd pass the Carrickdale Hotel outside Dundalk and there would be hundreds of cars there for the disco. The whole thing had changed by then. People stopped going out to country dancing and not too many of us survived. There was no one new breaking through then.[23]

The vast majority of the showbands broke up, although some survived as pop and rock bands, while others broke into smaller units and played the cabaret and lounge-bar circuit. Some mutated into country bands of different hues. Showbands were no longer 'cool', with a new generation raised on rock, as Sam Smyth outlines:

Showband fans were seen as admirers of people in lightweight business suits, clean cut folk who nurtured an image of being a good neighbour. The younger folk let their hair grow long, played their music very, very loud and sneered at their older brothers and sisters.[24]

Not all audiences wanted to hear pop music, however. Many rural audiences, in particular, were still more attracted to the country songs of Larry

Cunningham and Tom McBride. Thus, some of the Irish country music bands played on and have done so to this day.

Country music was always there, albeit less visible at some times than at others. It has not just appeared over the last decade, as some media commentators are wont to suggest. It has also continued to develop its sound from those early days. Over time there has been a move away from the use of a tense throat and the nasal 'drone' typical of early American country music towards a more rounded vocal style typified by artists like Daniel O'Donnell. In more recent times there has also been a move among many of the younger artists towards a more contemporary American-style – some would say homogenous – sound, but there is still plenty of distinctive Irish country music. The showbands, with their emphasis on copying the pop and rock hits of the day, may have overshadowed and outnumbered the country music acts for a period but, unlike the showbands, the country artists never disappeared; the candles flickered, but the lights did not go out.

It is time to look at a few of the now-deceased innovators – those who first performed country music in Ireland and paved the way for the many who make their living in the industry today.

4

SEARCHING FOR THE PIONEERS

Father Frank Bradley read the homily at the church in Killyclogher, County Tyrone, at Shay Hutchinson's funeral. He finished by speaking about the deceased singer's contribution to country music: 'His up-beat nature was what drew generation upon generation to the man and his music. I hope that American Country and Western music has reached heaven before him – otherwise they're in for a big surprise!'[1]

All the experts interviewed throughout the course of this book agreed that Shay Hutchinson (1930–2004) and his band, the Melody Aces, were true pioneers and deserving of the title of the first purveyors of country music on the island of Ireland. An article by Michael Commins in 2004 provides a signpost. Only eleven months before Hutchinson's death, Commins had seen him perform in the Royal Hotel in Roscommon along with two other former members of the Melody Aces, Gene Turbett and Edward McNamee:

Shay Hutchinson, regarded by many as one of the great original pioneers of country music here in Ireland, was joined by Gene Turbett and Edward McNamee for a night that will long be cherished by those who were privileged to see some of the great 'masters' of the showband scene.

I had heard much about the Melody Aces over the years and the huge popularity they enjoyed around the country. So when the chance came to see some members of the band for the very first time, I was not going to let it pass by.

You could sense the star quality associated with this band in their heyday. Shay, for all the world like an actor from an old western film, performed country songs from the 'roots' tradition and there was no need for hype or cover-up. This was the real thing. His versions of 'Gypsy Woman' and 'You're My Best Friend' had admirers standing in front of the stage showing their appreciation.[2]

The proliferation of technology sometimes comes in for much criticism, but the presence of a video camera in Killyclogher in 1994 and the fore-thought to put the material it captured on YouTube for posterity have provided valuable footage of Shay Hutchinson for the uninitiated. In that year the people of Killyclogher celebrated Shay's contribution to country music in Ireland with a night of entertainment in the local Cappagh Parish Community Centre. Singing stars Philomena Begley, Gene Stuart and Brian Coll, along with Father Brian D'Arcy, were among the many important figures of the Irish country scene present at the evening function entitled 'A Man and His Music – A Tribute to Shay Hutchinson'. It was like an entire series of the television show *This Is Your Life* rolled into one episode, and was a credit to the organisers – a celebration which reflected the tight community bonds in Irish rural society and the world of Irish country music. It lasted for more than four hours and included traditional music and country music performances; umpteen interviews and video clips of cousins, friends and musical stars; comedy sketches; and banter of all descriptions – above all else, it showcased the pride the people of the area had in their native son.

Pio McCann – a revered country music DJ on Highland Radio, Donegal, and a native of Tyrone – spoke proudly of his memories:

Once you heard him sing you never forgot him. He was something special.

Wherever you went it would make you proud to think you were from the same area. It was like being friends with some of the great Tyrone footballers of the time. This man has such a good voice that he should be still out singing every night of the week.[3]

Father Brian D'Arcy spoke of the love the locals had for Shay Hutchinson and described him as 'an originator' of country music in Ireland, who highlighted the musical links between the United States and Ireland:

He wanted to sing and make people happy with this other American music which in turn had been got from the Irish anyway ... so country music and Irish people ... it's natural that we would want to be part of country music because it was our music originally. It came out from the Celtic nations, from Scotland and Ireland, went out to America to the bluegrass hills and they still play bluegrass as Irish music to this very day ... people like Ricky Skaggs and Bill Monroe are indistinguishable from Sean McGuire [a famous fiddle player from Tyrone] playing the fiddle.[4]

In D'Arcy's opinion, the Melody Aces 'undersold themselves' and could have achieved greater success if they had been marketed better, particularly in comparison with the Clipper Carlton. Their contribution 'to country-music dancing' was, he believed, 'immense'. He presented a piece of crystal to Hutchinson, addressing him as 'the first, the original of the all-time country singers that ever stood on a stage in this country, the man who started it all' and 'the man who pioneered country music for other people, the greatest of them all, the high priest of country music'.[5] Shay, with his trademark crooked smile, graciously accepted the gift, looking like a cowboy who had been given a new horse.

My research into the life of Shay Hutchinson was to be given an invaluable boost by Henry McMahon of The Mainliners, who rang late on a Sunday night, saying:

I was up in Letterkenny at a dance last night and this man walked up to me and said he knew who I was but I wouldn't know who he was. He said that I was a friend of his father's from the old days. It was John Hutchinson, Shay's son. I told him what you're at. Give him a ring.

Before I had time to thank him, he was gone to check on his latest managerial protégé, Gerry Guthrie.

John Hutchinson turned out to be a fervent keeper of his father's musical flame and an encyclopaedic authority on his life and music. We spoke on the phone for fifteen minutes before John intervened: 'I'll tell you what. I've put together a book myself on my dad and my family. It hasn't been published, but I'll send it to you. Read it and we'll talk about things after that.' 'Shay Hutchinson: The Making and Breaking of the Mould' arrived a few days later. This beautifully produced, thirty-four-page book is a loving testament to the life and music of Shay Hutchinson. It brings together a wealth of factual data otherwise difficult to find.

Born on 30 October 1930, one of nine children, to parents Bridget and Joe, Hutchinson grew up in Killyclogher surrounded by traditional Irish music. His father spent much of his life working in Scotland and England, like others of his generation. In turn, Shay – aged just sixteen – left home to put in his time on British building sites, before signing up for a seven-year stint with the British Merchant Navy in 1949. After an initial nine-month training period, Shay set off to travel the world, working as a stoker mechanic. He never let go of his love of music: having brought his beloved piano-key accordion on board for his travels, he formed a band called Hutch's Hot Shots and regularly performed for his fellow sailors. Hutchinson learned to play guitar while in the navy and, in an era when pop and rock music were dominant, concentrated on country music, a genre that traditionally found favour with merchant seamen. John takes up the story:

What a sound, what stories, he just couldn't be content until he could learn this new type of music, so he purchased a guitar and somehow taught himself to play. He would strum his guitar to the sounds of Hank Williams, Eddy Arnold, Hank Thompson, Ferlin Husky and Hank Snow. When I recall him playing in the Melody Aces I can recognise that distinct rhythm of those old boys of Country Music. This was a sound that he really loved and felt very comfortable performing.[6]

When Shay returned to Tyrone he continued to play. Peter Fox, a former barman in Grugan's Bar in Campsie, Omagh, told John of how he first heard Shay playing:

One day this big guy strolled into the bar and ordered a bottle of Guinness … After a couple of Guinness he started singing and playing the guitar. He sang a song called 'The Spinning Wheel'. It was out of this world. I can still see it clear as day. What a voice. After that he came in the bar a couple of times a week. He would be singing away and he would say to me 'What song would you like me to sing for you now Peter?' I felt privileged to be asked and I used to say 'The Spinning Wheel' or the 'Blackboard of my Heart'. I loved to hear those notes when he sang way down low. I would ask Shay if he was coming in on Saturday night, if he said yes I used to tell everybody. They were people sitting up the stairs and everywhere. He just loved singing and entertaining the customers.[7]

Shay also played in McBride's Bar in Omagh, and it was there that the owner, Dessie McBride, after hearing Shay sing, contacted his brother-in-law, John Devine, the manager of the Melody Aces from nearby Newtownstewart. Hutchinson sang and played the guitar over the phone to the knowledgeable Devine, who knew a good thing when he heard it and immediately invited him to join the band.

The Aces, the resident showband in the Star Ballroom in Omagh, later had the honour of being the first to play in future taoiseach Albert Reynolds' Cloudland Ballroom in Rooskey, County Roscommon. (Reynolds went on to own a string of ballrooms across the Irish midlands and become a major player in musical-event management, later gaining the unofficial title of Ireland's first 'Country and Western Taoiseach'.) John described the career progression of the band:

> The Melody Aces took the country by storm in the late 50s and early 60s with a unique mix of Big Band, Dixieland and Dad's Country Music setting them apart from other showbands. The Melody Aces spent their time delighting the dance crowds all over the country and Dad had introduced the people of Ireland to Country and Western music and the big names of the *Grand Ole Opry* were becoming household names in Ireland thanks to the pioneering work of Shay Hutchinson.[8]

Hutchinson, as Michael Commins noted, sang in a 'roots' tradition; his vocal style was unadorned and direct, like that of his American musical heroes. The Melody Aces toured the United States three times – in 1959, 1961 and 1963 – and packed out venues in Boston, New York, Chicago and Philadelphia, a first for Irish country musicians. They found similar success on their annual tours to Great Britain, where they played in Birmingham, Manchester and London.

Unlike the Clipper Carlton and other showbands of the time, the Melody Aces did not include a cabaret section in their stage act, preferring to stick to a straightforward musical presentation. While band member David Coyle sang a variety of material, it was Shay Hutchinson who delivered the country numbers the band had as part of their repertoire.

Hutchinson's smoky-voiced, American-accented singing style is heard to great effect on 'Highway to Nowhere' (1965), 'From Nowhere at All' (1965), 'Lay My Head Beneath a Rose' (1966) and 'We Met in a Field of Flowers' (1969); the lack of the accoutrements of much of later Irish country music is immediately evident. The melodious element of the band's music is amply demonstrated on 'Highway to Nowhere' (Shay's first release, on the B-side of which David Coyle sang a beautiful version of 'Oft in the Stilly Night'). The Aces' traditional 'real country' format found particular favour in the west of Ireland and in their native Ulster, and they achieved huge success, commanding £200 a night in the 1950s, when a well-qualified tradesman would typically earn £30 a week. The Melody Aces, all lifelong wearers of Pioneer pins as abstainers from alcohol, were an unlikely slice of Americana touring the lonesome byways of rural Ireland.

In an interview, Henry McMahon – songwriter and long-time saxophone player with Big Tom and The Mainliners – remembered the way Shay Hutchinson hung on to the microphone when he performed: 'I'd never seen anything like that before. He was really something.'[9] McMahon wrote 'A Tribute to the Melody Aces' – released by Donegal singer Gary Gamble – referring specifically to the country music singing of Shay:

The man who sang the country was Shay Hutchinson
And that was long before Brian, Larry or Big Tom
With his arm around the mike stand he stood there tall and still
As he sang the 'Blackboard of my Heart' and 'The Mansion on the Hill'

In his impressive book, John Hutchinson notes the changing social scene and the resultant effects on the live music scene:

Time waits for no man and a new venue was growing in popularity, the lounge bar. Dad's local bar, The Village Inn, Killyclogher was among the first to start the new trend. The owner Eddie McGinn approached Dad and asked him to sing a few songs and play his guitar along with their resident piano player which he did willingly. The lounge was filled to capacity each night he played. The scene was now set for all professional and non professional musicians to form groups of three or four to entertain pub goers throughout Ireland and it is safe to say that this trend was to signal the end for the big dance halls and therefore limit the dates available for the showbands.[10]

The Melody Aces played their last date in February 1972. Shay Hutchinson, Gene Turbett and Edward McNamee then formed their own pub-group called the San Antones and John notes that 'they had a full diary of dates for lounge bars, wedding receptions and dinner dances'.

Shay Hutchinson passed away on 17 January 2004. Father Frank Bradley summed up the feelings of the congregation at the singer's funeral:

> For it is the soul of his voice and the touch of his hand that will be missed most by everyone. Certainly, God will not find Shay wanting in the area of talent – he buried nothing of the things God gave him but rather shared them out. In an era of wastefulness and neglect, we would do well to take a leaf out of his book today.

Gene Turbett, the last surviving member of the Melody Aces, passed away at the age of eighty in 2012, severing the link with a group of men who took music in a new direction in Ireland. The very last page of John Hutchinson's beautifully prepared book contains a message in cursive script with an important emphasis: 'Although he may not have realised it at the time, Dad was without question *the* pioneer of Country Music in Ireland.'

***

Narrative is central to country music, and Johnny McCauley (1925–2012) is universally regarded as the father of Irish country music songwriting. The importance of McCauley became truly apparent at his funeral. Big Tom McBride spoke movingly:

> He had a brilliant brain, simply brilliant. Johnny was one of the first to

write Irish country music and he put a lot of Irish singers on the map with his songs. He was a gem, a poet and a musician all wrapped into one. Some people can write words but can't put the music to them, but Johnny could do both with ease.[11]

Irish country music superstar Daniel O'Donnell also praised McCauley:

People will be amazed by how many classic songs this one man wrote. His songs will be sung in pubs after closing time and the airs whistled by postmen on their rounds – in this business that's the sign of a brilliant song and a brilliant songwriter.[12]

Henry McMahon, a prolific songwriter himself, reckons McCauley was a 'genius': 'When you think about lines like "from the land of my heart to the heart of my land" you realise how important he was. It's a rare thing to be able to come up with lyrics like that.'[13]

Born in Limavady, County Derry, on 23 April 1925 and brought up in Fahan, County Donegal, Johnny McCauley moved to London at seventeen. There, as well as working as a painter and decorator, he became heavily involved in the music scene. In 1953 he formed the Westernaires. The band was famous for its cowboy clothes and pure country and western sound, and it held a residency in the Galtymore Ballroom in Cricklewood for many years. McCauley later established the Denver Records label, which counted Big Tom as one of its recording stars, and, along with Paddy Kelly and Johnny O'Shea, released songs on this label as the Johnny McCauley Trio. He was the first to combine the sound of country music with Irish themes in his songwriting.

McCauley's songs were instrumental in the careers of stars such as Larry Cunningham, Big Tom and Daniel O'Donnell. Cunningham took McCauley's 'Among the Wicklow Hills' (also later recorded by Christy Moore) to number two in the Irish charts in 1966, while another McCauley composition, 'Pretty Little Girl from Omagh' (apparently inspired by the sight of so many beautiful women from Omagh when McCauley was a resident musician in the Galtymore Ballroom in Cricklewood), reached number ten in 1969. Later, Big Tom scored one of his biggest-ever successes with McCauley's 'Four Country Roads', which reached number five in 1981, while he was with the Travellers. McCauley accompanied McBride on a trip to the United States aboard the liner *Queen Elizabeth 2* (*QE2*), famously writing twelve songs en route 'to pass the time'. Daniel O'Donnell's first recording was 'My Donegal Shore', composed by McCauley in 1983, and was to be a key foundation stone in the young singer's success. (Big Tom had first covered the song on his 1980 Nashville-recorded album *Blue Wings*.) Brian Coll, another pioneering singer in Irish country music, had a big hit with the McCauley-penned 'Hometown on the Foyle', and 'Any Tipperary Town' was recorded by Cunningham, O'Donnell and Pat Ely, amongst others. Interviewed by the *Derry Journal* in 2004, McCauley said, 'It's always nice to know that songs I wrote many, many years ago remain as popular today as they did when first released.'[14]

Johnny McCauley died in his adopted home of London on 22 March 2012, one month short of his eighty-seventh birthday. At his funeral, mourners placed a wreath in green, white and gold in the shape of a guitar on the altar.

***

The music industry has always been a more difficult environment for women than for men. Traditionally, female fans followed the male stars and dictated which artists had a greater following. Most men in the audience were in the company of – or in pursuit of – the female fans, and hence many of the male singers and bands found it easier to acquire success on the circuit. Combined with the state-mandated role of the wife as a stay-at-home mother, this made it even more difficult for women to make a successful career in Irish live music.

Despite these challenges, one woman who managed to make a significant contribution to the early days of country music in Ireland was Maisie McDaniel. McDaniel, by universal consent of those able to remember back that far, was the first professional female Irish country singer in Ireland, but her musical beginnings – like those of so many artists who found success on the Irish country scene – were in traditional Irish music. Lisa Stanley, Maisie McDaniel's daughter, and a successful singer and television presenter based in the United Kingdom, spoke to me at length about her mum's life while on a short holiday to her native home.

Mary Anne 'Maisie' McDaniel was born in London in October 1939 but came to Ireland as an infant. Lisa explained:

My grandparents were both originally from Sligo and had been working and living in London for a number of years when Mum was born. World War Two started and my granny decided to take her back home to escape from the trouble. My granddad followed them back a few years later.[15]

As a teenager, McDaniel won awards for her ballad-singing at high-profile competitions in Sligo and Swinford, and at the prestigious national ballad-singing competition at An Tóstal in Drumshanbo, County Leitrim. (An Tóstal, inaugurated in 1953, was a series of festivals held in various centres in Ireland as a celebration of Irish life and culture, and continued until 1958. Drumshanbo was the only town in the country to continue holding the festival after 1958; it still does so.) Lisa spoke about the important role played by her grandfather in the development of her mother's career:

My mum's father, Paddy McDaniel, encouraged her to sing. He was more into the ballads and the republican songs, but he backed her all the way. He was a great help to her. He encouraged her and her sister to enter singing competitions and all that.[16]

Paddy's encouragement paid dividends; Maisie and her sister Deirdre's photograph appeared on the front page of *The Sligo Champion* newspaper in August 1958, when they won first place in the ballad-singing competition at the Cootehall Feis in neighbouring County Roscommon, just a month after Maisie had captured the honours at the Strokestown Feis.

Maisie McDaniel came to national prominence in 1961 when, after signing up with manager George O'Reilly, she released her debut single 'Forty Shades of Green', written by American country singer Johnny Cash while he was touring Ireland two years earlier. 'Lovely Armoy', a staple of Maisie's ballad repertoire, featured on the Beltona-recorded B-side, but it was to be country-oriented material that would bring the Sligo singer to greater heights. O'Reilly, who also had Dermot O'Brien and his Clubmen, the Victors and the Nevada showband in his stable of stars, encouraged McDaniel to pursue the country angle. He proved an astute promoter; McDaniel's career quickly took off. Lisa Stanley acknowledged the role played by O'Reilly:

> George told her she had a great voice for country. It was a new thing at the time and he thought she would be perfect for it with her voice and her looks. She hadn't thought of it herself but he encouraged her. She was the first to put on the cowboy gear and all that. She thought she would look silly but the people loved it from the very start.[17]

Dressed in her trademark fringed skirt and calf-length, white leather boots, McDaniel first joined the music circuit with the Fendermen before becoming the lead singer with the higher-profile Nevada showband. In June 1963 the Fontana record label released the singles 'Something Special' and 'This Song Is Just For You', both excellent country songs. Later in the same year the label released an EP (extended play release record) of country standards, which included 'Jambalaya', 'I Fall to Pieces', 'Pick Me up on Your Way Down' and 'Someday'.

The Nevada had achieved moderate success with Brian O'Brien as lead singer, but from McDaniel's debut in the Premier Ballroom in Thurles, County Tipperary, on St Stephen's Night 1964, the band's career path moved into higher gear, with hits 'Pick Me Up On Your Way Down', 'Room Full of Roses' and 'Blackboard of My Heart', all released in 1963. McDaniel's high voice and distinctive phrasing had echoes of Patsy Cline, but there was no denying the Irish character of her music.

In 1965 McDaniel was to have represented Ireland in the Eurovision Song Contest, but a broken hip sustained in a car crash outside Kells, County Meath, resulted in a two-month stay in hospital. It was a terrible crash and, by all accounts, she was lucky to have escaped relatively unscathed. 'There were so many calls to the hospital in Navan where she was recuperating enquiring about Maisie's welfare after her accident that the switchboard became jammed,' according to Lisa.[18] Her place in the Eurovision was taken by Butch Moore, who came sixth with 'Walking the Streets in the Rain'.

McDaniel appeared regularly with Dermot O'Brien on the RTÉ television programmes *Country Style* and *Jamboree* during the early 1960s, and was a regular feature on Maureen Potter's radio show on Radio Éireann. She was also the first Irish female country star to be awarded her own television show. *Billboard* magazine reported in its 25 May 1963 edition that in a poll organised by Noel Andrews on RTÉ Radio 1, the listeners had voted her the 'top singer' in the country and approved of her appearances on *Country Style*. In 1964 *Spotlight* magazine voted her the 'Top Female Singer'.

In May 1965 McDaniel married well-known accordion player Fintan Stanley – widely acknowledged as one of the greatest exponents of the five-button version – and moved to England, where they achieved considerable success on the cabaret circuit. The couple returned to Ireland in 1969, spurred on by the opportunity to join *Hoot'nanny*, a new show on RTÉ Television hosted by Shay Healy. The programme proved a success, and

Maisie and Fintan formed the Ramblers showband – which soon changed its name to the Nashville Ramblers – and had a hit with the Merle Haggard standard 'Okie from Muskogee' in 1970. It was a competitive marketplace, but the band carved out a niche and toured Great Britain, appearing on the highly regarded BBC programme *Country Meets Folk*.

By then, however, Maisie McDaniel had had enough of the live-music circuit. In the 2 October 1970 edition of *Spotlight*, the couple announced that they were leaving the circuit to return to settle down on their farm in Tully Hill in County Sligo. Following this move back, the couple played occasionally at local venues on the cabaret circuit, but they made no full-time commitment to the business. Then, in 1973 their daughter, Lisa, was born and she explained:

> Three weeks after I was born she [Maisie] was back on the road. I was brought up by my grandmother for a time when we came back to Ireland first. My mum would often be on the road seven days a week. Later on I lived for a time with my aunt's family. That's why I started late in music myself because that was a very busy house with a lot of children in it and there wasn't the time to give to things.[19]

It was a hard life. While McDaniel shone in the spotlight, her confidence was always brittle and the tough life of the music circuit wore her down. She told her daughter Lisa that she loved performing but was always worried she would disappoint the audience, never felt comfortable with fame and did not like travel. McDaniel always carried rosary beads and prayed before taking the stage. Lisa said:

> I don't think she realised she was as good as she was. She'd get very nervous and would be peeking out at the crowd to see if they were nice or that. She'd be at the side of the stage saying prayers and that. She was just one of those people who found performing very nerve-racking. The thing was

once she got started they always warmed to her very quickly. She was very good, but she never had enough confidence in her own abilities.[20]

Maisie McDaniel's later years were to prove difficult. Her marriage to Fintan broke down and the couple split, after which Fintan emigrated to the United States. Maisie 'made a few comebacks, but there were issues with alcohol addiction and it never got off the ground for her. She tried to sort herself out, but there were difficult times,' according to Lisa.

In 1986 McDaniel came out of retirement to record a fourteen-track album of her former hits (with the help of Gerald O'Donoghue of Greenfields Studios) – *The Maisie McDaniel Collection*, re-released in 2006 by Chart Records. She made a few occasional appearances, but continued to live a quiet life until her untimely death on 28 June 2008 at the age of sixty-eight. Lisa requested that 'Room Full of Roses' be played as her mother's coffin was carried from the church; it was Maisie McDaniel's favourite song. The funeral witnessed a huge gathering, as Paschal Mooney – 'a long-time admirer of the country and western singer' – told Liam Collins of the *Sunday Independent*: 'It was the ordinary fans who turned out in their hundreds to touch the coffin and say a last goodbye.'[21]

Michael Commins summed up her life well in *The Mayo News*:

Maisie knew life from all sides. From the highs of being a national celebrity in the 1960s to the lows that followed her accident and the spate of private tragedy she had to deal with over the years, her own story began to resemble some of the story lines she sang about in her country songs.[22]

In 2009 Lisa Stanley released an album of her mother's hits. The huge love and respect Lisa has for her mother is evident in the way she speaks of her.

During her career, the Sligo singer had shared stages with Cliff Richard, Johnny Mathis and Jim Reeves. Reeves reckoned she was the best singer he had heard during his time touring Ireland in 1963, and he was not the only American superstar impressed by McDaniel's voice. Bing Crosby, a friend of her manager, George O'Reilly, heard her recording of 'Christmas Candles' – a song written specially for her – and was so moved that he made his own recording of the number for inclusion on an album. While other female artists, such as Bridie Gallagher, Rose Tynan, Nita Norry, Eileen Donaghy and Eileen Reid of the Cadets showband, touched on country music in their repertoire, it was Maisie McDaniel who was the first professional female country singer in Ireland.

***

Of all those Irish country stars who have departed for their eternal reward, one man is consistently mentioned by the experts as one of the greatest natural country voices Ireland ever produced. That man is Gene Stewart (1944–2016) – stage name Gene Stuart – who was known for his deep voice and exceptional phrasing.

Stuart was from Killeeshil near Dungannon, County Tyrone, a region of Ireland which could well be considered the centre of the Irish country music heartland, such are the number of singers who have originated there. He left school at thirteen and, after spending time as a barman and sales representative, emigrated to Britain, where he worked in construction. In 1969, back in Ireland, he secured work with *The Dungannon Observer* as a photographer and successfully auditioned for the Mighty Avons when Larry Cunningham departed. In the same year 'Before the Next Teardrop Falls' – his first recording with the band – reached number three in the Irish charts and they went on to have further successes with 'Just Lucky I Guess' (1969), 'Don't Go' (1971), 'I'd Rather Love and Lose You' (1971), 'Kiss an Angel Good Morning' (1972) and 'Christmas in My Hometown' (1973), all still hugely popular songs with fans of the music.

Stuart embraced a relentless schedule, but in 1973 he became ill with tuberculosis, which forced him off the road for six months. By the time he had recovered some of the band had decided to go their own way, but a new band, Gene Stuart and the Homesteaders, arose from the ashes of the Avons to even greater acclaim. What followed was a hugely successful career, which included the release of twenty albums.

When Stuart died in February 2016, after a long battle with cancer, Northern Ireland Arts Minister Carál Ní Chuilín paid him a fine tribute:

Gene Stuart was a fantastic singer with a rich, distinctive baritone that brought real emotional depth to his songs. He honed his performance and vocal skills at the height of the showband era, spending long periods on the road and playing shows virtually every night. Gene blazed a trail that is being followed by many country musicians today. He remains an inspiration to many and leaves behind songs and music that will provide pleasure to music fans for years to come.[23]

A Facebook post by Michael Commins, a personal friend of Gene Stuart, was widely quoted in the media:

Gene was an absolute legend to those of us who love real traditional country music. To me, Gene held iconic status in Irish country music. He was always a tremendous ambassador for Tyrone and one of the finest and noblest people on the country circuit … I am heartbroken at the loss of a truly special friend. We will all miss our beloved hero.[24]

Commins also wrote of his friend in his column in the *Irish Farmers Journal*:

Gene was hewn from the natural fountain of country music. The roots of his raising ran deep. The crystal clear voice was a real blessing in Irish country music for four and a half decades. His monologues album, *Once Upon A Time*, is, without question the finest album of its genre ever recorded in Ireland. His 'Tribute to John Wayne' is special but his version of 'The Bronco Twister' is the best ever recorded in this world. The greatest

Shakespearian actor on the planet could not surpass the majesty of Gene's rendition of this classic.[25]

Commins' journalistic colleague Willie McHugh also paid tribute to Stuart in *The Mayo News*: 'Gene Stuart, were he born in America, would have been an international singing star. Because few, if indeed any, had a naturally cultured singing voice like Gene Stuart and that lovely Ulster timbre, synonymous with singers from that region.'[26]

McHugh recalled listening to a final radio interview with the great singer:

[A]nyone listening attentively enough between the words could clearly hear Stuart saying he was singing the last few notes in the key of life. There was no air or pretence to Gene Stuart … Gene was answering the last encore and taking his final bow. As Gene left the stage of life he took some of the happiest memories of all our yesteryears with him. We will always cherish his memory.[27]

Having read Willie McHugh's poignant words I was moved to contact him. He elaborated on his love for the music of Gene Stuart:

I loved the singing of Gene Stuart since first I heard him on my parents' old Pye radio after he joined the Mighty Avons. I regard him as the finest Irish country singer I ever heard. I am sincere when I say was he born in America he would be up there among the greats like Merle Haggard, Waylon Jennings, Willie Nelson, Tom T. Hall, Ed Bruce and Johnny Cash.[28]

He spoke further of the last visit Gene Stuart made to the radio studio in Midwest Radio:

The tidings he got in a northern hospital earlier that day were a final diagnosis for him and a sudden realisation that precious time was slipping away. I knew from listening more to what wasn't being said, as against what was, by Gene that the real purpose of his trip was to personally thank his legion of followers in this region and also as a special last and fond farewell to Michael Commins and a public acknowledging of their close friendship over many decades. He was tying up a few important loose ends if you like.

Willie McHugh noted that he had only met Gene Stuart once but that 'even then he left a great and lasting impression on me as a man of genuine sincerity and bereft of any airs or graces – except for his perfect singing airs'.[29]

Michael Commins finished his tribute in the *Irish Farmers Journal* beautifully:

Gene Stuart, or Eugene as he was always known in the family circle, recorded some of the best country music on this island and his place among the greats is set in stone. His memory will endure as long as people love and respect real and genuine country music. Gene, you were top shelf, an absolute legend, and your friendship is engraved on my heart until the day that I die if we never meet again this side of heaven.[30]

Commins' deep affection for the artist is clear: 'The funny thing is a lot of people didn't know how great he was until he was gone.'[31]

***

The dedication of these artists to the country sound helped popularise the music in Ireland during a time when it was given little promotion by the media. They were true pioneers in the Irish country music industry. They made differing contributions and paved the way for those who followed.

However, there was one artist who burned brighter and longer than any of these. The biggest of them all – in every way – is the subject of the next chapter.

5

HOW 'BIG TOM' BECAME THE 'KING'

Never forget your roots and the old friends of yesterday. No matter how successful you are it's important to remember where you came from.

Big Tom to Brian Carthy
in *The A–Z of Country and Irish Stars*[1]

Tom McBride, universally known as 'Big Tom' – a nickname he acquired on the Gaelic football fields of Monaghan in imitation of Cavan footballer Big Tom O'Reilly – was the quintessential Irish country singer. His unique singing style, distinctive Monaghan accent and physical size made him the greatest star in Irish country music for decades. Within the industry and among fans he was and still is a revered figure; once heard, Big Tom McBride could never be mistaken for anyone else. In the same way that Hank Williams Senior could evoke the starkness of the lost highways of the United States, McBride could cut to the core of emotional issues which resonated with his listeners; his simple, unadorned style was the perfect vehicle for relating songs of heartbreak, emigration and loneliness.

Big Tom always divided the critics, as Tom Gilmore noted in *The Blackwell Guide to Recorded Country Music*:

> To many country 'purists' in Ireland Big Tom represented Irish country music at its worst – they loathed his records and his live shows ... he attracted a lot of criticism along the way from those who dislike the sad country songs about dead mothers, dead dogs, broken marriage vows, lost love and loneliness.[2]

However, Gilmore immediately pointed out that Big Tom 'was the "King" of country to thousands of fans who packed every hall and marquee in Ireland to see him perform'.

Although McBride was on the road for more than fifty years, his ascent to fame was not immediate. Having left school at fourteen, he got his first job working on a neighbouring farm for five shillings a week. Later, having spent a decade going between Ireland, Scotland, London (where he spent eighteen months working for Wall's, the ice-cream makers) and Jersey (where he worked picking tomatoes for a time), he settled down to a mixture of steel fixing, farming and music back in his native Oram outside Castleblaney. It was in Jersey that he heard the music of a band called The Mainliners, a name which he would later assume for his own group.

When his younger brother died of meningitis at the age of seventeen, McBride came home, at his parents' request, to look after the family farm; in his free time he played with the local Fincairn Céilí Band. At first he concentrated on the rhythm guitar and saxophone, before reluctantly taking over singing duties. Some members left, others joined and a new band, The Mighty Mainliners, was born.

From the beginning, the McMahon brothers, Henry (sax player) and Seamus (guitar), Ginger Morgan (bass and vocals), Ronnie Duffy (drums and occasional vocals), John Beattie (keyboards), Cyril McKevitt (trombone) and Big Tom were determined to make their way in the Irish music industry. Indeed, many commentators over the years have suggested the popularity of Big Tom had a lot to do with the unique sounds made by his backing band, especially the organ sounds of John Beattie and the lead-guitar play of Seamus McMahon, while numerous experts interviewed in the course of writing this book also referred to the technical ability of Ronnie Duffy on the drums. Henry McMahon recalled a time when he was taking a flight from Dublin airport and met the band Bagatelle, who were at the height of their fame on the Irish popular-music scene. They were lavish in their praise of Duffy, reckoning him to be one of the best drummers they had ever heard. Perhaps the most amazing thing of all, as Henry McMahon noted, is that they were all from the local area; 'The Band With the Magic Beat', with all the skills and abilities required to become Ireland's greatest country band, were all from a small area around the town of Castleblaney.[3]

It was not easy for the band and for three years they laboured away, often making only £5 a night. Then John McCormack, owner of the Maple Ballroom in Rockcorry, spotted them playing at a 'teachers' dance' at the Riverdale Hotel in Ballybay, County Monaghan. He was so impressed he immediately booked them for a date for the then-princely sum of £25, and offered to become their manager. Bookings followed in Cavan and Leitrim, and they soon spread their musical net to the capital, where they played at the famous Ierne Ballroom. In May 1966 the band got a lucky break when they were invited to appear on RTÉ Television's popular *Showband Show*. Ginger Morgan performed lead singing duties on 'Let the Four Winds Blow', while Ronnie Duffy led a rendition of 'Johnny B. Goode', but it was a song included in the set as a time filler and sung by McBride that was to launch the career of The Mainliners into a higher orbit. Manager John McCormack told the story to *Spotlight* magazine in 1976:

We had recorded a couple of songs for Phil Solomon's Emerald label, one featuring Ginger which was to be the 'A' side and the flip featuring Tom. Ginger, naturally, was to be given the TV spot to plug the single, but

Adrian Cronin [producer of *The Showband Show*] told us he had an extra few minutes and could we come up with another number from the band. The obvious choice was the 'B' side featuring Big Tom so that's what went out on TV. Neither the Mainliners nor RTÉ were prepared for the result. Literally thousands of letters poured into RTÉ asking for details about the Big Tom song.[4]

'Gentle Mother' caught the public attention when it was beamed to black-and-white televisions all over Ireland on Saturday 26 May 1966. It was an iconic moment in the history of Irish country music and indicated the listeners' huge desire for songs of home and sentimentality. With the release of 'Gentle Mother', Big Tom and The Mainliners had found their niche and were never going to let the punters down.

The story of the song, like all great country songs, is straightforward. The lonely churchyard where the singer's mother is buried is beside a clear, crystal fountain under a willow grove, and her tombstone is decorated with primroses. Her love can never be recovered and from this we can take a lesson: 'Some children take a liking to their parents/While some others fill their mothers' hearts with pain/But some day they will be sorry for their blindness/When the crying will not bring her back again.' It is a simple but devastating message, all the more affecting when heard with McBride's singular phrasing and voice.

McBride first heard the words and tune of 'Gentle Mother' from a flatmate during his time in London. The two were playing guitar and singing one evening when his friend sang a verse and the chorus of the song. Big Tom liked it and asked him to continue, but, finding out that his friend did not know any more, McBride prevailed upon him to write home to his sister for the rest of the words. It was to become the song that launched his career into the stratosphere, and it remained a constant on his set list to the end.

After the television broadcast, the lives of the seven young men from

Monaghan were changed forever. The song went to number seven in the Irish charts, stayed in the top thirty for forty-eight weeks, and sold more than 50,000 records in its first year – making Big Tom the brightest star of Irish country music.

McBride and The Mainliners had further hit singles with 'An Old Log Cabin for Sale', which reached number four in December 1967 and stayed in the charts for fourteen weeks; 'The Old Rustic Bridge' in June 1968; and 'Flowers for Mama' in June 1969. In the early 1970s they found success with 'The Sunset Years of Life' (1970), 'Back to Castleblaney' (1971), 'Broken Marriage Vows' (1972), 'I Love You Still' (1973) and 'Old Love Letters' (1974), the last three of which were consecutive chart toppers. Successful albums included *A Little Bit of Country and Irish* (1969), *From Ireland* (1970) and *I'll Settle for Old Ireland* (1974) – all released by the appropriately named Emerald Records – but it was the landmark 1972 release *Ashes of Love* which was to become the first-ever Irish-country LP to sell more than 50,000 copies. Although Big Tom's versions of the Waylon Jennings and Willie Nelson standard 'Good Hearted Woman' and the Harlan Howard-penned 'Sunday Morning Christian' were not universally praised by the critics, the punters flocked to the tills to buy them. It was Irish country all the way, music mostly played in quickstep or waltz time, and Big Tom reigned supreme.

Social commentator and journalist John Waters was intrigued by the singer. He found it difficult, he wrote, to believe Big Tom was real:

> He was a strange phenomenon to look at – a mountain of a man with blonde hair, dressed in incongruously coloured clothes, who sang a succession of odd songs without saying much else besides, rarely communicating at all other than by means of the occasional theatrical wink.[5]

Paschal Mooney described the negative images some elements attempted to perpetuate:

A growing intolerance among the more pop music oriented sections of the industry fuelled by prejudiced columnists in the media cast Big Tom, Larry Cunningham and their ilk in the role of musical morons. Stories began to circulate that Big Tom could not answer for himself in interviews, that his manager had to do all the answering, he could not sing – the truth is he rarely sang out of tune – and that his first big hit 'Gentle Mother' was perpetuating an obsolete image of rural Ireland, not in tune with the pulsating beat generation of the sixties.

But, as Mooney went on to point out, 'such criticism did little to stem the popular tide in favour of country music and by the end of the seventies country music was in the ascendancy around the nation's ballrooms'.[6]

Big Tom's success inspired parodies. RTÉ journalist Derek Davis – who went under the name 'Mean Tom' for a period when he joined Cork-based band Pat Lynch and the Tree Tops – set one parody to the melody of Buck Owens' 'Crying Time':

It's laughing time again, I'm making millions
You can see that twinkle in my eye
And the only thing that makes me most unhappy
Is the other people's records you still buy.

Davis bore a remarkable resemblance to McBride, but his musical success was limited. He went on to have a successful career as a television and radio chat-show host.

In 1976 RTÉ Television screened a well-regarded documentary on Tom McBride and his native Castleblaney, presented by Tom McGurk and Aine O'Connor. In it, locals spoke with quiet pride about having a star in their midst, praising his musical ability and humility. The documentary portrayed a man of the people, shy in front of the microphone. When the camera moved to a dance hall, however, and he started to perform, the magnetism between singer and audience was immediately obvious. Women stared adoringly into Big Tom's face as he sang songs of emigration, failed relationships and heartbreak.

A 1982 RTÉ Television documentary series, *Secret Languages: Folk Art*, sought to explain the popularity of Big Tom and his version of country music in rural Ireland. The introduction began thus:

> Ireland is a predominantly rural country. The homespun philosophy of Nashville strikes a chord in farmers' hearts that was never struck by Mozart or Motown. Identification is immediate but the secret language is there as well. Country music manages to combine the earthy realities of family life with quasi-religious parables of sin, redemption and all-forgiving love. Life is a vale of tears, home is heaven, heaven is home and Big Tom McBride has sold a million records.[7]

As the narrator spoke, dancers jived and waltzed in a smoky hall to McBride's huge hit 'Four Country Roads' – one of the great songs of Irish country music. It has the classic elements of an Irish country song: emigration, death of parents, lost love and a love of the home town. The four roads leading into and out of the town are the four 'dusty byways' to the singer's heart and mind. One leads to the school he attended, another to the churchyard where his parents are buried, a third to the site where he walked with his now-lost love, and the fourth was the way he left town. The amount of imagery and emotion built into a few short lines is an example of country music songwriting at its best, and a lasting tribute to the song's composer Johnny McCauley. It had a profound resonance for Irish people at home and abroad, too long used to seeing the damage caused by emigration. The song spoke to the people; so many of those interviewed through the course of this book said great country music is music that speaks to the people.

Big Tom made an unlikely appearance on the cover of the culture and music magazine *Hot Press* in November 1983. Founded in 1977 by Niall

Stokes, the publication still provides a fortnightly analysis of the musical, social and cultural life of the nation. Country music had rarely come under its spotlight – the magazine is primarily oriented towards rock and pop music – so putting McBride on the cover was an unusual move. He sat on a chair on an American-style front porch, with two dogs in attendance, a black Stetson on his head and wearing a blue silk, western shirt and black trousers with a red stripe; the caption beside him read: 'So what's Big Tom doing on the cover of Hot Press? Confessions of an Irish showbiz legend'. John Waters wrote in the article:

> On stage, Big Tom, dressed in a red jacket, white pants and a white open-necked shirt is surrounded by half a dozen men half his age wearing black pants, red shirts and bright sequinned waistcoats. Big Tom, singing country, alternates at a mike with a man with white pants and an indoor hairdo who sings the 'pops' and does all the introductions. Big Tom rarely speaks, if at all … Big Tom is all business. He hardly ever moves his big frame, except to walk up to, and away again from the microphone. He's cheerful, winking in his odd slow way at the odd punter, mostly the women. But, overall he has the look of a man who would be much happier behind the wheel of a muck spreader than a guitar … he gave the people what they wanted; songs about their own joys and sorrows, their exiles and reunions, their lovers and their mothers. Plus, Big Tom looked perfect. He wasn't a star symbol, but the opposite. Like John Wayne, he looked ordinary, only indestructibly so … Big Tom's face resembles the side of a mountain.[8]

Fans were shocked and the world of Irish country music was rocked in April 1975 when McBride announced he was leaving The Mainliners to form a new band called the Travellers. (The Mainliners played their last date together at the Lilac Ballroom in Enniskean, West Cork, on Sunday 4 May.) For some time there were criticisms that the new outfit could not match the sound created by The Mainliners, but the new recruits bedded down and Big Tom's success continued undiminished. John Glenn was recruited to take his place in The Mainliners and went on to have a very good innings.

In 1980 McBride recorded his first album of original material in Nashville. He travelled by boat because of his fear of flying; he returned unimpressed by the Nashville Sound pioneered by Chet Atkins. McBride later said he believed the album – *Blue Wings* – would have been better if it had been recorded in Ireland with producers and musicians used to the Irish country sound. McBride later built his own recording studio in Castleblaney and never again changed from his own production code, having further hit singles in the 1980s with 'Streets of Dublin City' (1981), 'If I Needed You' (1984) and 'Jealous Heart' (1984).

McBride has had personal difficulties, all of which he has managed to surmount. In 1992 he was accused of sexual abuse by Geraldine Shields from Crossmaglen, County Armagh. She claimed they had commenced a sexual relationship when she was fourteen and that it had only ended ten years later, when she became pregnant. Shields contended they had a child together and, according to her initial submission to the court, McBride paid for an abortion. But the case eventually fell apart and Shields apologised for making false allegations. It was a difficult time for McBride and his family, but with huge support from his fan base he got through it. Following the collapse of the case, McBride's star shone even brighter, and he continued to perform in Ireland and in emigrant centres throughout the world to adoring audiences.

Journalist Michael Commins, a long-time friend of McBride, saw the singer perform in the Galtymore Ballroom in London in 2004. He wrote about the show in the *Western People*:

It was a throwback to the golden years of the showband era. A swaying crowd in the Galtymore as the famous Cricklewood venue echoed once more to the sounds of one of the most famous bands that ever played the venue … Big Tom and the Mainliners. The Monaghan combination were back in town and it was celebration time for the Irish exiles. This was a night to cherish and the followers came from many parts of England … On a night when even the walls were sweating, happy faces reflected the happiness of a people who came to give thanks and pay homage to a man who has touched the lives of so many since back in the mid-1960s.[9]

Commins was enthralled by the welcome given to his friend:

How can you fathom such unswerving loyalty over four decades? It has to go beyond the ordinary bounds of 'followers'. Big Tom has managed to maintain an extraordinary bond with his friends that goes right to the heart. I would challenge anyone in the country, and especially those who don't like his music, to spend a half an hour in the company of Big Tom and to come away not liking the man. In the virtues of tolerance and patience, he has hardly any equals.[10]

The Galtymore, first opened in 1952, was – along with other venues such as the National in Kilburn, the Blarney Club in Tottenham Court Road, the Innisfree in Ealing and the Hibernian in Fulham Broadway – a haven for the Irish in London. As Ronan McGreevy wrote when it closed, it 'marks the end of an era as the Irish emigrant community in London has dwindled and gotten older while the younger generation has sought out more cosmopolitan venues'.[11] Big Tom spoke to McGreevy about the change:

It's gone, that London as far as the band is concerned. There is nowhere left that would pull a crowd that would justify us going over there in the first place. We noticed things started changing 12 or 14 years ago when people started to move back home, but the Galtymore always seemed to be the one holding its own. It was the one that stood the test of time down through the years. The ones that used to go to the dances in the Galtymore have married and settled down and their families are all reared. They would not be as anxious to go dancing as they might have been 10 or 20 years ago.[12]

McBride spoke again of the night to Mary Kennedy on RTÉ Television's *Nationwide*, in an episode marking his eightieth birthday:

> It was probably one of the saddest nights I ever played. That night the place was packed full. The people were dancing around and coming near the end of the night they were dancing around with tears in their eyes because they knew the club was going … it was a sad night, a very sad night.[13]

Despite suffering a heart attack at the age of seventy in 2006, Big Tom still continued to perform. In 2009 he completed a tour of Ireland to packed houses. Sadly, two days after the last concert in Ennis, County Clare, trombone player and vocalist Cyril McKevitt died of a heart attack.

In 2011 Ronan Casey went to The Marquee in Drumlish music festival in County Longford, made famous by country singer Declan Nerney. It was McBride's first appearance there in more than forty years. Casey commented:

> When introduced on stage by Nerney the roar is like that accompanying a last-minute winning goal. Delighted to be on stage, the beaming singer is still a giant of a man, his large frame shadowing that of the rest of the band. … There can be no doubt that age has left its mark on Tom, the face more wrinkled than that of old, the voice an octave or two lower and he doesn't sing every song (one in every three), but he still possesses the quintessential Irish country and western voice and the Castleblaney man's enthusiasm and gentle manner on stage would put many's the more youthful act to shame.[14]

Early in 2016 the residents' committee of Cong, County Mayo, announced that Big Tom, along with fellow Irish-country singer Daniel O'Donnell, would have his hands cast in bronze and mounted as part of the Cong 'Hands of Fame' project later in the year. The evening of Friday 8 July was wet and cold in Cong village. The crowds waited expectantly in the grey drizzle for the appearance of the two stars. Despite the weather, the mood was jovial and celebratory, with music provided by local artists. The Balla Pipe Band led the singers and a procession of dignitaries to the 'Wall of Fame' located beside the famous statue erected in acknowledgement of the Hollywood film *The Quiet Man*. It was a beautiful setting for the evening's proceedings, despite the rain. All agreed the sculpted bronze impressions of both singers' hands were excellent, and then the freedom of Cong was conferred on the singers – an honour which allowed them the right to exercise their ducks around the streets of Cong for the rest of their lives if they so desired. Daniel O'Donnell amused the crowd when he expressed his delight at having the prospect of a future with a constant supply of duck eggs. Big Tom entertained the crowd with renditions of three of his most iconic songs: 'Gentle Mother', 'Four Country Roads' and 'Going Out the Same Way You Came In'. The fans were delighted and many danced in the rain that evening in Cong. It was a truly Irish celebration of Irish country music and it was clear to all that Big Tom was still the king.

There is a general consensus among all those interviewed for this book: there may be critics but even the harshest acknowledges the lasting contribution the Castleblaney man has made to country music in Ireland. As the music strays ever more away from the roots, it is likely the music of Big Tom will become more valued and will be seen as the bedrock of a unique cultural folk music. Surely it is worth a wager that a song such as 'Lonesome at Your Table' will stand the test of time in what is increasingly becoming a disposable and, in the words of singer Brian Coll, 'synthetic' product.

In May 2017 Big Tom released 'A Love That's Lasted Through the

Years', a duet with fellow long-time-Irish-country-music-artist Margo. The unwavering worship that Tom McBride instilled in so many fans for so long is fittingly reflected in the words:

> Darling I still love you more than words can ever say
> The years we've spent together seen our love grow more each day
> I guess we are the lucky ones to find a love so true
> It seems like only yesterday that we both said I do.

So many said yes to the Monaghan man and his fellow troubadours and have followed them for so long that to tell the story of country music in Ireland without mentioning Big Tom would be like discussing the Catholic Church without mentioning the pope. Everyone seems to have an opinion of, or a story about, Big Tom and his music.

Paschal Mooney has an interesting story about the clash of Irish rock and roll and Irish country music. He was tasked with driving Phil Lynott and the other members of rock band Thin Lizzy from Dublin to a gig in Limerick. On the way back to the capital they passed a marquee where Big Tom was playing. Phil Lynott, long jaded by the excesses of the rock lifestyle, asked Mooney to stop. He told Mooney he did not like country music but made an exception for McBride, because 'he wasn't trying to copy anyone else and he seemed a humble man'.[15]

Charlie McGettigan – the highly regarded singer-songwriter, former Eurovision Song Contest winner and radio presenter on *Shannonside Northern Sound* – has had a bird's-eye view of the Irish country music scene for decades. His songwriting has crossed genres, but a number of country artists have recorded his songs with success. Ray Lynam alone recorded three ('A Bed for the Night', 'Until the End of Time' and 'I'll Never Get over You'), while Daniel O'Donnell has had success with 'When Hope Dawns at Sunrise', and Mary Duff with 'If Anything Happened to You'. McGettigan is also a board member of the Irish Music Rights Organisation

(IMRO), a body which administers the performing rights in copyright music in Ireland on behalf of songwriters, composers and music publishers. His take on Big Tom McBride, which he gave to me in September 2017, is illuminating and a good summary of the views expressed by many:

> I didn't get Big Tom until I went to see him and stood down in the crowd. He is one of them. He doesn't apologise for what he is. What you see is what you get … he is exactly what it says on the tin. I could see the physical reaction of the people to the songs like 'Gentle Mother'. You have to be there to know. People would stop and look up at Tom and you don't often see that. The vast majority of the time everyone dances. The songs are sentimental but everyone has a mother and the people believed him when he sang and knew that he felt the same way. It's very hard to fully understand why a song works for people and why a singer can get a message across. Big Tom is able to get into the mind of the listener. He is the genuine article. Whatever 'it' is, Big Tom has it.[16]

Gerald O'Donoghue, owner of Greenfields Studios, has been at the forefront of the Irish country music industry for nearly forty years and is eloquent in his thoughts on Tom McBride:

> First of all there was the sound. They had that perfect dancing beat and the musicians could all do their piece well. Secondly the thing about Tom McBride is the massive respect he had for his fans and they responded to that. After a Big Tom concert you'd see him sit on the edge of the stage and talk to people for a few hours. Who else would you see do that with the exception of one or two? They were special.[17]

Nationwide's eightieth birthday celebration show for McBride was substantially filmed in his capacious house – a house dominated by the themes of family and music. The singer brought the show's presenter,

Mary Kennedy, into his 'trophy room', where reminders of his long career covered all the surfaces and most of the walls. 'Music is the prayer the heart sings' scrolled across the wall above a painting of the man himself. Kennedy asked the singer about the many fans who come to visit him. 'We get people coming from all around the country,' he said. 'They're all awful nice people. I think you'll find that with people that like country music, there's no badness in them.'

Kevin McCooey, long-time manager of The Mainliners, had a unique take on the appeal of the Monaghan man for the presenter: 'I think it's the fatherly figure that he is … people felt like he was a dad to them.'

The show finished with Kennedy asking McBride about the appeal of country music, to which, after a few moments' thought, he eloquently replied:

> There's a tear in country music and even to this day I sing songs that you could feel a lump in your throat because you're picturing what they were all about down through the years. I love singing those songs and I can sing them from the heart and I love to think that I put a feeling into them … I don't think there's anything else I like more than the music because the music has been very good to me. I hope to do it for a while more.[18]

Big Tom McBride, the king of Irish country music, departed to his eternal reward on 17 April 2018, having been predeceased by his wife, Rose, the previous January. His death brought down the curtains on a singular era of Irish culture and the outpourings across the nation of both grief and appreciation for his life were remarkable. He had left his mark on the genre like no other artist before him. There is no doubt his likes will not be seen again. His funeral, with its lengthy graveside musical tribute by top artists from the Irish country music world, was the very definition of a happy type of sadness.

6

THREE QUEENS OF IRISH COUNTRY MUSIC

It wasn't God who made honky tonk angels
As you said in the words of your song
Too many times married men think they're still single
And that's caused many a good girl to go wrong.

From 'It Wasn't God Who Made Honky Tonk Angels'
sung by Kitty Wells[1]

On the 2017 *Late Late Show Country Music Special*, host Ryan Tubridy introduced three women to the audience as the 'Queens of Irish Country Music'. Between them they had spent a total of 149 years on the circuit in Ireland and further afield: Philomena Begley had been plying her musical wares for fifty-five years, Donegal's Margo O'Donnell for fifty-three and Susan McCann for forty-one. These three grand dames of the scene entertained the audience and viewing public with their bawdy good humour, throaty laughs and tales from the world of Irish country music. When Tubridy asked them about the difficulties for women in the industry, Margo told a story about a time she was performing at the Moylough Carnival in County Galway, where she went outside the tent to try to find a toilet. One of the organisers asked if she was looking for something, to which she replied she was 'looking for the ladies'. She was given a short and simple instruction: 'Put your bum to the wind.'[2]

The three women flirted with Tubridy and intimated that all types of shenanigans had been taking place backstage during the course of the evening. When Margo praised Tubridy for his good looks, he questioned her motives and she replied sharply: 'I don't want to have to spell it out to you but any Friday night … although you'll have to take a back seat if Big Tom is around!' Big Tom, a long-time friend and occasional singing partner of Margo, was sitting in the front of the audience and smiled broadly.

The women told Tubridy, who was looking worried as to what they might come out with next, that they all would have liked to have been nurses if circumstances were otherwise.

'Imagine the sort of hospital that would be,' the nervous-looking host said.

'At least we'd have been able to sing them all to sleep,' Margo chimed in. Then the Donegal singer started to tell him that she could tell all sorts of stories if she got talking about the times the three women were in Nashville. Tubridy looked increasingly discombobulated, but in the end Margo told a benign story about having to lie on a floor to show Philomena Begley the lyrics of a song she was having difficulty committing to memory.

'Aye, I was always a bit of a slow learner,' replied Begley, chuckling.

From the interaction and joking among the three women it was clear they had a deep sense of collegiality; they were a trio who had travelled the same dusty highways and byways for many years. All were in agreement about the significance of Irish country music in binding together Irish communities overseas, and they spoke movingly of the contribution of the British ballrooms – particularly those in London like the Galtymore and the Hibernian – to keeping the spirits of Irish people up when times were tough. They explained that their music forged a link with Ireland for those Irish who were in the unfortunate position of not being able to come home if they wished to, because of the prevailing economic conditions in Ireland. Big Tom had earlier echoed their sentiments when asked by Tubridy to explain the appeal of the music. The women talked and agreed about the great times to be had in Britain, particularly during Lent because of the Catholic Church's decree that there should be no performances throughout those six weeks in Ireland. They were singing off the same musical sheet, albeit a country one.

For much of its history, the journey for women in country music has been more challenging than that of the men. The first ever number-one *Billboard* country hit for a female country artist in the United States was Kitty Wells' 1952 hit 'It Wasn't God Who Made Honky Tonk Angels'. This song was a response to Hank Thompson's 'The Wild Side of Life', in which he criticised a former female lover lured to the 'glamor of the gay night life ... where the wine and liquor flows'.[3] Wells' song said that women would not be submissive to men any longer, nor would they accept men's crooked ways. Women who did go wrong were led astray by married men looking for flings and affairs, not through their own lack of morals. It was a show of strength and a call to arms, and, falteringly, it led the way for other women to enter the male-dominated country music industry: among them Dolly Parton, Patsy Cline, Loretta Lynn and Tammy Wynette.

'It Wasn't God Who Made Honky Tonk Angels' was a daring statement to make in a conservative era when women's liberation was only a distant dream for many. The NBC radio network in the United States banned the song for being 'suggestive', and Wells was prohibited from performing on the *Grand Ole Opry*. This did not hold back her career, however, and she died the American 'Queen of Country Music' at the age of ninety-two in 2012.

Like Wells, the three queens of Irish country music successfully overcame the challenges the music industry presented. With its late hours and frequent travel, the life can be difficult to sustain over a long period, but Margo, Philomena Begley and Susan McCann have, in the spirit of many Irish country music artists, forged remarkably enduring careers.

***

Songs in praise of fellow artists have always been a popular subgenre of American country music; when Waylon Jennings sang 'Are You Sure Hank Done It This Way' or Johnny Cash launched into 'The Night Hank Williams Came to Town' the audience response invariably confirmed the respect which fans of the genre hold for the greats. So when Susan McCann released 'Big Tom Is Still The King' in 1977 – a reworking by Michael Commins of the Waylon Jennings song 'Bob Wills Is Still The King', which praised the Texan singer known as the 'King of Western Swing' – she had a surprise hit, selling more than 100,000 records and announcing the arrival of a huge new talent in the Irish country music industry. At home relaxing after a few tough gigs, her voice sounds a bit strained, but other than that she feels great, she says. She is happy to talk on the phone, and Susan McCann can talk as well as she can sing.[4]

Patricia Susan Mary McCann – the 'First Lady of Irish Country Music' – was born in 1949 in Carrickasticken, Forkhill, County Armagh. Before coming to national prominence, she had been playing with her husband, Dennis Heaney, around Newry, County Down – first in the John Murphy Country Céilí Band and subsequently with a group called the Fairylanders. The show-business impresario Tony Loughman, who also managed Philomena Begley, had been impressed by Susan's singing and invited her to join his group of artists at Top Spin Records. Loughman had previously had the name Fairylanders registered in his office with a singer from Cavan called Ian Corrigan, according to Susan. His band had just broken up and Loughman transferred the name to McCann's newly formed group of musicians.

McCann's distinctive, strong and driving northern voice was a perfect vehicle for country music and soon brought the fans out in huge numbers.

Her 1977 single 'Big Tom Is Still The King' was a stirring, upbeat tribute to her near neighbour, by that time the long-time undisputed premier artist in Irish country music. It launched her career when it went to number one in May of that year. The upbeat anthem placed Big Tom at the pinnacle of country music in Ireland:

> I'd drive one hundred miles to hear that voice so warm and kind
> And I can still recall now the first time I heard him sing
> I feel proud to be from 'Blaney where Big Tom is still the King
>
> You can have your Waylon Jennings or Nashville's Charley Pride
> They boast of all their superstars but for us it's Tom McBride
> Oh Nashville is so far away it scarcely means a thing
> But when you're in old Ireland Big Tom is still the King.

McCann pointed out a factual inaccuracy in the song: 'I was managed from an office in Castleblaney. I never actually lived there, despite what the song says.'

During her illustrious career McCann has appeared at the Grand Ole Opry House and the Royal Albert Hall, performed five times at the Wembley Country Music Festival, entertained United States Presidents George H. W. Bush and George W. Bush, and appeared three times on *Good Morning South Africa*, a hugely popular television programme. Her rise to popularity in South Africa was whimsical:

> My husband, Dennis, was at a record conference in France and he met an agent from South Africa, who invited us over. The first time we went to go over there we had to turn back halfway because the plane had gone into some airspace it shouldn't have. We got there the next time. Anyway for some reason my music took off over there. It was a strange place with the apartheid and that. I haven't been back there in years, but I might get there yet.[5]

She also spoke about meeting the younger Bush: 'He was a nice man, yeah. I gave him a copy of a CD and told him to have a listen to it if he got a chance. He's from Texas so he must know a bit about country music,' she said, once more accompanied by a throaty chuckle.[6]

Despite a life-threatening car crash and problems with her throat, McCann – in true country music fashion – has persevered and gone from success to success. In 1980 she recorded *Susan McCann in Nashville* in Fireside Studios, Nashville, which was owned by American country music stars Porter Wagoner and Dolly Parton. She also appeared on Wagoner's syndicated country music programme while there. Winning the European Gold Star, Europe's premier TV country music talent contest, in 1982, with the song 'While I Was Making Love to You', provided her with a further major career boost. In 1988 McCann had the honour of being the first non-American to perform on stage at Dollywood – the entertainment park established by Dolly Parton. She was also the first non-American artist to headline the famous Strawberry Festival in Tampa, Florida, when she played alongside superstar American artists Garth Brooks and Travis Tritt in 1991.

Susan McCann discussed her show-business life with Lisa McHugh on *On the Road with Lisa*, on the now-defunct Irish TV cable station, in 2015. She recalled filling dance halls with more than 1,000 people at the height of the showband era. Termon, County Donegal, had a capacity of 900 people, she said, and they 'would be hanging from the rafters'.[7] When I'm talking to her, she bemoans the recent lack of females in the Irish country music industry: 'It's funny but there were more women in it in my day than there is now, although it was never easy. There's a lot more to distract people nowadays too. Technology has changed everything.'[8]

In March 2006 McCann told Paddy Kehoe of the *RTÉ Guide* how her father used to give out to her for her talkativeness when she was a child: 'Susan would you ever shut your mouth. You've a tongue for ten rows of teeth.'[9] But her natural communication skills and homespun loquaciousness have paid off handsomely. Her biggest-selling singles include 'When the Sun Says Goodbye to the Mountains' (1983), 'Fantasize My Freedom' (1986), 'Old Dublin in My Tears' (1988), 'Broken Speed (of the Sound of Loneliness)' (1989) and 'The String of Diamonds' (1991). In more recent times she had a hit with 'Old Man on the Porch' (2014). 'When the Sun Says Goodbye to the Mountains' – written in 1936 by Harry Pease and Larry Vincent – had the distinction of reaching number one in Holland, where country music has always had a strong following. When sung by McCann in her crystal-clear voice, this country gospel number is far removed from her famous tribute to Big Tom, but the international attraction is immediately evident.

During the 1990s McCann teamed up with singer Sean Wilson to record 'King & Queen of Irish Country Music', a record which sold more than 250,000. In June 1994 she sang to 5,000 people in Saint Petersburg, Russia, as part of a 'White Nights Festival'. The year 2016 was her fortieth on the Irish music circuit.

When asked by author Brian Carthy in 1991 for a 'star comment' for her biographical pen-picture, she expressed a desire to see an end to the Troubles in Northern Ireland: 'I long for peace in our country and wish health and happiness for everyone.'[10] It is great to see her wish come true and that times have moved on from the dreadful era when artists and bands from the Republic of Ireland would not travel to Northern Ireland to perform.

Nowadays McCann spends as much time as she can with her five grandchildren: 'My granddaughter Laura is starting to get involved with the singing so I help her along. Her mother Linda is the Head of Music at the local school so they all have a bit of it.' She would have no problem, she says, encouraging any of her grandchildren to get involved in the music industry. 'There's no reason they shouldn't just as long as they have someone to look out for their best interests. I was lucky because I had Dennis from the start, so they'd definitely need a hand there.'[11] One senses that with Susan McCann, they would have a formidable presence in their corner.

***

Margaret Catherine O'Donnell – universally known as Margo – was born on 6 February 1951 in Kincasslagh, County Donegal, and is widely known as the 'Queen of Irish Country Music'. Brian Carthy wrote in 1991 that she was 'as much a part of the Irish entertainment scene as the mountains and rivers are part of her beloved Donegal'.[12] Margo is unapologetically the most quintessential Irish country singer of the three queens discussed in this chapter, and is the nearest female equivalent to Big Tom McBride in her preoccupation with themes of home and hearth. Margo's voice is a perfect vehicle for telling stories of love and loss. Her enunciation is clear; the inherent sadness in much of the music comes through without any need to over-adorn the production. Like Big Tom's, once her distinctive northern voice is heard it will never be mistaken – another direct link to the bedrock sound of the Ulster Scots lineage of the music.

Only fourteen when she first performed with local showband the Keynotes, Margo had just turned seventeen when her first single, 'Bonny Irish Boy/Dear God', was released in 1968. It was at a gig in the Mulroy Ballroom in Kerrykeel in Donegal that she acquired her name. When the band arrived for the show they were confronted with a sign reading 'Appearing tonight, Margo and the Keynotes'; Margaret was no more. Her intention of becoming a nurse was sidelined and, with the blessing of her parents, she took to the road with the band. Her second single, '(If I Could See the World through) the Eyes of a Child/Road by the River' (1968), brought her to wider attention, but, tragically, her father died on the weekend the record was released. This, she later often said, affected her deeply and aggravated personal problems.

In 1969 Margo joined the Country Folk band; her younger siblings were dependent on her for financial support and she was offered the then substantial sum of £100 a week, as well as a car and a driver to take her to her shows, to move to the new band. Very shortly after she joined, they had a number-one hit with the old Irish ballad 'I'll Forgive and I'll Try to Forget' (1970) – her weekly wage doubled immediately. In 1971 she was voted the Irish Female Vocalist of the Year. The following year she was invited to play at the Wembley International Festival of Country Music alongside such stars as Loretta Lynn, Conway Twitty and Tom T. Hall.

In 1973 Margo left the Country Folk and, after a short-lived stint with another band, Margo and Co., she joined Mattie Fox to form Country Pride. Following some health scares, she joined Larry Cunningham and his Country Blues Band in 1975 and they had the hit 'Yes Mr Peters'. Eventually she went on the road with her own band.

During her career, which has lasted for more than fifty years, Margo has had problems with alcoholism, depression and financial mismanagement. In 2006 she told Joe Jackson that her father had asked her to look after the family after his death – a request which proved a heavy psychological burden and, she reckoned, contributed to her alcoholism. She also told the journalist of her memories of her father working in Scotland. Even though her parents were married for twenty years, her mother said that she had only lived with him for thirteen months, because of his coming and going.[13]

Margo had a mild heart attack in 2014, just two weeks after her mother died; later in the same year she published her autobiography, *Margo, Queen of Country & Irish: The Promise and the Dream*. In it she described how her then-manager John McNally sold all her previous recordings to Outlet Records in Belfast for £37,500.[14] The transaction was made from the boot of one car to another and the singer was never consulted. Margo later took the case to court. It was settled in her favour in 2002, but she had lost out on substantial royalties in the meantime.

Margo also revealed in her book that she had been the victim of a sex attack in 1970 at the age of twenty. At the time she had regular blackouts as a result of a serious car crash. She explained:

After singing one night, I felt dizzy and had one of my blackouts and as I was coming round, this man, whom I knew, was performing a lewd act in my presence and though I was never physically raped, I was forced to perform a sex act on this person.[15]

It destroyed her self-esteem, she wrote, and she described herself as 'feeling dirty' for a long time afterwards. She went on to outline the effects of the attack: 'Abuse can take many forms and this event affected me very badly. I couldn't sleep and was prescribed sleeping pills which I took for a long time to blot out these horrible memories that raged inside me.'

On an appearance on *The Late Late Show* Margo was asked about her sexuality by Ryan Tubridy – over the years there have been unsubstantiated rumours that Margo is gay and also that she has had multiple abortions. She memorably replied that 'bread on bread is dry eating … if you have a slice of bread and put another slice on top of it without something in the middle it would be kind of dry'.[16]

In 2014 Margo O'Donnell celebrated fifty years in the Irish music industry. In an interview with *The Irish Sun*, she addressed the long-circulated rumour that she is Daniel O'Donnell's mother (he is her brother):

I first heard it after a concert when a fan said to me, 'Your son isn't as good a singer as you'. I felt so sad for my mother over it, wondering about how it made her feel with people saying these things. I said to my mother before she died last year that I was going to address it and she told me I should.[17]

Margo would have had to have given birth at ten years of age to be Daniel's mother.

In 2007 Margo was proud to receive the 'Donegal Person of the Year' award. She is still on the road. She has always had a huge fan base among the Irish community in Britain. Being from Donegal, an area which has long suffered from its geographic remoteness, her songs of exile and longing for the home country are particularly credible and moving. The long list of songs she has recorded on themes of emigration include 'Goodbye Johnny Dear', 'Back Home to Donegal', 'The Green Hills of Sligo' and 'Isle of Ireland'. Like Big Tom, she is a shrewd analyst of the contribution of Irish music to exiles; following the closure of the famous Galtymore Ballroom she spoke to the *Derry Journal*:

> People do not realise the importance of the Galtymore to many Donegal people and indeed people from all over the country. This was one of the few places that people who were forced to emigrate could meet with their friends and find a small 'piece of Ireland' in a strange city. It really saved lives – people from remote areas of Donegal, Mayo, Galway and Kerry lived for the weekend at the Galtymore. Without that all important Friday and Saturday night many would have felt totally alone and many would [have] fallen into depression. It was their home from home and kept the spirits high in difficult times.
>
> Younger people today do not realise the impact of the Galtymore on the Irish community. These were pre-Ryanair days when you went to London, you probably went for good. It was not just a matter of hopping back and forward for the weekend or to work as it is today. Many people never saw their native shores again – all they had was their memories and the Galtymore kept those memories alive …
>
> Many met at the Galtymore and many married in the same venue – the Galtymore was an Irish institution. It was ironically probably the only place in Ireland which did not recognise borders or religious differences even though it was located in Cricklewood. It crossed all boundaries and if you were Irish you were Irish and that was it. That was the only criteria needed.[18]

Contemporary Irish country singer Declan Nerney paid tribute to Margo in a 'What Others Say' chapter in her autobiography, highlighting the significance of her music to emigrant communities and substantiating the thoughts she expressed to Ryan Tubridy. He had, he said:

> … come to realise how important those melodic tones of Margo were back then … to the thousands of our fellow Irish emigrant brothers and sisters in nurturing their sanity, their calling from home, their dietary musical feed of all things Irish when they congregated to see her perform at dance venues in London, New York, Boston, Birmingham, and even Dublin …[19]

Nerney recalled a concert in the west of Ireland where Margo had performed:

> She instantly had the audience in the heart of her hand. Her connection and her charisma with the assembled company is something the books and the learned men of top proficiency don't possess. There is no doubt about it that my good and lifelong friend is the true Queen of Country and Irish music.[20]

Father Brian D'Arcy noted the similarity between Margo and Big Tom McBride:

> They both became superstars by being themselves. What you see is what you get. They were successful entertainers because we knew they believed what they were singing – indeed the songs they sang so passionately retold stories they could identify with.[21]

As a family friend D'Arcy knows the triumphs and tragedies of Margo's life:

> [W]hen she stood on the stage and entertained the thousands who came to see her, they accepted her as one of their own. Her music, her storytelling

ability, her sincerity, mean that she communicated at a deep level with her fans' own experiences. They were at one.[22]

Big Tom McBride also spoke about Margo, putting it straight, as is his style:

Margo was the first Irish & Country singer I ever listened to … she has always picked songs with a nice story and, like myself, there was always a tear in the story of every song she sang. Margo has a beautiful touch of feeling for the old Country music and it is a touch of magic that she has in her voice. Margo sings a song like no other, I think the word I'm looking for is – unique.[23]

Margo O'Donnell has made a huge contribution to Irish country music and popular culture, and, as long as she continues to perform, she is guaranteed a devoted and loyal following. She is quite simply, as Big Tom said, unique. It is appropriate to leave the last word to Margo herself:

I can honestly say that Margo has stood the test of time. Margo the singer or entertainer or whatever people want to call me is still in big demand to this day and that, I think, says it all. My ever-loyal fans and friends keep me going and I'm always so very grateful. Margo, the Kincasslagh lass born on 6 February 1951, is doing okay; she is rich with friendship and loves the simple life.[24]

**

Philomena Begley, born in Pomeroy, County Tyrone, in 1942, was the fourth of eight children. She is widely regarded as having one of the very best authentic voices in the history of Irish country music. She is, after all, from the very heart of the original home of the Irish dimension of country music – the land of the Ulster Scots, which American superstar Porter Wagoner said provided the best country voice he had heard outside the United States. Following a short spell working in Fishers' hat factory in Cookstown after she left school at fifteen, she started her singing career with the Old Cross Céilí Showband in 1962 – another country singer who cut her teeth in the céilí-band scene. Her first gig arose from a dare in a local hall, an event she recounted to Brian Carthy as her 'abiding childhood memory'.[25] She sang a duet with her friend Mary McConnell at Clarrie Hayden's Travelling Show, winning ten shillings. The band and the audience were impressed, and she was offered a job full time; the Old Cross released three records in 1968 and 1969 with limited success. Following a change of name to the Country Flavour – in keeping with the country music boom of the late 1960s and early 1970s – in 1971 their fortunes changed, when 'Here Today, Gone Tomorrow' reached number seven, spending nine weeks in the Irish charts. It was country music all the way after that, and Philomena and her band took to the highways and byways of Ireland with increasing success. In 1972 they had a further hit with 'Never Again (Will I Knock on Your Door)', which peaked at number fifteen and spent a total of four weeks in the charts.

In 1974 Begley formed The Ramblin' Men, and in the same year married Tom Quinn, the piano and accordion player in the band. The band was under the shrewd management of Tony Loughman, who would go on to be a big player in the music management and promotion business, bringing American stars such as Porter Wagoner and Tom T. Hall to Ireland. Shortly after their formation, the band was invited by Hank Locklin to Nashville, where they recorded three albums. Locklin – a classic honky-tonk singer whose hits included 'Send Me the Pillow That You Dream On' and 'Please Help Me, I'm Falling' – had a loyal following in Ireland; in 1963 he recorded an album called *Irish Songs, Country Style*, which included 'If We Only Had Old Ireland Over Here', 'I'll Take You Home Again Kathleen', 'When Irish Eyes Are Smiling' and 'The Old Bog Road'. Until his death in 2009 at the age of ninety-one, he was the oldest member of the *Grand Ole Opry*; an obituary in British newspaper *The Times* described him as 'the last remaining link between country music's hillbilly roots and the lusher, modern pop sound of Nashville'.[26]

Begley had further hits with 'Light in the Window' (1973), 'Wait a Little Longer Please, Jesus' (1974), 'Once Around the Dance Floor' (1976) and 'For the First Time in a Long Time' (1977). She also recorded a number of successful and poignant duets with fellow Irish country artist Ray Lynam, of which 'My Elusive Dreams' is the best known. Begley and Lynam are perhaps the two purest country voices on the Irish scene and Shane MacGowan of The Pogues, viewed by many as the most gifted Irish songwriter of his generation, famously referenced the duet in his song 'A Pair of Brown Eyes'.[27]

In 1975 Begley had the biggest hit of her career with a rollicking version of the Billie Jo Spears song 'Blanket on the Ground'. Even though Spears released her version of the country classic at the same time in Ireland, it was Begley who had the greater success. The song stayed in the charts for five weeks, topping out at number five – a significant achievement as the charts were musically undifferentiated, with all genres under the same heading. Begley received a standing ovation for her performance of the song at the Grand Ole Opry when invited to perform there by Porter Wagoner in 1978. A few years later she met Spears at a country music festival in Peterborough and, according to the Tyrone woman's often-repeated account, it was not a pleasant encounter. Philomena did not recognise Spears at first, but when the American heard Begley's name her reply was abrupt: 'Are you the bitch that stole my song?' However, they soon settled their differences, became close friends and later toured together as the 'Queens of Country'. After Spears' passing in 2011, Philomena Begley released 'My Friend Billie Jo', which was played at the deceased singer's burial.

On 13 April 1987 RTÉ Television broadcast an episode of *Evening Extra* profiling a day in the life of Begley. She had been twenty-five years on the road at that time. The day began at 8.30 a.m., when she was getting her children ready for school. Sometime later in the day, she drove to Dublin to prepare for a performance that night. When her two-hour show in the Ierne Ballroom ended, she drove back to her home in Tyrone, arriving there well after 4 a.m. She would do the same the following day. She told presenter Patricia Murphy, 'I love it. It's my life really. I couldn't give it up. If I had to give it up I do believe I'd be wrecked. It wouldn't suit me at all. I thrive on it.'[28]

Begley went on to explain that she could never see herself as a star and for a time stardom caused her to have an 'inferiority complex'; she was 'more comfortable in herself' by the time the documentary was made, although she still felt uncomfortable in front of the television camera and meeting 'important people':

I could never see myself as different from anyone else. To me I was just Philomena Begley. I do believe I will always feel the same way … I wouldn't be one of these people that have to keep up with the Joneses. I do my own thing and if they don't like what they see, I couldn't be bothered trying to live up to a big star's image.[29]

Begley also spoke of her regrets at having left school early, a fact she has mentioned a number of times over the years.

Begley sang a highly praised version of her hit 'The Way Old Friends Do' at the funeral of fellow singer and Tyrone native Gene Stuart. The song had originally featured on ABBA's album *Super Trouper*; Begley's version was her biggest-selling song in Great Britain. She was asked by Tom Gilmore about the song, and explained:

My brother Kieran bought an ABBA album with 'The Way Old Friends Do' and I just kept playing it and playing it. I got the idea to put a wee Country feel to it and we tried it out with amazing success. It went down really well, especially with audiences all over the UK at the theatre shows and as the old saying goes, the rest is history.[30]

It was a fitting farewell to Gene Stuart.

In her long singing career, Begley has appeared on stage with many American country stars, including Roy Acuff, Ernest Tubb, Minnie Pearl, Marty Robbins, Don Williams, Charley Pride and Charlie Daniels. Tom Gilmore even recalled an occasion where she played on the same bill as the Bay City Rollers:

> It was back about the time that Phil was at the peak of her popularity for songs such as 'Ramblin' Man' or 'Truck Driving Sweetheart' that she was also voted by readers of Irish Pop magazine *New Spotlight* as the Top Female Country singer and booked to appear on the same stage with Teenybopper stars The Bay City Rollers. When the Scottish stars were late in arriving at the Pop awards concert in Dublin Philomena was given the onerous task of taming the teenyboppers who were surging towards the stage screaming for their Pop idols. Other singers might have flinched from this task, but not so Philomena. She went out centre stage and belted out some of her biggest Country hits and won the hearts of the teens too.[31]

Begley had her most recent hit singles with 'She Sang the Melody' in May 1985 and 'Dear Santa' in December 1988. The latter reached a respectable number eleven and stayed in the charts for three weeks.

Philomena Begley is thus far the only star of the Irish country music scene to be inducted into the British Country Music Hall of Fame. In 2013 she became the thirtieth inductee. These days she still plays the occasional gig and short tour.

***

The trio of Margo, Philomena Begley and Susan McCann have had startlingly long careers. Their origins are in keeping with the heritage of country music, with Begley and McCann from Northern Ireland and Margo from neighbouring Donegal, providing further evidence that the wellspring of the genre lies north of the Irish border and in the adjacent areas. None of these women are prolific touring artists any more, but they continue to entertain from time to time in differing circumstances and all make appearances on an ongoing basis. Each has left a substantial mark on the Irish country music landscape. However, it was to be a member of Margo O'Donnell's family who would rise to levels never seen before in terms of record sales and popularity in country music in Ireland and Britain combined. From the periphery of the Donegal coast, a man came to the centre of the Irish country music world and, as was the case with his sister, only his Christian name had to be mentioned to evoke a response – albeit mostly in a quiet way and largely among an older female demographic. The man's name came from the Hebrew meaning 'God is my judge'. The people sat in judgement and found him a worthy successor to those who went before him. He was the anointed one: his name was Daniel.

7

THE RISE AND RISE
OF 'WEE' DANIEL O'DONNELL

You could hear the screams from miles around
The night Daniel O'Donnell came to town

From 'The Night Daniel O'Donnell Came to Town'
by Louise Morrissey[1]

If imitation is the best form of flattery, then Daniel Francis Noel O'Donnell must be the happiest singer ever born in Ireland. He has almost single-handedly kept a generation of impersonators and comedians in business; his ultrasoft-spoken manner, distinctive Donegal accent and smooth-limbed movements have long been imitated for cheap laughs. O'Donnell has been parodied in the media as, amongst other incarnations, country singer Eoin McLove in the popular Channel 4 comedy series *Father Ted* and Irish singer Donald O'Daniel on the BBC sketch show *Chewin' the Fat*, and is a perennial favourite on Today FM radio sketch show *Gift Grub*, where he is brought to life by comedian Mario Rosenstock.

Despite these parodies, Daniel O'Donnell still has probably the biggest fan base of all country music singers in the British Isles. His success is staggering and his musical presentation's uniqueness is such that, according to many commentators, his output might best be called 'Daniel music'. It is difficult to describe fully in words to the uninitiated O'Donnell's unique style – he has a sound that has to be heard to be fully appreciated. When he sings of home and place – and he has hundreds of such songs and scores about Donegal alone – as is the case with his sister, Margo, and with Big Tom McBride, the sound will never be forgotten. When the Donegal man brought out an album of Hank Williams songs, the renditions were the polar opposite of the raw, nasal sound of the original hillbilly hellraiser. O'Donnell's versions were soft, gentle and soothing, just like the singer himself. While he consistently mines the Irish country vein, O'Donnell is equally at home with gospel music, movie classics and his version of rock and roll. Whatever the song is, he reinvents it in his inimitable style: there really is no phrase for his prodigious output other than 'Daniel music'.

Born in 1961 in Kincasslagh in the Rosses, a beautifully elemental coastal region of County Donegal, Daniel O'Donnell was the first true megastar in the modern era of Irish country music. The youngest of five and a self-confessed mother's pet, particularly after his father died from a sudden heart attack at the age of forty-nine when he was just six, O'Donnell's memories of his father are limited and he has said that the death did not have the impact on him that it had on his older siblings, particularly his brother James – who was ten at the time – and his famous singing sister, Margo. He was brought up in his cousin's house without an indoor toilet or hot water until the age of six, but his experiences were not unique. Kincasslagh, like so many other villages on the west coast of Ireland, saw hard economic times; O'Donnell has mentioned that there was only one house in his village that had a bath and proper indoor toilet.

Whatever facilities the homesteads may have lacked, the cohesion and community spirit are what O'Donnell speaks of most fondly when asked about his early life. From the age of nine he worked in a local shop; this, he has often said, helped him become comfortable with people of all ages.

Any chance he got to sing, he took. The local Catholic church, where he sang in the choir, played a central role in the life of his family and he has consistently credited his love of inspirational music to this early experience.

'Wee Daniel', as he is affectionately known among his family members and legions of fans, remembers the moment he realised he wanted to sing professionally. He was fifteen and got up to sing 'The Boys from the County Armagh' – one of Irish singer Bridie Gallagher's best-known songs – in Ostan Na Rosann, a local hotel. O'Donnell told Barry Egan of the *Sunday Independent* about the occasion: 'I was looking at the people. They were all dancing. They were singing along with it. I could see a smile, happiness. I thought, "I'm really happy doing this. Wouldn't it be great to do this all the time?"'[2] It was a few more years before he was to fulfil his wish.

Following secondary school, O'Donnell went to the Regional Technical College in Galway (now the Galway–Mayo Institute of Technology) to take a course in business studies, with the intention of pursuing a career in banking, but dropped out before the end of the first term. He performed with his sister Margo from 1981 to 1983, before going solo. She advised him to think carefully about entering the music industry.

O'Donnell paid £1,200 to have four songs, including 'My Donegal Shore' and 'Stand Beside Me', professionally recorded in Big Tom's studio in Castleblaney in February 1983. He then sold all the copies himself, an early indication of the determination which was to bring his career to such heights. He famously sold copies to a group of pilgrims on a bus journey to Knock Shrine in County Mayo – even, as he has frequently said, to those who had no way of playing a copy. Despite the reservations of Margo and his great friend Philomena Begley, who told him to 'stick to the books', O'Donnell formed his own short-lived group called Country Fever, quickly followed by an outfit called the Grassroots, both of which met with limited success. It is difficult to imagine that Daniel O'Donnell ever had lean times, but his memories of the early days are bleak:

We had so many bad nights to begin with where we wouldn't get paid. You wouldn't get any money because no one turned up for the dances. You'd be taking the door as they termed it, and that meant what people paid in was your fee. But there were times when you'd be better taking the door that was hanging than what you got, because it would be worth more.[3]

In 1985 Sean Reilly, manager of Ritz Records, saw Daniel perform at an Irish festival in London and signed him up immediately. He remained O'Donnell's manager until his retirement in 2015, when he was replaced by Kieran Kavanagh.

Speaking to Barry Egan, O'Donnell recalled that on New Year's Eve 1985 he had played in the Farnham Arms Hotel in Cavan town, where he collected £163 on the door: 'There were only 40 people at the most.' But then something changed – O'Donnell himself can't seem to explain it: '"But then all of a sudden" – he clicks his fingers – "in 1986 …"' He recalls playing in the Milford Inn in Donegal in March 1986: 'I could hear people chanting my name. I was nearly frightened to come out. One of the band looked out and said to me, "Daniel, there's people everywhere." Stuffed. And from then on, that was how it was.' On the following year's New Year's Eve he was playing to 1,400 people. 'It was quite amazing. I had thought about giving up before that, before it started to happen for me.'[4]

Daniel O'Donnell's success has been phenomenal. After his first number one in Ireland with 'Take Good Care of Her' in 1987, his career moved into a higher orbit; by the end of the same year he had reached number one in the United Kingdom country chart with the album *Don't Forget to Remember*. Since then his career has gone from strength to strength.

In 1991 Brian Carthy wrote about the singer's career to that date and how he had changed the face of the industry:

Daniel O'Donnell is the 'Quiet King' of Country and Irish … he has transformed what some people had regarded as dated and old fashioned

… into the thriving industry it is today. The quiet and unassuming young man from the hills of Donegal has in the space of a few years captured the imagination of the dancing, concert going and record buying public and is unquestionably the success story of the eighties on the Country and Irish music scene … It is no overstatement to suggest that Daniel O'Donnell is likely to go down in history as the man who altered the thinking of a whole generation of Irish music lovers.[5]

Since his first appearance on *Top of the Pops* on the BBC in 1992 with the single 'I Just Wanna Dance With You' – which the singer considers a highlight of his career – O'Donnell has had twenty top-forty albums and fifteen top-forty singles in the United Kingdom. In 2015 he became the first artist to have a different album in the British charts for twenty-eight consecutive years, and over the course of his career he has sold more than ten million records there. There may be knockers of his laid-back, mellow style, but no other Irish country artist has come anywhere close to his level of sales or popularity.

The awards have come thick and fast for O'Donnell: Irish Recorded Music Association 'Entertainer of the Year' in 1989, 1992 and 1996; 'International Artist of the Year' at the British Country Music Awards in 1991, 1992 and 1995; and an 'Ambassador Award for Outstanding Services to Country Music' by the same organisation in 1997. In 2002 he was awarded an Honorary MBE (Member of the Order of the British Empire) for services to the music industry (Irish citizens cannot be awarded a full MBE).

O'Donnell has also had considerable success in the United States – a notoriously difficult market for foreign acts in the country music sphere – where, to date, he has charted an amazing eighteen albums in the top twenty of the United States *Billboard*'s world music album chart, along with several entries in the independent album charts; he has also starred in seven concert specials on the Public Broadcasting Service (PBS).

American superstar Jim Reeves on tour in Ireland, June 1963. *Courtesy of James Reddioch*

Larry Cunningham, who had a huge hit with 'My Lovely Leitrim', despite being from Granard, County Longford. *Courtesy of Tom Gilmore*

Shay Hutchinson, Ireland's first male country star. *Courtesy of John Marion Hutchinson*

Maisie McDaniel, Ireland's first female country star. *Image courtesy of RTÉ Archives*

Gene Stuart and the Homesteaders, who came from Tyrone, the heartland of Irish country music. *Courtesy of Colin Stewart*

Big Tom and The Mainliners. *Back row*: Ginger Morgan, Seamus McMahon, John Beattie and Henry McMahon. *Front row*: Ronnie Duffy, Big Tom and Cyril McKevitt. *Courtesy of Karen McMahon*

Ray Lynam and Philomena Begley. *Image courtesy of RTÉ Archives*

Susan McCann, the
'First Lady of Irish
Country Music'. *Courtesy
of Susan McCann*

Daniel O'Donnell, the first superstar of Irish country music.
Image courtesy of RTÉ Archives

Margo, Donegal's finest and sister of Daniel O'Donnell.
Image courtesy of RTÉ Archives

Garth Brooks, global superstar. © *Shutterstock*

The Cotton Mill Boys: Ireland's first big bluegrass band. *Courtesy of Gerry Madigan*

Phil McLaughlin, CEO of Keep it Country TV. *Courtesy of Phil McLaughlin*

Paschal Mooney presents an award to American singer Don Williams. *Courtesy of Paschal Mooney*

John Hogan, the 'Prince of Irish Country Music'. *Courtesy of Tom Gilmore*

The boy from Ballinamuck, Mick Flavin. *Courtesy of Mick Flavin*

In 1995 American music magazine *Billboard* ran an article mentioning O'Donnell, in which journalist Ken Stewart marvelled at the queues standing 'in line for hours' outside the house of the 'Celtic Cowboy' waiting patiently to meet him.[6] In 1994 *RTÉ News* correspondent Eileen Magnier went to Kincasslagh for Daniel O'Donnell's annual tea party and spoke to the singer about the origins of the celebration, held each year at his home in conjunction with the local Mary from Dungloe Festival. In his inimitable, relaxed style, O'Donnell, with the queues seemingly snaking for miles through the barren landscape, discussed the beginnings of the annual event:

> About four or five years ago I told them [the audience] on the second night of the show that I would be here on the Wednesday, you know, at a given time and I wasn't working that night and a lot of people came and we just held it and every year more people seemed to come and today there's quite a lot.[7]

Six thousand cups of tea were served on the day that Magnier and the RTÉ cameras attended.

In 2000 O'Donnell held his last tea party, and Eileen Magnier was back to cover it for *RTÉ News*. The event had become too big, with too many people and consequent issues of health and safety. The pictures of snaking queues, mostly of female fans, amidst the landscape of bare rock and stone walls under frequently grey skies were coming to an end. The singer spoke about the ending of the tradition:

> I think it's too hard to control. Yeah, I think this is the last open day we're going to have. It's getting too big so I think it's best. Rather than havin' a few people, ya know, unhappy, it's better not to have them … but we will enjoy this but I think this will be the last one.[8]

Magnier interviewed an English woman who had just been released from a coronary care unit and was unlikely to have been passed fit by her doctor to be there: 'I'm on every tablet under the sun … cholesterol tablets, heart tablets, sprays … but anyway I'm here, the sun is shining and I'm happy for Daniel … I'm happy.'[9] Looking back on it afterwards with Ryan Tubridy on *The Late Late Show*, O'Donnell jokingly agreed that the 'tea orgies' were his equivalent of the wild parties given by other musical artists and that they had come to an end purely because of the singer's immense popularity. In his inimitable style, O'Donnell told the television host that the only orgy he was likely to be involved in was 'bingo or Ludo'.[10]

Also in 2000 O'Donnell was honoured by the *This Is Your Life* BBC television programme. The show recalls the life and achievements of the guest and brings to the stage significant people from his or her upbringing and passage to fame. It was an amazing achievement for an Irish country singer from the periphery of Donegal to make it onto a show so central in British popular culture, and a reflection of his popularity among the emigrant Irish community and those hundreds of thousands of Irish descent who have championed his music. O'Donnell could not have got to the top of the business without support from some of the British native population as well.

In 2002, at the age of forty, O'Donnell married Majella Roche from Thurles, County Tipperary, whom he had met two years previously in her parents' bar in Tenerife. Roche has two children from a previous marriage which ended in a divorce sanctioned by the Catholic Church. She is a woman of substance, has become a respected advocate for those with mental-health difficulties, and has spoken movingly about her depression and breast cancer.

Another event that illustrates Daniel's close relationship with his fans occurred in 2011. In December of that year O'Donnell was due to turn fifty. He had scheduled a concert for October in Dublin's O2 arena (renamed the 3Arena in 2014) to celebrate the occasion, but decided to cancel it because of the difficult economic circumstances in the country, knowing people would come who really could not afford it. He has a legion of 'super fans' who try to get to his concerts wherever he plays – a level of relationship between performer and fans rarely seen. It is unlikely the economic depression has dealt too severe a blow to O'Donnell's bank balance; in 2014 his company made a profit of almost €3 million.

In 2012 the Daniel O'Donnell Visitor Centre opened in Dungloe, where fans can see an impressive collection of O'Donnell's awards, a selection of his stage clothes and the wedding outfits of O'Donnell and Roche. Visitors can finish the experience by looking through merchandise and having a cup of tea in the attached Stepping Stone Bar. The centre isn't owned by O'Donnell – locals Anne and Pat Gallagher are the proprietors – but the singer is happy to lend his name to any enterprise in his home area. It is, as he has often mentioned, an area with limited employment and constant outward migration; any jobs created are valuable commodities.

When O'Donnell was awarded the 'Freedom of Donegal' in 2012 by Donegal County Council, the chamber was full to overflowing and *RTÉ News* cameras were once again in attendance. Graciously accepting the award, he joked: 'As I listened to everyone speaking … it's like a privilege not many get to be actually alive for their own funeral … it's the only time people are praised unreservedly.'[11] O'Donnell's mother, in attendance with his sister Margo, got the last word with RTÉ presenter Eileen Magnier: 'It's herself in the corner that gives all the orders,' said Margo, to which her mother added, 'I'm the one that should have got the medal.'[12]

There is no doubting O'Donnell's love of, and commitment to, his native place. 'Destination Donegal' is an iconic song for natives of the county and one of O'Donnell's best-known numbers. It describes an emigrant pining for a list of named places in his native county: Malin, Bundoran, Raphoe, Portsalon, Killybegs and many others. In 2013 O'Donnell joined Donegal Gaelic football manager Jim McGuinness in a rousing rendition of the song on an open-air stage in the Diamond, the main square in Donegal town. In front of an estimated 25,000 crowd, the duo serenaded the victorious All-Ireland-Football-Championship-winning team. Many had been waiting for six hours in incessant rain for this truly Irish country music celebration.

In 2015 O'Donnell took part as one of the celebrities in the popular *Strictly Come Dancing* BBC Television show, but was eliminated halfway through the contest. His nervousness was a surprising sight for such a normally self-assured performer. He could not, he said, even feel his legs, and in the end he was happy to be voted off the show. Later that year O'Donnell further endeared himself to members of the viewing public with *Daniel and Majella's B&B Road Trip,* a television programme made for Ulster Television (UTV). The couple toured the Republic and Northern Ireland, staying at family-run accommodation providers and engaging with local communities. Despite being caught twice for speeding, the O'Donnells were delighted with the series and it is scheduled to appear on American television. Such was the popularity of the show that the participating accommodation providers were inundated with enquiries and tourist authorities noticed an increase in the number of people in the country using B&Bs as a holiday option.

An incident on a St Valentine's Day special episode of *The Late Late Show* on RTÉ Television in February 2016 provided an amusing reminder of O'Donnell's enduring popularity. When presenter Ryan Tubridy announced Daniel O'Donnell as the next guest, audience member Molly Kate Sloyan rose from her seat with a look of delighted anticipation; however, when impersonator Mario Rosenstock emerged from the wings in typical O'Donnell pose, the camera caught the wave of annoyed disgust which washed over the young woman's face. O'Donnell was quick to react to Molly Kate's disappointment – on the following Tuesday he rang Tubridy on his RTÉ Radio 1 show and spoke to Molly Kate, inviting her to an upcoming gig in Killarney:

I hope you'll be able to come to Killarney to one of the shows in August and it will be lovely to meet you. Good on you. You have great taste ... I'm sure you've done more good for my street cred than I've done yours.[13]

Molly Kate Sloyan is definitely a 'super fan', based on what she told Ryan Tubridy:

Since I was three years old, I would've listened to him and went to a few concerts with her [Molly Kate's mother] when I was in Cork. I always liked him, but then when I saw him on the *B&B Road Trip* with Majella, I thought they came across great. I'm delighted I can go see him again.[14]

Molly Kate was just twenty-three at the time this programme was broadcast.

Daniel O'Donnell has been an iconic figure in Irish culture for more than thirty years now, but for many he has come to represent what they do not like about country music in Ireland. In 2012 Gail Walker of the *Belfast Telegraph* produced an interesting article entitled 'Why it's time for the begrudgers to leave Daniel O'Donnell alone'. She wrote about the attitude of many Irish people towards the singer – particularly those from the wealthier classes:

Daniel is the voice of unfashionable Ireland, north and south ... Because Daniel's face just doesn't fit. He's a reminder of a stubbornly untrendy place that BTs 7 & 9 and Dublin 4 [the postcode addresses of some of the richest parts of Belfast and Dublin] would rather forget about, or sneer at. In a world where any old dross can reap critical plaudits as long as it's badgering us, lecturing us, is 'edgy' or 'controversial', Daniel is just too ... ordinary. A 'lovely fella' straight out of Fr Ted central casting, he's an old Ireland parody. ... It's sad, though, that Daniel's success is barely accorded any respect here. Why? Because he recalls an Ireland that is supposed to be dead and buried ... *Ireland's Own*, daffodil teas, Tidy Towns, traybakes, never giving cheek back to the priest and of the need to be comforting and 'nice'.[15]

She argued for a different perspective:

Isn't there something profoundly rock 'n' roll about Daniel and all that he represents. After all, he's taking an American genre and making it his own, defying the self-appointed arbitrators of taste and not giving a hoot what anybody else thinks. The more I think about it, the more of this I'm sure, to quote Merle Haggard: 'I'm proud to be an Okie from Muskogee, A place where even squares can have a ball …'.[16]

Despite his detractors, O'Donnell is a character to be underestimated at the peril of the critic. Patrick Freyne interviewed the 'national treasure' and some fans attending one of his concerts at the Mullingar Park Hotel. Ger McGarry was there to celebrate her sixty-third birthday: 'Daniel's the sacred heart of country music,' she said. 'He's the king, next to Elvis. He's next to God really.' Ger's sister said, 'I'd do more than kiss him. I'd let him scatter crisps on my bed.' Ger, looking at a picture of O'Donnell, exclaimed, 'Ah, wouldn't you smother your mother for him?' Freyne asked O'Donnell himself if he thought there were any misconceptions about him amongst the public. 'Maybe people don't think that I'm as cute as I am – and I don't mean cute to look at, I mean cute up here.' The singer tapped his head. '[I'm] cleverer than people give me credit for.'[17] When you look at his success, it would be hard to disagree.

8

IN THE COUNTRY
OF 'REAL' COUNTRY

While the man from Donegal has largely stuck to the Irish country tradition, other Irish artists have taken the sometimes difficult path of staying true to American country music. One of them is Niall Toner, musician, radio presenter, songwriter, author, journalist and venerable authority on bluegrass music in Ireland. On RTÉ Radio 1 Toner has presented *Country Heartland*, *Sunday Best* and *Orange Blossom Special*; with the help of producer Aidan Butler, he is now the presenter of *Roots Freeway* on the same station. This programme broadcasts as wide a range of roots music as possible, and includes bluegrass, old-timey, blues, ragtime and singer-songwriters.[1] He is also the author of the book *The Nuts and Bolts of Songwriting*, 'a guide to writing better songs'. Toner was a founding member of the Lee Valley String Band, widely regarded as one of the most talented outfits of its nature ever to take the stage in Ireland. He has played in the Sackville String Band and Hank Halfhead and the Rambling Turkeys, and since 2001 has led his own group – the Niall Toner Band. His composition 'Nuns Island Reel' has been included in the biggest-selling video game in history, while his music has been recorded by Bill Wyman, the Nashville Bluegrass Band, Albert Lee, The Fleadh Cowboys and Special Consensus.

Now resident in Myshall, County Carlow, in the foothills of the

Blackstairs Mountains, Toner defines 'roots' as 'almost anything that has a strong connection to the great body of music that has been created over the past two hundred years, like The Carter Family, Hank Williams, Bill Monroe, Earl Scruggs and gazillion others'.[2] He is in a prime position to judge the division between country music in its original American strands and Irish country music:

> In order to make the performing of country music a commercial proposition here it had to be given a local label, and that's how it gained its own recognition. It's probably also true to say that the skill and ability required to play Bluegrass instruments convincingly is very challenging, whereas the basic skill required to play and sing a Buck Owens or a Hank Williams or a Johnny Cash song is something which is a little easier to learn. This more simple approach was something that many of the thousands of players who came up through the Showband system could easily adapt to playing 'country-style', and so the market was created for country and Irish.[3]

He mentioned the divisions that emerged:

> Those of us who came to Bluegrass and Country Music from the Folk-Music side of things were alienated, and a divide, or a rift, grew between the two 'camps', which still exists to this day. This is not in any way intended to denigrate, but to point out that one side stems from a love, a passion and a respect for the real thing, while the other stems from a commercial approach.[4]

Bluegrass music has a strong following in Ireland, and although there are no big stage acts active on the scene now, this was not always the case. During the 1970s and into the early 1980s the country witnessed a surge in the popularity of big bands with a bluegrass sound. While none of them have survived, they were significant parts of the musical landscape in those times, when, arguably, country music was interpreted in a broader way in Ireland.

The most successful of these bands was the Cotton Mill Boys, which was, founder member Gerry Madigan claims, the first band to feature the five-string banjo – 'the core of bluegrass music' – on stage in Ireland: 'We were also the only Irish band capable of playing live on stage "Foggy Mountain Breakdown" or "Duelling Banjos", known throughout the world through the films *Bonnie and Clyde* and *Deliverance*.'[5] The Cotton Mill Boys survived from 1968 to 1985 in varying forms. Gerry Madigan and Brian Dowling began their careers playing in Dublin clubs as a duo specialising in close harmonies, with a particular affinity for the music of The Carter Family. Madigan explained how the band acquired its name:

> We used to sing a song called Cotton Mill Girls. One evening, on the way into the 95 club in Harcourt Street, Mick Moloney and Paul Brady [who were later members of The Johnstons folk group] said, 'Here come the Cotton Mill Boys,' and the name stuck.[6]

The Cotton Mill Boys played their very first gig as a seven-piece electric band in the famous Crystal Ballroom in Dublin on Friday 23 May 1969. Their first single, 'Joey Moroney' (1969), brought them an appearance on *The Late Late Show* at a time when such exposure provided a significant career boost. In 1970 'That Silver Haired Daddy of Mine' and the double-sided single 'Goodbye My Darling'/'Little Liza Jane' brought their country sound further into the public consciousness. The Cottons also had a special attraction: 'the dancing fiddler' Mick McManus. Success came quickly, as Gerry Madigan explained from Calgary, Canada, where he is now resident:

> We were very lucky, as the constant airplay with 'Joey Moroney' generated massive numbers, and by the end of September of 1969 we were beginning to attract record-breaking crowds. We started out with a Volkswagen van and

trailer, with just a standard Philips PA, 2 Crazy boxes, and the mandatory Binson Echo, of course. Within a year we had the latest Mercedes Coach, fully converted with airplane seats, two roadies, a Soundcraft mixing desk, the latest microphones from Austria, 2,000 watts of PA, Vitavox horns, great speakers and bass bins, and top-quality stage and strobe lights.[7]

Fiddle and harmonica player Charlie Arkins, a musician equally as adept as McManus, joined the band in 1975. Arkins could play both instruments in the country style.

Military personnel based in United States air force bases across Europe often longed for the sounds of home, and this was a niche market in which the Cotton Mill Boys found success. Such was their popularity, they had the high honour of playing at the Supreme Headquarters of Allied Powers Europe (SHAPE) in Belgium, as Madigan fondly recalled.

The year 1976 was the band's red-letter year. They entered the hugely popular Thames Television talent show *Opportunity Knocks* and were invited back three times, a measure of their significant following. This heightened their profile in Ireland, but more importantly it brought their music to a wider British public. Like many others before them, they played to a full house in the Galtymore Ballroom on a number of occasions:

We were doing record crowds at all of the Irish clubs in England but *Opportunity Knocks* opened the door to the very lucrative country-music clubs and working-men's clubs in England. We headlined most of the major music festivals throughout the UK, including Peterborough, the Isle of Wight and, of course, Wembley Festival. Vince Power brought us to the Mean Fiddler in London on many occasions. He told us we were the most popular band, according to the staff.[8]

Madigan thinks the success of the band has been overlooked in recent times:

In those recent TV shows remembering the good old days of the country-music bands, it's amazing the Cotton Mill Boys don't get much coverage. Yet the band was one of the biggest attractions in the entire country, especially in Galway and Northern Ireland. We were huge at the carnivals. Oranmore Carnival in Galway was a huge carnival, and it had us on the opening night and the closing night. No other band ever warranted two appearances in the same carnival. I remember in December 1980 doing twenty-one nights on the trot from Christmas to the middle of January, and we never had less than 2,000 people at any of the gigs. We started in Claremorris on Christmas night, and did twenty-one straight nights of record crowds.[9]

The Cotton Mill Boys appeared at the International Country Music Festival in Wembley and in the Landmark Hotel, Las Vegas, and in 1976 set a new record when they became the first Irish band to hold the first and second positions in the Irish charts simultaneously: 'The Wedding Song' was at number one and 'Rainin' in My Heart' at number two. The bluegrass standard 'Orange Blossom Special' – on the B-side of the latter – went on to become their most famous number. In the summer of 1977 they had another number two on the Irish charts with a cover version of the Kenny Rogers song 'Lucille'.

On 30 May 1978 the Cotton Mill Boys' version of 'Orange Blossom Special' debuted as the soundtrack to bawdy and vaudevillian comedy programme *The Benny Hill Show* on BBC Television – a major achievement, given the immense popularity of the show. In the same year the band had a six-part series on RTÉ Television; Paul Brady and Marianne Faithful appeared as guests, and a live album taken from the series proved a significant hit. Sadly 1978 would be their last year of real success: 'Heaven's Just a Sin Away' reached number twelve that year, but this was to be the last time the band charted with a single.

As the ballroom circuit began to dry up, the environment for live music became increasingly difficult. Despite the introduction of female vocalists to the band – first Kim Newport and later Sharon King (real name Colette O'Hanlon) – the hits stopped coming. The addition of female singers did allow the band to widen their material:

> Sharon King made a huge difference. She was an absolutely dynamic performer, super singer, and added that glamour to the band, making us more appealing for a wider selection of gigs. It was great for concerts and cabarets. Her rendition of 'Blue Bayou' got standing ovations at concerts.[10]

In 1979 Gerry Madigan left the Cotton Mill Boys to form Mash with George Kaye and Dermot O'Connor, who had had a number-one hit ('The Wind in the Willows') with his band Spud. Mash signed a one-album deal with Polygram Records and toured Great Britain and Ireland before going their separate ways.

The Cotton Mill Boys continued to have some success in Britain and on American military bases across Europe, but by 1985 the game was finally up. During their sixteen-year career they had released fifteen top-selling albums and more than twenty-five singles. At their peak in the mid-1970s they were the biggest 'real' country, bluegrass-oriented music band in Ireland.

Gerry Madigan is happy with his lot these days and recently released a new CD of all original songs, entitled *Wild Bird, Fly Free*. He explained:

> I left the music business, went into the world of financial services, then into teaching, and then wrote three books, became a corporate trainer, and then a keynote speaker on the international speakers' circuit. In 1979 I also managed Bagatelle, secured them a recording contract with Polygram Records, launched them on *The Late Late Show* with 'Summer in Dublin', and then let them go to another manager. I know, what was I thinking? Now I'm doing music as a hobby, but the market is ripe for my original songs, and the folk-music circuit is perfect for me at my age.[11]

In late 2017 Gerry Madigan and George Kaye took to the stages of Ireland in the hope of reigniting their Irish careers.

These days Charlie Arkins runs a music studio with his son David in Athboy, County Meath, as well as occasionally playing with the Jimmy Buckley Band. He also contributes to country gospel music as a session player. Arkins is still most famous for his time with the Cotton Mill Boys and owns the right to the name.

***

Naming a band after a mountain range along the Tennessee–North Carolina border considered to be a sub-range of the Appalachian Mountains – the home of bluegrass music in the south-eastern United States – is a fair indication that a band wants to stay true to the spirit of original American country music, and so it was with the Smokey Mountain Ramblers. The band's debut single 'Ballad of Amelia Earhart' was a moderate success, but their hard-core-bluegrass style, with many instrumental numbers, did not find immediate favour with the dancers of the Irish music circuit, who preferred the Irish country sounds and rhythms and the words of Big Tom and his compatriots' Irish country songs. At this remove, the original recording of the 'Ballad of Amelia Earhart' could have been recorded in the Tennessee hills, such is its lack of any semblance of the Irish country music style. The level of musicianship and tightness of the band is exemplary and bears favourable comparison with contemporary acts on the American circuit.

The remarkable story of Jerzy Kryzanowski – better known as George Kaye – is central to the development of the Smokey Mountain Ramblers. Kaye now resides near Essen in Germany with Sabine, his partner for twenty-one years, from where he recounted – on a rather poor phone line – his life story and that of the band. Kaye's father was from Belarus and had joined the Polish army in the 1940s. He had met Kaye's mother before the war, but after the fighting ended he was unable to return to his home due to his opposition to the Russian invasion of the country and was subsequently deported to a Siberian work camp. He managed to stay in contact with his lover – who was related to the composer Chopin – and through a circuitous route they were reunited and eventually settled in England, where George was born. Kaye's father and Sabine's grandfather fought on opposite sides in the Second World War and, amazingly, Kaye subsequently found out their opposing units had engaged in direct combat.

Kaye remembered his first exposure to American bluegrass:

> I first heard the music on an American airbase near where we lived in England. I thought it was magical and knew straight away it was something I wanted to do. Once I got involved in the music I never looked back.[12]

Kaye came to Ireland to busk after having played in a number of outfits on the folk circuit in Britain. Shortly after his arrival, he got involved in the Irish pub-music scene and formed the Mitchell County Ramblers with Clive Collins. His talent was soon recognised, and he was approached by Des Kelly – formerly of the Capitol Showband and, by then, an important figure in the Irish music industry – to see if he was interested in being part of a serious bluegrass outfit. Kelly saw the end of the showband era coming and the increasing popularity of country music. He did not want to have another Irish country band, instead aiming to put together an outfit that would attempt to play country music as it was being played in the United States. George Kaye was happy to go along with this idea – 'whether it was the right thing or not' – and the Smokey Mountain Ramblers were formed in 1967. Kaye stayed with them until 1970. His athletic fiddle-playing, like that of Mick McManus in the Cotton Mill Boys, brought an added touch of glamour to their stage shows:

> When I played with the Smokies, I tried to project that traditional blue-grass feel into the music. Apart from fiddle, I also picked a little banjo

which we regularly featured. The Cotton Mill Boys also had the banjo and fiddle. The whole thing exploded so quickly. I remember we had a residency in a hotel in Leixlip in Kildare. They were always in trouble with the fire authorities because there would be twice the number of people that there were supposed to be. It was an unbelievable time for a few years.[13]

Kaye believes he was the first musician on the ballroom circuit in Ireland to front a full band playing electric fiddle. The Smokey Mountain Ramblers found chart success with 'Little Folk' (1968), 'But You Love Me Daddy' (1970) and 'Just Beyond the Moon' (1971). While their albums never sold in huge numbers, they toured relentlessly. When Kaye left the band in 1970, having collapsed on stage the previous year, he declared himself burnt-out and later reported that the band had played sixty-four nights in a row at one point.

The addition of frontman Pat Ely to the Smokey Mountain Ramblers changed the overall sound of their music, and brought them a little closer to the normal Irish country band of the time. Typical of the direction the music moved was Ely's rendition of 'Ladies Love Outlaws', which was reminiscent of American great Waylon Jennings.

Like the Cotton Mill Boys, during the 1970s the Ramblers found success on the United States military bases, where the forces longed for the genuine sounds of home. While the Smokey Mountain Ramblers' star shone brightly, they were not to have the same lasting power as the Cotton Mill Boys. The band went through numerous line-ups before finishing up subsumed in the inevitable wave of disco and Irish country music.

Subsequently Kaye formed the Rocky Tops with Pat Ely, and went on to have many adventures, among them the establishment of a band called the Permanent Cure:

I founded it in the late 1970s with Dermot O'Connor and we had an offer to tour the newly opened lands of East Germany. This was in 1993, and without realising the second language in the East was Russian, we blithely set off with our humorous songs and stories. Fortunately, we had a German accordion player who was able to translate, but the show would often turn into a fiasco.[14]

At that point the phone link with George Kaye went dead and the interview ended.

***

Contemporary bluegrass in Ireland may be vastly overshadowed by the Irish country acts popular on the circuit, but it still demands a loyal following and attendances at bluegrass festivals around the country are continually on the rise. Uri Kohen, who was raised in an Israeli kibbutz, is now the director of the annual Westport Folk and Bluegrass Festival, which, in the years since its foundation in 2006, has grown to become the second-biggest bluegrass festival in Ireland. Fittingly, Omagh, County Tyrone, hosts the most eminent gathering each September, in the Ulster American Folk Park. Kohen's company, Electric Cave Productions, is named after a popular Israeli children's short story and is indicative of the crazy pathway that brought about the birth of the festival. Kohen explained: 'I wanted to run a music festival here but didn't know what to try. Someone said bluegrass. I didn't know anything about bluegrass, but it didn't stop me.'[15]

When asked about the perception some might have of bluegrass artists outside Ireland as pale imitations of the real thing, he laughs and mentions one of his early headline acts, a Dutch bluegrass outfit:

You could say that about any type of music. Hey, it's crazy. I tell people that it takes an Israeli to bring a Dutch band to play American music in Ireland. The thing is I hit the jackpot the day I chose bluegrass.[16]

In 2017 the festival had twenty-five individual shows in eleven locations. From being met with indifference, the festival now engenders enormous respect among the locals. Kohen said he was 'lucky' when he picked Westport, County Mayo:

> The people are great. The other day a woman came up to me in SuperValu and gave me €20. She owns a bed and breakfast and thanked me for all the business we have brought to the town. It's a win-win situation.[17]

One of the Irish bands which performed in the 2017 festival was 'The Rocky Tops String Band' (a different outfit from the band set up by George Kaye), a staunch, traditional bluegrass outfit based in Killawalla outside Westport. Hubie McEvilly and his sister Sarah are the driving force behind this band. Hubie, who plays the five-string banjo, is eloquent in his descriptions of his deep-seated love for the music and the culture of bluegrass. It is the 'communality and sense of a family' above all else that define the bluegrass genre for him. 'When I meet fellow bluegrass musicians it is like we speak the same language,' he says.[18] McEvilly is at pains to emphasise that his music is a world removed from what he terms 'new country', the music of Nathan Carter and his compatriots, and acknowledges that this leaves him and his band largely outside the contemporary commercial loop. 'We play in the pubs and at birthday parties. We go to the festivals and that's about it,' he says. While McEvilly would like to work at his music full time, he is realistic about the prospects:

> My sister Sarah ... works as a secondary-school teacher but would love to make it full time in music, but the market isn't big enough for that in this country. I know musicians who play full time who might play a bit of bluegrass and a bit of something else. That would be the only way to do it.[19]

Sarah is a staunch traditionalist and recently refused to sing 'Folsom Prison

Blues' when requested; it was not in the traditional canon of the music. McEvilly points out the limits this imposes on her chances of making it full time. But he constantly emphasises the family nature of the music and the pride he feels to play with another member of his own family:

> I suppose we harmonise well because our voices aren't unalike. There's a long tradition of families playing bluegrass music together and we're just adding to that tradition. One of the things I love about the music is the fact that it is unselfish. We play for each other. It's not for show.[20]

Another 'local' who has performed at the Westport festival is Tim Rogers, originally from Stamford, Connecticut, and now one of the best-known musicians on the Irish bluegrass circuit. By a circuitous route (through a high school called 'New Canaan', a 'crunchy' third-level experience at Goddard College in Vermont, where students design their own curriculum, and a host of jobs, including working as a lighting rigger for cult rock band Phish), Rogers ended up living in the west of Ireland, where he is now employed by the Probation Service. He says of bluegrass:

> I often say bluegrass is about the argument. I gave up trying to explain what it is or isn't to people years ago. Music is not for dividing people. Just because people have a banjo and a mandolin doesn't mean they can play bluegrass. Too many people can deliver a drug called stagecraft. Bluegrass music is certainly not a hereditary condition. No one owns it.[21]

With such passionate supporters for this music style out there, there can be no doubt that bluegrass will continue to make its mark on the Irish country music scene.

***

When you ask the experts about the artists who have ploughed the furrow of more traditional American country music in Ireland, one name comes from every mouth: Ray Lynam.

Born in Moate, County Westmeath, in 1951, Lynam is considered by many to be the purest country voice in country music in Ireland. He has stayed true to his vision of the genre – a pure sound with no Irish element – and has frequently been compared to the American star Buck Owens. Many commentators have suggested that, had he been born in the United States, Lynam would have had a chance at international stardom, such is the quality of his voice.

While still in secondary school, Lynam began playing saxophone with a local group, the Merrymen. In 1969 he became frontman for the Hillbillies, another outfit from the area, whose intention to stick to original country music is reflected in the name they chose for the band. After signing with Mick Clerkin of Release Records in 1970, the Hillbillies embarked on a professional career. Their earliest release clearly announced their intention to stay true to American country music: a full-voiced version of the Harlan Howard song 'Busted' – most often associated with Johnny Cash. While it did not trouble the charts, it was a solid start.

'Sweet Rosie Jones', released later in the same year, languished just outside the top twenty for a month and was a further step in the right direction. The Dolly Parton-written 'Gypsy, Joe and Me', released in early 1971, had a similar fate, but Lynam and his band were becoming established on the circuit. The following year their second album, *The Selfishness of Man*, spent two weeks in the Irish top twenty. The direction country music was taking in Ireland was demonstrated by a poll organised by *Spotlight* magazine to establish Ireland's favourite 'country and western' acts. The Hillbillies finished fifth behind Big Tom, Gene Stuart, Dermot Henry and Dermot Hegarty, although Big Tom, the leading purveyor of Irish country music, was miles ahead of the posse.

Ray Lynam and the Hillbillies had further hits with 'Brand New Mister

Me' (1972), 'I Can't Believe That You've Stopped Loving Me' (1973), 'Borrowed Angel' (1973) and 'Second Handed Flowers' (1974), all of which showcased Lynam's smooth, subtle style of delivery. Other singles that brought him success included the great Waylon Jennings classic 'The Door Is Always Open', 'I've Loved You All Over the World', 'You're the One I Sing My Love Songs To' and 'Sweet Music Man'. All were sung in his melodic, laid-back and mellow tones, in sharp contrast to much of the typical sound of Irish country music.

Lynam had the honour of appearing at the highly regarded International Festival of Country Music at Wembley Stadium in London in 1973, and repeated the achievement when he appeared with Irish country singer Philomena Begley in 1974 – the year in which the pair were voted 'Top European Duo' by the British Country Music Association.

Paschal Mooney discussed the issue of the limited commercial appeal of Lynam's music in *Spotlight* magazine. He praised the technical ability of the Hillbillies but expressed reservations about the limitations of their playlist. An all-country programme, he wrote, 'could endanger their bid for wider popularity. Many people get bored if they listen all night to the same type of music, no matter how good it might be.'[22] Despite Mooney's reservations, Lynam's talent was recognised by music critics in 1973 when he was voted the number one country singer in Ireland by fans in the National Showbiz Poll in *Spotlight* magazine. In 1974 Lynam made it to Nashville to record the album *Someone Special* and returned in 1984 to record *Music Man*. He even released a single called 'There Ought to Be a Law' on the American market – a rare achievement for an Irish artist. Lynam's partnership with Philomena Begley was a fruitful one; they had a major chart success with 'My Elusive Dreams' in 1974 and a British hit in 1985 with 'Mona Lisa Lost Her Smile'.

In 1979 Lynam released a single entitled 'I Don't Want to See Another Town', which, according to Tom Gilmore, is one of the best of all his releases. Even though it only reached number thirteen in the Irish charts, this country-rock style song, written by Kevin Sheerin, is reminiscent of Californian superstars the Eagles at their best. (There is also an excellent version of the Americans' 'Lyin' Eyes' on the album.) Gilmore provides a good summation of Lynam's part in the Irish country music industry in *The Blackwell Guide to Recorded Country Music*:

> Lynam was Ireland's answer to George Jones and his band was almost all brilliant country musicians. He was always the 'respectable' sound of Irish country to those who would deride music of this genre. In the early 1990s when, as the teenagers went wild for the sounds of Garth Brooks, Billy Ray Cyrus, Travis Tritt and other 'young fellows', Lynam always remained respected by even pop and rock critics in Ireland as a purveyor of new country as well as being acclaimed by older fans too.[23]

In 2013 the Hillbillies staged a reunion in their hometown of Moate and have continued to perform regularly since. Their concerts over the last number of years have garnered rave reviews, with audiences consistently noting that Ray Lynam's voice is as good as ever it was. The band continues to carry the torch of traditional American country music in Ireland.

It has never been easy for Irish acts – if they are seeking to make a living in the industry – to stick solely to classic interpretations of country music in the 'roots' mode of American greats such as Hank Williams, George Jones, Tammy Wynette or Patsy Cline. The Irish country music scene is so overwhelmingly based on dancing that the market for slow ballads in the 'honky-tonk' or 'pure country' tradition is limited. At best, such songs can be accommodated as part of a concert, or brought up-tempo to provide a platform for dancing. For some purists, this is the difficulty they have with much of what is termed 'country music' in Ireland. To them it is strictly 'country and Irish', used solely as an accompaniment to dancing and a world removed from the Tennessee hills and the bar rooms of Texas.

However, in recent times there has been an increase in the number of sit-down concerts, and it is largely in such an environment that 'hard country' can thrive. But it is hard to see it ever challenging the popularity of the real, live American who changed the face of country music across the world and also had a profound effect in Ireland. It is time to go to 'Garthland'.

9

GARTH BROOKS' HAT CAN SING: GARTH BROOKS AND IRELAND

> When you hear them singing your stuff in Croke Park, it's like heaven.
>
> Garth Brooks to Neil McCormick of *The Telegraph*[1]

The 1990s saw country music change dramatically in America. Handsome men in hats, pretty girls in boots, and flashy music videos saturated the airways. The terms 'hot country', 'new country' and 'hat acts' – the last of these supposedly coined by country singer Travis Tritt – gained currency in the United States to describe the arrival of Garth Brooks and his friends.

Troyal Garth Brooks, the best-selling solo artist of all time in the United States, is a central figure in this change. With the addition of rock pyrotechnics, wireless microphones, climbing ropes and trapeze wires, he brought the music to new audiences during the 1990s and is frequently cited as the artist who single-handedly invented 'stadium country'. His mix of styles hit the industry like a bomb. The mishmash of musical sounds and cultural symbols was a revelation; rock and country, cowboy clothes, rock posturing and electronic trickery combined to bring country music into a new dimension.

Like many of the previous greats, Brooks – born on 7 February 1962 in Tulsa, Oklahoma – would quickly become known to his legions of fans by his first name. For the music industry he was a godsend, but for many purists, including author Nick Dawidoff, his style was not 'country' at all:

Hot country is really pop music for a prospering, mostly conservative white middle class. It's kempt, comfortable music – hyper-sincere, settled and careful neither to offend nor surprise. A lot like Disneyland, in some way its model, country music thrives because it is sleek and predictable, a safe adventure in a smoke-free environment.[2]

American writer and journalist Kinky Friedman – a fan of traditional, honky-tonk country music – called Brooks the 'anti Hank': 'Anyone who likes Hank for any reason would not like Garth Brooks. Country music crossed over and never came back.'[3] Brian Hinton expressed similar reservations: 'This is music for people with too many records in their house and has been put together with the precision you'd expect from a well made vacuum cleaner: a slow song, then a fast song.'[4]

Johnny Cash certainly did not appreciate the new generation of artists: 'I think a lot of it is sex. These guys wear these tight jeans. They work out with a trainer three times a week. I can't see a lot of good country music coming out of it.'[5] Fellow singer Emmylou Harris was equally scathing when she called it 'bloodless cookie cutter music'.[6]

However, millions of people would beg to disagree: Brooks' high-energy, rock-style stage shows – inspired, he has frequently said, by his hero Chris LeDoux, a former rodeo rider who went on to become a country-rock artist – filled his audience with millions who had never before been to 'country music' concerts. He may have been different to Hank, George, Willie, Waylon and the boys, but he was to change things forever.

Following a childhood playing music, Garth Brooks trod in the foot-steps of Jim Reeves by going to college on an athletics scholarship, where he specialised in the javelin. Unlike Reeves, he completed his studies and holds a degree in marketing and advertising, a qualification which has stood him in good stead in his career. Brooks' rise to fame was far from meteoric. He spent time working as a bouncer and playing music in local bars in his native Oklahoma, and when he first went to Nashville in 1985 he disliked it so much he returned home within twenty-four hours. He subsequently thought better of his decision and returned two years later with a band called Santa Fe. They split up, but Brooks persevered and was spotted playing at the famous Writers Night in the Bluebird Cafe by a music executive.

In 1989 he made his breakthrough when his self-titled album was released by Capitol Records. Unlike much of his later work, there was a significant element of traditional country music on *Garth Brooks* – including fiddles, steel guitars, honky-tonk rhythms and lots of his Oklahoma twang. With its success, his career quickly took off, and two singles – 'If Tomorrow Never Comes' and 'The Dance' – went to number one. His second album, *No Fences* (1990), reached number one on the country chart and number three on the pop chart; it contained monster hits 'Friends in Low Places', 'The Thunder Rolls' and 'Unanswered Prayers'. No country album had gone multi-platinum before; it eventually sold thirteen million copies. Country music had entered a new frontier.

Garth Brooks had it all: the Oklahoma accent, carefully maintained small-town humility and an excellent rapport with the media. He was open and given to self-disclosure, willing to discuss his personal difficulties and speak out in support of his lesbian sister. He took a stance against the recording industry by offering his albums directly to the audience at below-market prices. Brooks was the perfect project for the media age. His rise to fame was helped by the boom in line dancing; his music was the perfect fit.

Brooks has never been shy about speaking of his musical influences. Rock characteristics of 1970s bands such as the Eagles and Journey are immediately evident in his work, but he also likes weepy ballads written by James Taylor, and he even covered the Billy Joel song 'Shameless' on his album *Ropin' the Wind*. Each of his albums has power anthems, party tunes and sentimental ballads. With this mix and his hyped-up honky-tonk sound it was as though 'he'd pressed all the right buttons at the same time, and the public just started salivating on cue', according to Kurt Wolff.[7]

By 1994 Brooks was the biggest-selling country star in history. When tickets went on sale for planned Irish concerts in Dublin, an estimated 130,000 people came into the city centre to purchase them (it was the pre-Internet era). In less than two and a half hours, all four concerts were sold out and gardaí had to help disperse crowds. It was at these concerts in Dublin's Point Depot that Brooks' love affair with Ireland began. Brooks was also thrilled to be able to walk around the city centre; something which would not have been possible in America, he said. Photographer Kyran O'Brien was tasked by the *Irish Independent* to take pictures for music magazine *Q*, which was planning a first-ever feature on country music to highlight the wave of new interest in the genre. It was to have been a sixteen-page special on the artist, but American rock star Kurt Cobain died shortly after the photo shoot, and the feature was shortened and the photographs omitted. When eventually released in 2014, the photographs showed the remarkable relationship between artist and fans.

The year 1994 also brought an infamous appearance on the British Channel 4 television programme *The Big Breakfast*, on which he spoke to presenter Paula Yates. Objectors took issue with Yates' introduction: 'Country singers always seem to be weeping over the dead dog and things ... I thought you'd come in here and twiddle your pistol around and be impressed.'[8] The channel received scores of complaints objecting to the crude stereotype, but Brooks simply observed that Yates did not seem to know much about country music.

Channel 4 was not the only media organisation to incur the wrath of country music fans. ITV's *London Tonight* news programme introduced a feature on Brooks by describing the singer as 'a top-selling, rooting-tooting, cotton-picking, country-and-western star, yeeha!'[9] Despite the simplistic media commentary, Brooks sold out the Birmingham NEC Arena.

The following year Brooks included a song called 'Ireland' on his album *Fresh Horses*. It is difficult to say what the song – co-written with Stephanie Davis and Jenny Yates – is exactly about, but it may refer to Irish soldiers who fought for Britain in the First World War. However, it could also refer to the American Civil War. Many Irish immigrants joined the Confederate side, seeing a parallel in the desire of the south to break away from the federal government and the historical fight for independence in Ireland. The only thing known for certain is it involves fighting, where the Irish are outnumbered 'forty against hundreds'.[10] Brooks was asked about the meaning of the song in an interview with *Hot Press*. He replied:

> 'Ireland' is just a fantasy. It's a nod back to a country that took my music in when I probably needed it the most. It [Dublin] was the first city on the European leg of the world tour, the first time I ever felt the music reach out across a body of water.[11]

He even mentioned the difficulty of trying not to imitate an Irish accent on the album: 'For some reason I kept having this Irish burr and I had to get away from that as far as I could. It's still in there.'[12]

After his time in Ireland, Brooks' career continued on its upward trajectory, and by the end of 1996 he had sold over sixty million albums, a feat surpassed only by The Beatles and Billy Joel, although Brooks had achieved these sales faster than any other artist in any field of music. In 1997 he returned triumphantly to Ireland. According to polls, one in twenty Irish people wanted to go to see him. When tickets went on sale for three concerts, all 150,000 sold out immediately, surpassing the previous record set by U2 in 1992. Ireland had entered the digital age, so there were no crowd-control issues for the guards this time, but there were a lot of disappointed people.

Brooks mentioned his Irish blood through his maternal side at a press conference before the first of his 1997 concerts:

My mom's grandma's family is from Cork so my mom feels very proud to claim that she is Irish. Mom believes there are two kinds of people on the earth, Irish people and those that wanna be Irish. But the last thing I want people to think is 'Oh great, now Garth thinks he's Irish'.[13]

He went on to describe his conception of a good concert:

Every night must be an event; we owe that to the people. That was the theory long before these stadium gigs ever came along. When it was a club there had to be something that happened that night so you would remember it. If it meant pushing a piano off into the audience or running down the bar kicking bottles – whatever it took, you found it. That's what we do. We do events. But you gotta weigh the spectacle against the music. I tell the guys who make the place blow up and fly; you do your job and I'll do mine. My job is music, sincerity and honesty. I'll take care of that part.[14]

Neil McCormick was impressed by Brooks' handling of the press in Croke Park. The singer learned and remembered the names of all the journalists in the group. McCormick was also amazed by the honesty with which Brooks spoke about his marriage:

There have been tough times, tough times … still have them, even to this day. There's times when there's been no communication … lots of wondering what was going on when we were apart. I was the one that was probably doing 99 per cent of the wrong things, but it's like all marriages, you have times when you look at each other and think that sometimes it'd be better to start over … Which, God forbid.[15]

For the journalist this was a long way removed from the behaviour of typical rock stars, and he found Brooks' humility intriguing, even when he spoke of himself in the third person:

I'm not a big fan of myself; I'm a fan of real writers. I wouldn't say really I'm that much of an artist, because I'm not much of a fan of Garth's voice and I'm sure not a fan of how he plays guitar, but I sure like the fun that goes with the event.[16]

McCormick was unused to such direct and intimate interaction with a music star in a press conference:

Garth the guy is a father to three children, a husband to a wife, a guy that tries to keep a farm in balance back home and loves his mum and dad and just kind of hangs out. He's very much of a slob … very much of a regular guy. I can go out of the house as me, but if someone says 'Hey look, there's Garth Brooks' then you become that guy, the guy you saw on-stage last night. He's one of those big circle G logos. He's the whole thing, the Stetson and the ridiculously tight jeans.[17]

Used to seeing the trappings and attitudes associated with rock stars, the Garth Brooks experience reminded McCormick of 'a cross between a corporation and a religious cult':

One day, I feel certain, there will be a place called Garthland, a huge country and western amusement park for the whole family, where you can go and eat Garthburgers, drive around in Garthcarts, ride the Brooks bucking bronco and pay homage to a huge inflatable blow-up of the king of country.[18]

Colm Connolly set the scene for the Irish nation on RTÉ Television's evening news on 16 May before the first concert:

In case you haven't already heard, he's here, Garth Brooks that is, and the stage is waiting for him. It is 465 feet long and 65 feet high and the high-energy act will need every available square foot. Garth and his band jump, strut and run almost all night. It is probably the biggest stage ever seen in Ireland. The equipment for the event fills sixty trucks. Each show needs 4,000 amps of power in comparison to a normal house which runs on just 200 amps.

The concerts were a triumph, and cemented Brooks' place as a musical hero to swathes of the Irish public.

An NBC TV special, *Garth Brooks: Ireland and Back*, first aired on 5 March 1998 and attracted an audience of more than fifteen million in the United States. In one scene Brooks bodysurfed over the crowd at one of his Croke Park concerts, and later said Ireland was the only country where he felt safe doing this because he implicitly trusted the audience. This trust was exemplified by an extraordinary event shown on RTÉ Television's news programmes at the time of his Irish concerts: Brooks went out and about meeting his fans in Bray, County Wicklow, and ended up singing 'Friends in Low Places' from the roof of his van. The narrator was matter of fact in her introduction:

> It wasn't quite Nashville but it wasn't for the want of trying. The fans dressed country for Garth Brooks who was taking part in a live linkup between East Coast Radio and The Voice of America. Then it was Garth Brooks live and unplugged as the star climbed up onto the roof of his minibus and serenaded the crowd.[19]

The year 2014 was set to bring a triumphant Irish homecoming for Brooks. After seventeen years off the road, he announced a comeback to the world stage and declared Croke Park as his venue of choice to launch his new show. There was delight and pride in Ireland. He had promised to come back and he was doing so. Of all the possible locations in the world he had chosen to come to Dublin to reboot his live act, a true affirmation of his love for Irish audiences and an indication of the special place the country held in his heart. Suzanne Byrne of RTÉ asked him why he chose Dublin. He replied:

> If we're going to show ourselves to people again I sure would like the venue to be perfect and for everything to be like it was and to show them no time has passed. If you want a place like that I think it would have to be Croke Park.[20]

In 1997 the stadium was under reconstruction, but this time, he said, if he got his way, there would be twice as many people to see him which would make it 'twice as much fun'. Earlier he had met with fans outside Croke Park, and Byrne had asked him what that had been like. Brooks said: 'Well the girl that killed me … cause everyone always says "Welcome to Ireland Garth" and she looked at me and said, "Welcome home." Oh my God, I love this place.' Byrne asked him if he had an outstanding memory from his 1997 concerts in Croke Park, to which he replied mystically:

> There was this white film over everything, kind of like a haze. I thought it might have been some of the stuff that made the lights work … but it was something much deeper than that … it was almost like we were communicating without saying anything at all.

He pointed to his heart: 'It was a beautiful feeling inside of here and I really, really want to taste that kind of feeling again.'

Alan Hughes interviewed Brooks for *Ireland AM*, the morning-television programme on TV3. Brooks praised the Irish people: 'I just can't explain how good you guys are at welcoming people. When they go "Explain Ireland to me", it's easy. When you land, your fists … they just relax. It's the greatest land of love. I just love playing over here.'[21] Hughes reminded Brooks that he had said playing in Ireland was almost like a religious experience, and that the only person who had commanded a bigger Irish audience was Pope John Paul II when he came to the country in 1979. Brooks laughed:

Let's be sure we all understand each other. I'm not coming back here to relive what was there. We're coming back here to do bigger and better things than we did last time and it won't be us that do it … it'll be you guys that will do it. It's always you guys that take it to something historic. That's why I love coming here.[22]

When Brooks told his band they were going to launch his world comeback tour in Ireland some of them cried, he said. He reinforced this message in his Croke Park press conference, where he spoke in the third person: 'I just know this has always been a wonderful place for us and if Garth Brooks is going to step in and do a comeback special this would be the place to do it.'[23] He spoke about his connection to Ireland through his mother's ancestry. 'Coleen Carol McElroy is my mom's maiden name.' He asked if there was a Gerry Kelly in the audience; there was. Brooks went down into the audience and gave him a hug and some of the spectators clapped. 'Gerry was very sweet to my mother and got her a family crest from here and everything,' explained Brooks, 'so that might be one of the answers when you say Garth and here [Ireland] … it might be.' The greatest time in his mother's life, he said, was when she came to Ireland. On his previous tour he had received a call from his parents to tell him his mother's cancer had come back, and even this was a further connection to Ireland. He felt, he said, like an 'adopted son'.

When tickets for two Garth Brooks concerts on 25 and 26 July 2014 at Croke Park went on sale, they sold out in twenty minutes. A third date was added for 27 July; this sold out in fifteen minutes. A few days after an announcement that there would be no extra shows, Brooks added a fourth date for 28 July. Tickets went on sale on 6 February at 9 a.m. and sold out in twenty-five minutes. After selling out the fourth date, Brooks announced he would play a fifth date, and tickets sold out in fifty minutes. In total 400,000 tickets with a value of €28,600,000 were sold, bringing the artist to a new level. But it was all too perfect, and cracks soon started to appear. Residents of the area around Croke Park started to express opposition to the number of concerts and notified the event's organisers, threatening legal action because it was breaking the terms of an agreement signed in 2009. On 3 July 2014 Dublin City Council refused permission for concerts on 28 and 29 July. Brooks was adamant: it would be five concerts or nothing. The situation soon began to descend into farce. It was, according to Emer O'Toole, a journalist with *The Guardian* newspaper, 'a social and political meltdown'.[24] An 'unbelievable' sequence of events was triggered, she wrote:

> [There were] public protests, calls for the Taoiseach to talk with Brooks, an offer of diplomatic help from the Mexican Ambassador to Ireland, politicians gearing up for talks, and the Lord Mayor of Dublin claiming that residents planned to ask President Obama to step in.[25]

The White House politely informed an *Irish Independent* journalist they would leave it to Mr Brooks and the city of Dublin to resolve the problem. If the Taoiseach could see his way to a meeting with Brooks, the singer said he would 'crawl, swim and fly to get there'.[26] Letters were sent to Taoiseach Enda Kenny from members of the public who wanted him to take action. One read: 'I want to ask you to do something to save this country from a complete shambles. The chance is there and you need to grab it … We listened to you when you were begging for votes and granted your wish, now it's time for you to pay us back.' Another noted: 'I am writing to you in desperation to ask you to intervene in this disaster … you can't stand idly by and let it fall away.' A third argued that 'changing this law … would bring great happiness to many and the country as a whole'.[27]

Disappointing the fans would be like 'asking to choose one child over another', Brooks said. He issued a statement to the 'Irish people':

> I have always been advised to NEVER send a message in 'the moment.' It is said it is best to take a walk, wait awhile, and think about it. With that said, I just received the news the Dublin City Council cannot change their earlier ruling to not allow the licenses for all five shows. To say I am crushed is an understatement. All I see is my mother's face and I hear her voice. She always said things happen for a reason and for the right reason. As hard as I try, I cannot see the light on this one. So it is with a broken heart, I announce the ticket refunds for the event will go as posted by Ticketmaster. I want to thank the Irish authorities for going the distance for all of us who wanted to share songs and dance together. I really want to thank all the people around the world that continued to think good thoughts that this would actually happen. Most of all, to Peter Aiken [of Aiken Promotions] and those 400,000 people who believed enough to go through what they have been through to get to this point … I love you, always have, always will. I encourage any and all of them that can come see the show, at some point around the world, to bring your Irish flags and wave them proudly at the concerts. I will be looking for you.[28]

Arts Minister Jimmy Deenihan said the 'saga' was an embarrassment for the country: 'It is a huge disappointment and when you consider 400,000 people were going to come to Dublin for these concerts, it's a huge loss as well to the city … it will result in reputational damage to the country as well.'[29] He added the point that 70,000 of the tickets had been sold to customers overseas, and if all these people decided not to come to Ireland now, it would represent a one per cent drop in tourist numbers over a calendar year.

Dublin Lord Mayor Christy Burke described the incident as 'a funeral without a corpse' and spoke about the 'sadness throughout the nation' on TV3 News.[30] Hundreds of fans in Dublin signed their names on a 'Save Garth' van which moved around the city. Burke spoke about a seventeen-year-old girl who had rung him and asked him to plead with the leader of the government to intervene. She had been counting on three days' work with the catering company in Croke Park. The Lord Mayor appealed to Garth Brooks and his team: 'Please reconsider. Please consider the fans. Please consider the small businesses and the community and indeed all of those who have bought tickets.' Business interests claimed Ireland would lose up to €50 million as a result of the cancelled concerts. Donal O'Keefe, chief executive of the Licensed Vintners Association, spoke to *Six One News*, the premier news programme on state television:

> We're shocked and dismayed by this. It's a disaster for the pubs in Dublin. It's a disaster for the wider hospitality sector in Dublin, including restaurants and the hotels and for the image of the city. Our reputation as an events centre and our famousness for hospitality have been damaged by this decision.[31]

He too called on the taoiseach and government to try to do something to get the concerts to proceed as planned. Gina Quin, Chief Executive of the Dublin Chamber of Commerce, also spoke to *Six One*:

> We are damaged by this. You can't avoid that. What we have to do now is to actually change how people think about Ireland. Events are part of our tourism product so we need to address all of the planning issues.[32]

On the same programme Lord Mayor Christy Burke said, 'Ireland is saddened, Europe is saddened and further afield is saddened,' but he did not want to get into 'the blame game'. He termed the legislation pertaining to the holding of concerts in Croke Park outdated and instructed the chief of the Dublin municipal authorities to consider bringing in revised rules. A resident of the area adjacent to Croke Park who took an injunction against all five concerts was sent a death threat and 'was in absolute bits' in the Lord Mayor's office, according to Burke. Taoiseach Enda Kenny had received more than 1,000 emails on the subject, according to TV3, which had sought the information under the Freedom of Information Act. *The Journal* website calculated Garth Brooks was mentioned 103 times in the various organs of government.[33]

Marian Finucane interviewed performer Sandy Kelly on RTÉ Radio 1 on 13 July 2014 and asked her to contextualise the happenings from a music perspective. 'I don't think,' said Kelly, 'it's a country music thing … Garth Brooks is a little bit outside the box of traditional country music. If you look at the audience coming to see him, they wouldn't necessarily be country music fans … they are Garth Brooks fans.' Big artists in Nashville would, according to Kelly, now think twice if they were offered work in Ireland following the Brooks episode.

Fiona Looney, journalist with *The Irish Times*, wrote a play centred on the concert saga: *Are You There Garth? It's Me, Margaret.* In it, Margaret from Kinnegad has been through a terrible time because of the economic recession. Her husband, whom she met at a Brooks concert seventeen years earlier, has lost his job and she has been on her knees financially since then, trying to get the children through school. At the end of this bleak road stands the light of a Garth Brooks concert, but it is not to be. Looney spoke to Brendan O'Connor on his RTÉ Radio 1 show on 6 July 2007. He wanted to know if Brooks had let the people down. Fiona Looney was definite: 'Yeah I think he did, to be honest … I think he let down 400,000 people.'

At present Garth Brooks has no plans to return to Ireland.

10

'YOUR NEXT DANCE PLEASE': TRIPPING THROUGH THE WORLD OF COUNTRY MUSIC DANCING

Try everything once except incest and folk dancing.

Sir Thomas Beecham[1]

Garth Brooks was not the only country craze to sweep Ireland in the 1990s. The decade also saw the start of a dancing phenomenon that swept the country and briefly dominated the leisure time of a substantial number of the Irish people.

There is a long, documented history of dancing in various guises in Ireland: Druids danced around oak trees at religious ceremonies; the Celts imported their folk dances from central Europe; the Anglo-Normans brought with them 'carol' dancing from Normandy (performed in conquered towns) in which the leader sang surrounded by a circle of dancers who replied with the same song; and English colonists brought their own preferred dances in later times, including quadrilles, the two-step and the waltz. Historical accounts of life in Ireland frequently describe dances at social gatherings such as weddings, fairs and on holidays. Sir Henry Sidney visited Galway in 1569 and wrote a letter to Queen Elizabeth describing girls he saw dancing jigs as 'very beautiful, magnificently dressed and first class dancers'.[2] He observed the dancers performing in straight lines, which suggests they may have been performing a 'long dance' or *Rince Fada*, which – along with the 'Irish Hey' and 'Trenchmore' – was the most popular dance of the era. The Trenchmore was an adaptation of an old, Irish peasant dance, while the Hey was a forerunner of the present-day reel.

As far back as the early 1700s, travelling dance masters, professional educated men, moved around Ireland teaching step dancing – so called because it was executed in eight-bar steps. These dances were highly disciplined; they included the holding of hands, albeit loosely. The masters, typically flamboyant characters with bright clothes and staffs in their hands, tied straw or hay to the pupil's left or right foot and instructed 'lift hay foot' or 'lift straw foot'. Those pupils who showed the greatest abilities became soloists and were held in high regard in their community; doors were often taken off their hinges and placed on the ground for them to demonstrate their skills.

In the late nineteenth century dance masters modified traditional dances by making them more formal, with the adoption of a more rigid posture and less movement of the hand. High kicks and finger snapping were discouraged. The Gaelic League, established in 1893 to promote all aspects of Irish culture, further codified this form of dancing, which was becoming known as 'Irish dancing'. The dancing of the Munster region was promoted, as it was there that the dance masters were most active, while there was criticism of dances in the west and north of the country.

In 1904 a correspondent in the *Western People* wrote of local dancing: 'In some instances there was a tendency to clog-dancing and other displays more suggestive of English than of Irish style.'[3] Two years later the northern style was described as:

… a series of 'batters' – more batters indeed than the best Irish dancer would be called on to execute and the pity is that those whose wonderfully intelligent feet mistake the 'clog' for the real article should not have the opportunity of practising the real Irish hornpipe.[4]

The west Galway or '*sean-nós*' style, which was more 'flat-footed' than the Munster style and often featured the flamboyant arm movements frowned on by Munster dancing masters, was also rejected. A strict interpretation of the Munster style was presented as the national style and came to dominate the traditional style from that time on.[5]

No type of dancing can dominate a culture forever, however, and many shades and styles were to have their day. But nothing created as much of a media stir as the line-dancing boom of the 1990s. The Reverend Ian Paisley, head of the Democratic Unionist Party (DUP), said of the style: 'Line dancing is as sinful as any other type of sexual gestures and touchings. It is sensual, not a crucifying of lust but an excitement to lust.'[6] The Reverend David McIlveen of Paisley's Free Presbyterian Church's Morals and Standards Committee took it a step further, condemning dancing in general:

Well as far as we are concerned, we feel that dancing in any shape or form is incompatible with a Christian profession. We were mainly concerned about couples coming to our Church to get married who bring a very strong and a very sincere testimony of their saving faith in the Lord Jesus Christ. They could well go to a reception which included some form of dancing as part of that reception. We felt as a church that this was inconsistent with regard to their own personal testimony which was confirmed and spoken about in the Church.[7]

Mr McIlveen had only once seen line dancing – on a video – but was aware of the general danger of dancing from reading the Bible:

It very often does happen, as mentioned in the Bible, that dancing has a sexual outcome. When Moses came down from the mountain to find the Israelites dancing there was undoubtedly sexual activity going on.[8]

These comments were met by a strong response from the DUP's political opponents, including South Armagh Ulster Unionist Party (UUP) candidate David Burnside, who described them as an attack on a perfectly normal leisure activity: 'I'm calling on line dancers to say "No", to carry out a campaign against the Paisleys … who are trying to stop people having a bit of decent ordinary fun.'[9]

While out canvassing, Burnside had found the line-dancing issue such a hot topic of conversation among the public that he considered it worth using in his political campaign: 'This gives a warning to the voters if the Paisleyites get elected to Westminster or to local government. What sort of dictatorial regime would they impose on our lives?'

His opponent, Willie McCrea of the DUP, hit back:

It is pathetic at a time when the RUC [Royal Ulster Constabulary, the former police force in Northern Ireland] is being destroyed and Sinn Fein/ IRA is in Government and terrorists are being released on to our streets that David Burnside should attack me on a matter such as line dancing.[10]

But it was Burnside rather than McCrea who seemed to have tapped into the popular zeitgeist. The natives had also become restless over Paisley and his Church's comments. Rose Kilmartin, a line-dancing enthusiast from Belfast, spoke to BBC Radio Ulster's *Talkback* programme: 'What is the difference between dancing and singing or anything in which people enjoy themselves through music? I think it is quite ludicrous. Dancing is a different form of socialisation.' Kilmartin believed that line dancers were exercising their gift from God, and that line dancing did not fit a 'sensual' description: 'Line dancing's very name suggests that everyone is dancing in a line. As far as it being sensual, that is not a word you would attribute to country music.'[11]

Tony Devenney, chairman of the Western Dance Association of Ireland, and a line dancing teacher for seven years, was also not happy:

A lot of people have been seriously offended. We have 70 instructors teaching thousands of people every year, many of them committed Christians, who've made a lot of friends across the religious divide, and get a great deal of innocent pleasure from line dancing. What sort of social life do these Free Presbyterians have if they're not allowed to dance?[12]

Paisley and his Church were not the only ones to criticise line dancing. Irish writer Joseph O'Connor was also unimpressed, albeit for a different reason. In *Sweet Liberty: Travels in Irish America* he wrote about going to New York City nightclub Denim and Diamonds. It was the first time he had seen line dancing and he was not charitable in his description:

There must have been several hundred of them and they were doing something so ineffably strange, so truly horrifying, that if I had not seen it myself, and if I had not somehow summoned up the presence of mind to capture it all on several rolls of high grade Kodak film so that I could examine it later, in the cold light of day, and rub my eyes in numb and gaping horror, I would not have believed it was possible. I would have thought I had been slipped some potent hallucinogenic drug.[13]

He went on to describe the dancing:

Two hundred check-shirted and chubby New Yorkers all twisting and grinding and swivelling their hips and swinging their arses and smacking their corpulent thighs and yee-hawing, and doing it all with military precision, standing in lines, each in his or her own little defined space, not one of them ever touching another ... I remember thinking, as I gazed in abject dread upon this terrifying scene, that if the Nazis had succeeded in conquering the world, this is how everyone would dance.[14]

He saw a woman with all the usual symptoms of this 'scourge': 'the wide-eyed vacuous stare, the Stetson hat, the jeans so tight you could read the dates on the coins in her pockets'. O'Connor hoped line dancing would never take off in Ireland. Unfortunately things did not work out as he wished. Two years later he had settled back in Dublin where 'line dancing has caught on ... the way leather trousers caught on in 1930s Germany.'[15] When his nephew was asked to write down the name of his home town – Youghal in County Cork – O'Connor wrote that the young man spelled it 'Y'all'.

Despite the cynicism shown by O'Connor and other cultural commentators, line dancing went on to achieve huge popularity in Ireland when it crossed the Atlantic from the United States.

The origins of line dancing actually lie in the disco scene of the 1970s, not among cowboys in the 'wild west', despite the Stetsons, western shirts and boots. 'The Continental Walk' – a version of a previous dance called 'The Hustle' – is frequently cited as the first disco line dance. The 1977 movie *Saturday Night Fever* created a boom in coordinated disco dances, but it was Billy Ray Cyrus's single 'Achy Breaky Heart' which unleashed a line-dance craze in the early 1990s in country music circles across the United States. Written by Don Von Tress, the song was originally called 'Don't Tell My Heart' and was first performed by the Marcy Brothers in 1991, but when Cyrus covered it on his 1992 album *Some Gave All*, it became a worldwide hit.

Cyrus, a Kentucky-born artist who had been struggling to make it in the music industry for years, had unwittingly uncaged a rare beast. The record company released the single five weeks before the album, and it sold 500,000 copies alone. The album sold more than eleven million copies in the

United States and topped both the country and the pop charts. The singer became an 'overnight' success, having performed in small bars for nearly fifteen years previously. It is not a universally appreciated song; VH1, an American television music channel, lists it at number two on their '50 Most Awesomely Bad Songs Ever', and according to Kurt Wolff it is 'as dumb as they come'.[16] Wolff also criticised Cyrus for his 'decidedly unfashionable haircut' and 'Chippendale-style stage moves'; the singer's defining physical features were his mullet and chunky musculature. In his tight T-shirt or tank top, Cyrus was far removed from the cowboy image portrayed by the many 'hat acts' in vogue.

Despite the reservations expressed by many at the time, the music video for the song, choreographed by Melanie Greenwood, launched a dancing craze which soon spread to countries across the world. The launch of Country Music Television (CMTV) – the 'V' was dropped after a complaint from MTV – in the United States gave the video and song huge exposure. The combination of young, good-looking music stars and the pulsating rhythms proved a lucrative mix. To help with the promotion of the record, the production team also made an eleven-minute video outlining the dance steps, and distributed it to bars and clubs throughout the country. Even though Cyrus was not a particularly talented dancer, the moves designed by Greenwood were easy to follow and her choreography skills were much in demand; among her many creations were the 'Lambada' dance for Lorrie Morgan's song 'Watch Me' and the 'Four Star Boogie' for Marty Stuart's 'Now That's Country'. Many other singers got in on the act. Mary Chapin Carpenter had her 'Down at the Twist and Shout', Tracy Byrd her 'Watermelon Crawl' and Tim McGraw his 'Indian Outlaw', but it was Brooks and Dunn's 'Boot Scootin' Boogie' which came closest to the success of Billy Ray Cyrus. A 1995 version of the traditional American folk song 'Cotton Eye Joe' by Swedish band Rednex unleashed a further avalanche of line dancers on the world; it is a tune heard across the world in nightclubs to this day.

In Ireland, line dancing quickly gained traction and became a prominent feature of St Patrick's Day parades. In 1995 Sean Whelan did a feature on it for *RTÉ News*. The opening shots showed a group of line dancers on a rainy main street in a small town. Whelan reported: 'Line dancing is the craze that has swept the nation. If proof were needed, all you had to do was turn up at the parade today.'[17] The clip went on to show parades from around the country with Stetson-wearing, jeaned-and-booted cowboys and cowgirls stepping in unison to 'Cotton Eye Joe'. The presenter went into a shop and asked the shopkeeper: 'Boxes of Stetsons point to the growing popularity, but why do people do it?' The reply was that 'they like to get dressed up and they like to get into all the gear and it's a very healthy pastime'. The segment finished with the Dublin parade, where a dance troupe in full denim, black Stetsons and black boots stepped in perfect time. However, not everyone was happy, said Whelan, as he introduced 'the words of an expert' – Dustin the Turkey, a puppet frequently on Irish television at the time:

Absolutely scandalous … It's terrible I tell ya. If Saint Patrick was alive today he'd turn in his grave he would … ah this line dancing has been spreading, it's a terrible disease … spreading throughout the whole country and it's coming from places like Leitrim and Cavan and Longford … uneducated people goin' out and spreadin' this disease to the good people … even line dancing appeared in the Dublin parade and I don't know … it's a well-known fact too that snakes attend line-dancing classes regularly … that's why Saint Patrick got rid of them out of Ireland.[18]

Line dancing sounds straightforward. Each dance consists of a number of walls. A wall is the direction in which the dancers face at any given time: front, back or one of the sides. In a one-wall dance the dancers end up facing in the same direction as when they started, while in a two-wall dance the start of each routine alternates between two walls (almost always the front and back walls). A four-wall line dance is one in which, at the end the whole routine of dance moves, the dancers turn through ninety degrees, so that they face all four walls in turn during four repetitions of the routine. However, for those who are poorly coordinated and have tried some of the more complex steps, it is not as easy as it might look.

Liam Fay, of *Hot Press* magazine, attended an 'intermediate' line-dancing class in Break for the Border nightclub in January 1995. He could 'hear his hair turn grey' in the alcohol-free environment as he watched the participants struggle with the steps to 'If Bubba Can Dance (I Can Too)' by Shenandoah.[19] Fay interviewed country music journalist and broadcaster Howard Dee, who established Step in Line dance company with his partner Geraldine Halpin. Halpin had seen line dancing in the Rodeo nightclub in Nashville and thought it would work well in Ireland. She toured the United States to choose appropriate dances and settled on those popular on the west coast, because they were 'more stylish and less hick'. From this they derived the company motto 'We're Hip: Not Hick'. They hired Skip Jennings, an American dancer resident in Ireland, to teach classes around the country. Before Irish actor Colin Farrell achieved international success, he appeared on Irish language television channel TG4 as a line dancer as part of Jennings' troupe. Sporting a sleeveless western shirt, Stetson hat, tight jeans and cowboy boots, he was a good dancer but never looked as though he enjoyed it. Despite this, in television interviews over the years Farrell has frequently been reminded of his early career.

Dee told Fay he believed line dancing grew quickly in popularity for the same reason as country music did:

Baby-boomers had nowhere else to turn. They didn't find much solace in the beat-driven music which is all you hear in the nightclubs. They also got tired of the classic hits formula, 'Brown Sugar' rehashed a million times. They found shades of stuff like the Eagles and James Taylor in what Nashville is pumping out at the moment, and they liked it.[20]

He acknowledged the social dimension too:

> Not everybody in Ireland has a partner and, in Line Dancing, the whole floor is your partner. It's safe sex, dancing style. Women, particularly, are not preyed upon by guys just looking for a piece of meat for the night. The highest proportion of people going to Line Dancing are women, the gender balance is about 75 to 25.[21]

But Fay was unimpressed with proceedings and launched into a scathing criticism of line dancing:

> There is something horribly depressing about watching young folk waste the best years of their lives on a craze as mundane and moribund as Line Dancing. If these people wore red noses, revolving bow-ties and honked loud horns, they couldn't look like bigger clowns. It's not only that their hops, skips and jumps are so hopelessly prim and twee. It's that they have to labour so hard to make them that way. The scowls of humourless concentration on the dancers' faces are truly frightening. Not a single person smiles. They all just stare intently downwards, solemnly scrutinising every step as though they were tip-toeing through a minefield.[22]

Today Howard Dee lives in Athboy, County Westmeath, and is still involved in the country music industry as singer Kathy Crinion's manager. About the line-dancing world of the 1990s, he says:

> It was like the hula hoop. It was a craze. It snowballed. I suppose I would now say it was a bit of a gimmick. We had sponsorship from Coors and Wrangler and Country Music Television got involved. It was all over by the end of the summer of 1995 but it was great while it lasted. The pubs had enough of people coming in and only drinking water. For me it was always more about the music.[23]

Colin Farrell? 'Colin hated it but he needed the money at the time. I got him through Assets Model Agency in Dublin,' says Dee. 'In fairness I have heard he has been very gracious about me over the years. He's thanked me for helping him get used to performing in front of a live audience and for a look inside the world of show business.'[24]

Skip Jennings? He is now a motivational speaker in Hollywood.

***

Howard Dee was not the only person to identify the business opportunity that line dancing presented. Robert and Regina Padden from Crossmolina, County Mayo, established a line-dancing school called RnR in August 1994. It was the first such venture outside Dublin. The couple had been to Las Vegas the previous February and seen the genre's burgeoning popularity. In that pre-Internet age, the only forms of advertising RnR used were fliers and word of mouth. Within a month the business had expanded to two further venues and was catering for upwards of 350 people. From the start, eighty per cent of the attendees were female. Their classes went from strength to strength at an 'incredible rate', according to Robert. 'It was something new. It was before the Internet or anything like that. It was also something the whole family could do,' he said. 'You'd have children of seven and eight in the class along with their parents and grandparents. There had been nothing like that before. At the very height of it I remember having 420 people in the town hall in Ballina.'[25]

In February 1995 the couple organised an outdoor line dance in Castlebar for charity, attended by more than 1,000 people. 'At the time it was so busy I could have employed twenty people full-time teaching,' Robert remembered. In the same year a team from RnR travelled to the British Dancing Championships in Torquay, where they placed second.

In December 1996 Robert and Regina enjoyed a major breakthrough when they choreographed 'Electric Reel' set to the music of 'Cry of the Celts' from 'The Lord of the Dance', an Irish dance and music show put together by American dancer Michael Flatley. 'Electric Reel' quickly became an international sensation and was voted Line Dance of the Year in British magazine *Linedancer*. The couple were invited to judge competitions in Great Britain, Holland and at the famous Tamworth Country Music Festival in Australia. The following year they choreographed the 'Shamrock Shuffle' set to the song 'Tell Me Ma' by the band Sham Rock. Such was the popularity of the dance that the single was re-released.

By 2001 Robert reckons they were getting only ten per cent of the original numbers, so the couple tried to reinvigorate the scene by introducing couple dancing, East Coast Swing and West Coast Swing, but nothing achieved the same traction as the original. As well as there being too many substandard teachers and classes, things had moved on and the worldwide boom had died down. It was time to shut up shop, but by that time the couple had formed Wavelength, a successful covers band.

When asked to look back on the boom and explain its success, Robert takes a minute. 'There were a few things about it,' he says. 'All ages could come to the classes, like I said. It was great for fitness and it was cheap. Women felt comfortable in the environment. Things move on, but it was a great time.'[26]

Despite its popularity, perhaps surprisingly, the line-dancing craze did not necessarily benefit live country music. According to singer Declan Nerney, an astute observer of the country music scene in Ireland:

There were a lot of country music clubs that line dancing eradicated. That was another big blow, a huge blow … even though it would, so to speak, wear the hat of country music … the line dancing would … it definitely didn't go anywhere to enhance getting more younger people involved in coming into country clubs.[27]

***

While line dancing may have waned in popularity, country-music-led social dancing classes and evenings have exploded in popularity in recent years. Eunice Moran from Ballaghaderreen is one of the leading teachers on the circuit in the west of Ireland:

> People want to be able to dance the proper steps when they go to hear the bands. I teach four dances at my classes – the jive, the waltz, the quickstep and the foxtrot. The jive is very popular in recent times with the more upbeat country music, and some teachers just concentrate on that, but I like to cover all four.[28]

Jiving was introduced to Europe by American soldiers during the Second World War and, as with other things, it was associated with the United States so it was something to aspire to. John Waters memorably described the role of jiving during his younger years living in Castlerea, County Roscommon. According to Waters, if you wanted to meet girls, you had to go to see Irish country acts like Big Tom and Larry Cunningham, and you had to be able to jive:

> Much of the action and activity of the dance was performed by the female, but she remained at all times within her partner's control. The jive enabled the male to participate fully in a dance of apparently great intricacy while managing to appear totally disinterested in what he was doing. It allowed country men who felt uncomfortable in their Sunday suits to communicate with women without speaking and without losing their sense of composure.[29]

Romances grew, Waters went on, 'from a couple's ability to jive together as frequently as they did out of compatibility in other matters. The more permanent the relationship, the more complex and dexterous became their embellishments of the jive.'[30]

I asked Eunice Moran why jiving has become pre-eminent over other dances in recent times:

Well it's high energy and you can add a lot more things into it, a lot more fancy footwork and that. People like to show off new moves. With the other dances, you learn them and that's it. There's not much you can add to them. The thing I find is that many people will come to the classes just expecting to learn to jive, but really like the others when I introduce them. Also you can talk more with some of the slower dances, and some people get into the scene to meet people so I tell them you need to know the other dances as well.

Moran teaches classes seven days a week, both public and private:

It's a booming business. Younger people love it. They got sick of the nightclubs and the emphasis on alcohol. It's not just young people that come to my classes though. I get a mix of all age groups. I like the name social dancing because it is what it says it is – sociable.

I asked her if her classes are all about teaching? 'No, some people come in later just to dance after the teaching is finished. We even have live music some times. It's great.'[31]

Another well-known instructor on the social-dance teaching circuit is Roscommon man Gerard Butler. He too instructs dancers in the steps popular for country music dancing in Ireland and is particularly well known for teaching jiving in the northern half of Ireland. Teaching country music social dancing is, he says, all about effective communication skills: 'If you can put people at ease it is half the battle.'[32]

When Butler first started out, his classes were overwhelmingly attended by women, but this imbalance has changed over the years, and roughly forty per cent of his attendance now is male. Social dancing, he says, thrives in recessionary times. 'At the height of the boom people had more interesting and expensive things to do and attendances dropped off,' he explains, 'but with the crash there wasn't as much money around the place. The thing is, it's an affordable night out where people can meet friends and get exercise.'

There will, according to Butler, always be a future for social dancing and dance teachers: 'There'll always be people who like to learn new skills and socialise in an environment where it's not all about alcohol. ... Although things come in waves and the nightclubs might make a comeback yet.'

He points out that the new range of artists on the country music scene has been a huge boost for the dance-teaching industry. 'The thing about the likes of Nathan Carter is it makes things into a two-way street. I was talking to his manager John Farry recently and he agreed with me,' he says. 'When people go to the concerts they like to be able to dance properly, so they come to me first, so it's great for all of us at the moment.'

It is not only concerts where people like to be able to show their skills. On a wet Wednesday night in March in Westport, County Mayo, in the Westport Woods Hotel, dancing instructor Sean Joyce notes that some of his class that evening are there to brush up on their dancing skills before an upcoming wedding the following weekend. In the basement function room, roughly forty people are concentrating on learning the steps to what looks like a complex line dance.

Joyce, along with Kay Ryan, runs a weekly social-dancing night in the hotel. For him the social aspect of the dancing is what keeps people coming. Many people find it an easier environment than traditional nightclubs in which to talk to others, and 'there's more focus on dancing and less on drinking,' he says.[33] He compares the social-dancing environment with nightclubs: 'The music is easier to dance to. The lighting actually allows people to see each other. It's an outlet for people who had no suitable environment to meet people in the past.' It is also, he explains, a comfortable environment for people to come to after a separation or divorce, or the death of a partner. People can gradually ease back into a social life without being intimidated by the aggression and heavy drinking associated with other social outlets.

Sean introduces Kevin, an exceptionally sprightly 'over-65' from Mulranney, just over twenty miles from Westport. Although he is married, he comes on his own because his wife has no interest in dancing. 'Jiving was always my thing and I love coming to Sean and Kay's classes. It's mighty altogether, great that this type of dancing has taken off in such a big way,' he says. 'It's a funny thing, but a lot of people like to go dancing in places away from their own town or village,' he continues. 'There's still a bit of snobbery about it in some people's mind. The thing is,' he chuckles, 'the ones who criticise know nothing about social dancing at all.' Just then Sean announces the restart of the dancing and informs the crowd that this time it will be a jive. Within moments couples are flying around the floor, before the music changes to a Garth Brooks song and the dance to a slow waltz.

I ask Sean if social dancing is a way for people to meet potential partners. 'It has happened but it is not part of the agenda ... the place to go for that is the big live-country-music venues,' and he points to the McWilliam Park Hotel in Claremorris as an example.

The McWilliam Park Hotel is a mecca for Irish country music and social dancing in the heart of the west of Ireland. It is 'The Nashville of the West' according to its own publicity. On Tuesday 27 June 2017, American Robert Mizzell, a major star on the Irish country music circuit, is playing in the hotel. Before the concert Mizzell explained to me how he came to understand the centrality of dancing in Irish country music following his attendance at a gig by Offaly singer John Hogan in Kildare. It was a startling experience for the Louisiana man:

The one thing I couldn't get over was the fact that all these people herded onto the floor when the music started and then there was a space between songs where they all left the floor, reformed and came back out again, and I was trying to figure this out. For a long time I couldn't and I discovered that it was an actual set of dances, a set of jives, a set of waltzes, a set of foxtrots … the dancing is very particular and you have to do it in a certain way. Believe me, the dancers out there, if you don't do it the right way they'll tell you, they know how to dance, they know their style.[34]

Waiting for the music to start are the three McGintys – Sheila and her daughters, Triona and Laura – and their friend Ann, who have travelled from Achill to dance and will 'go anywhere for dancing'. They cannot wait for the music to start. 'The thing about coming here is that the people are courteous and mannerly … most of them, anyway. There's never any hassle. If you refuse a dance there's no problem,' Triona says.

Patricia and Janet are glamorous women in their fifties who have travel-led to the McWilliam Park Hotel from Galway city for the night. Patricia is eloquent about the attraction of social dancing: 'Dancing is good for the soul because you live in the moment. It is uplifting, a form of expression.' The ballroom is big, with plenty of places to sit and talk, unlike a conventional nightclub. The music is loud, but it is still possible to hold a conversation. The atmosphere is upbeat, and there is no sense of latent threat sometimes found in other late-night social events. Throughout the night the number of women dancing with other women is noticeable.

The McGinty sisters finally sit down after nearly half an hour of non-stop dancing. 'Well the music is great, anyway. I like Robert Mizzell. I only saw him once before. The men are no great shakes though,' Triona says. The other women are in agreement.

As the night comes to an end towards 2.30 a.m., those who came with the intention of having a few drinks are still going strong at the bar counter. Tom Nallen, a jovial man from Belmullet, is talking to the McGinty family. Tom, who is divorced, sums up his attraction to social dancing: 'I love the dancing. I go all over the place for it. It's a great way to meet people and get a bit of exercise at the same time.'

American sociologist Ray Oldenburg has a famous theory about the importance of informal public gathering places, which he calls 'the third place', for a functioning civil society and democracy and for civic engagement. Home is the first place, the workplace the second, and the third is the place where we meet other people and fulfil our social needs, meet and make friends, develop a network and unwind from the stresses of everyday life. In his book *The Great Good Place* he suggests the pub is an ideal third place.[35] Experience of 'The Nashville of the West' suggests that it may well be time for Oldenburg to add social dancing to the list.

Questions arise about how long the social-dancing scene will survive in its current form. Robert Mizzell believes it has a great future:

> You are the vehicle for people to have a great night. It's all about the dancing and the beat for jiving, waltzing and quickstep, and you have to structure the whole thing properly ... When you go to pubs and clubs, you're going into a dark room where you can't see anyone, can't get to the bar and can't talk. I don't find that entertainment, and a lot of people feel the same way. With country music you have a great night, meet your friends, and make new ones of all ages. What more could you ask for?[36]

Mick Flavin sees it differently:

> The dancing has gone back a lot in the last few years. I think it will be more or less gone in ten years' time. You just need to look at the number of venues now and the amount of them that there used to be. I think there are only four up north now. The thing is moving towards concerts. There's only a living in it for a handful of bands. Those few might be doing well, but there isn't the work to go around. Things have changed. The smoking ban and the drink driving legislation hit the scene and people are changing the way they live. They can buy cheap alcohol and go around to each other's houses. If you look at Christmas you can see the way things have gone. One time there was a great buzz around it with dances everywhere, but now it's

the same as every other weekend. Mayo and Donegal were the best two dancing counties in the country. You only need to look at how few venues there are in both of them now to see how things have changed.[37]

Only the future will tell, but one thing is certain; social dancing is still immensely popular in Ireland. Rachel Lavin wrote in the *Sunday Independent* of her attendance at a social-dance class in Roscommon:

Social dancing has all the old-fashioned Hollywood romance of being approached for the dance with old-fashioned chivalry, and all the fast-paced craic and increasingly complicated dance moves, as well as a unique local flavour you'll only get on the rural Ireland country and western scene. As I travel back to the city, I wonder if I can convince my Dublin friends to come down the country and experience the thrill of 'keeping her country'.[38]

For the time being, dancing is still at the very centre of the Irish country music scene and for many people across the nation it is their primary social outlet. If analysed more closely, it would prove, no doubt, to be making a decent contribution to the Irish economy. It is a hobby that brings happiness and health to many people. Above all else, it brings people directly into contact with others, an increasingly rare event in a world where technology continues to change the way we live. Whether Robert Mizzell or Mick Flavin is right about its future, only time will tell.

11

TRYING TO KEEP IT COUNTRY: THE MEDIA AND COUNTRY MUSIC IN IRELAND

Despite the popularity of the genre, the amount of coverage given to Irish country music by the national broadcaster has long been a bone of contention in certain quarters. Michael Commins agrees that the airtime for country music on RTÉ is lacking. Indeed, he believes it was 'virtually musical apartheid' for many years.[1] Occasionally a country song might be heard in a music programme, but that was very much an exception, and often a novelty.

During the 1950s and 1960s country music fans in Ireland had limited options for listening to their chosen music. Those lucky enough to receive the American Forces Network radio signal were able to hear the music regularly, but the signal was available only to those who lived in or close to Northern Ireland and those who had short-wave radio sets (as Michael Commins did). Other than the AFN and Radio Luxembourg, pirate-radio stations were the only consistent source of country music. Singer Mick Flavin spoke to me about their role:

The pirate radio stations were crucial for the music. The likes of me would never have got any coverage without them. I remember bringing around my cassettes to them. They led on to the creation of the legal stations then. They were so important.[2]

From 1965 Canadian 'Daffy' Don Allen was the voice of country music on pirate station Radio Caroline. Born in Winnipeg, Manitoba, Allen spent time working as a broadcaster in the United States before moving to England. He presented the weekly *Country and Western Jamboree* along with his daily programme *Big Wide Wonderful World of Daffy Don Allen*. He stayed with Radio Caroline until its closure in 1968. He then spent some time at Manx Radio in the Isle of Man, where a promotional advertisement for his show described him as 'the smooth-voice chief announcer, keen on country-style sounds'. In 1972 Allen moved to Radio North Sea International, which broadcast from a ship off the Dutch coast before it closed down in August 1974. He later moved to Ireland and spent time working at Radio Nova, Cavan Community Radio and Radio West in Mullingar. It was Allen, according to Michael Commins, who first gave Irish country music star Gene Stuart airplay.

However, RTÉ could not afford to completely ignore country music when its popularity rose in the 1970s and at that point the coverage increased to some degree. In early 1972 *It's Country Music Time* began broadcasting on RTÉ Radio on Saturday nights. It was introduced by Noel Andrews (a brother of Eamonn, who became a household name in Britain for his television show *This Is Your Life)*, with contributions from Paschal Mooney. Mooney, who became the face and voice of country music for many years on RTÉ Television and Radio, had begun his career working as an entertainment correspondent, writing about the Irish ballroom scene in London for *Spotlight* magazine, as well as writing a weekly column for London-based *The Irish Post*. Having been asked to cover the famous Wembley International Festival of Country Music a number of times, he developed a love of country music.

It's Country Music Time frequently topped the ratings published monthly by Television Audience Management (TAM) Ireland (whose managing board of directors represented all member broadcasters and agencies in the Republic of Ireland). During its lifetime the programme featured concerts from Dublin, Wembley and Nashville, and broadcast shows by Glen Campbell, Anne Murray, Chet Atkins, Bobby Bare, Waylon Jennings, Hank Snow, Loretta Lynn and the Glaser Brothers. When *Billboard* magazine interviewed its producer, Tony Gaynor, he explained:

> It's very popular, particularly outside the city. And we get a lot of fan mail from the North of England … For years country music was always popular, but it was generally because of a limited number of artists like Jim Reeves and Slim Whitman. In more recent times the field has broadened, so that it's now possible for Waylon Jennings to come here in May. Thirty years ago they'd have asked, 'Who?'[3]

Gaynor went on to tell *Billboard* about other developments in the Irish country scene:

> Irish artists have developed slowly but surely from country and Irish to a more refined country. There are better session men, better arrangements, better quality songs, musically and lyrically. Some of the better singers, such as Larry Cunningham and Ray Lynam, even prefer to go to Nashville to make records.

Gaynor pointed to country artists then popular in Ireland, who were previously rarely heard, including Charley Pride, Merle Haggard, Buck Owens, Hank Locklin and Johnny Cash. His programme, he believed, was a catalyst for the growing popularity of the music. 'A few years ago a lot of people liked country, but they didn't know what it was,' he said. 'The program encouraged people to go looking for lesser-known country artists.'

Performers who had previously not engaged with country music were now doing so, he believed. 'There's a bright picture here for the future. Dickie Roc's [sic] new album is country. Red Hurley and D. J. Curtin are singers who have big hits with country songs. The most popular Tom Jones disks here have been country ones.'[4]

The 1970s were to represent a high point in the coverage of country music by the national media. When RTÉ Radio 2 rebranded itself as 2FM in 1979, Paschal Mooney was asked to present *Keep It Country* twice weekly – between 8 p.m. and 10 p.m. on Tuesdays and Thursdays. RTÉ Television producer John McColgan noted the success of the programme and invited Mooney to present *Country Star Time*, a show which featured contemporary Irish country music bands and ran for two successful years. In the early 1980s Mooney presented a series of one-hour country music specials on television from various venues, including one filmed at the Rose of Tralee Festival; he also presented the first-ever National Country Music Awards broadcast live from Castlebar.

However, as Mooney points out in *The Swingin' Sixties Book*, a decision made by RTÉ Television in 1977 would effect a profound change in the Irish music industry and would adversely affect the future of country music in Ireland.[5] RTÉ 2 decided to start airing the BBC show *Top of the Pops*, the most successful popular-music television programme in Britain, at the same time as it was broadcast on the BBC. Within a couple of years the British Top Twenty had become the bible of the music industry in Ireland, displacing the Irish singles chart. The knock-on effect of this change was to make it virtually impossible for Irish artists to thrive, particularly country music performers. The acts, as Mooney said, 'lost the oxygen of their own publicity'. Acts began to disappear from radio and television, and the country music industry went into decline. Money became scarce and no prominent Irish country artist was to emerge until Daniel O'Donnell.

In 1984 RTÉ Radio 2 decided to orient itself towards pop and rock music, which resulted in Mooney's moving to RTÉ Radio 1, where he presented three weekly programmes. It was not a successful move, as Mooney explained:

> I think the decision taken in 1984 to drop *Keep It Country* and other pro-grammes of musical diversity from Radio 2 schedules damaged the station in the eyes of the Irish public. I strongly believe the decision taken then was wrong and has led to the slow decline of 2FM. The argument put forward, mainly by young producers from the Dublin pirate-radio scene, was that the original brief was for an exclusive pop-music station, and management at the time bought into it. I don't think the move was properly thought out. The programmes were spread across the schedules on different days and at different times. I lost the audience from *Keep It Country* and by 1987 I was presenting one forty-five-minute country music programme per week.[6]

Mooney remembers his time and many of his colleagues at RTÉ fondly, but he believes country music was not appreciated by all:

> RTÉ became ruled by a civil-service culture inimical to rurally orientated programmes. A snobby Dublin 4 mentality came to prevail. I remember my programmes being described as provincial by a senior management person at a meeting. They weren't seen as highbrow enough. Many of them had no interest in even trying to understand country music and what it meant to the people.[7]

Subsequently Mooney went on to script and present a series of country music documentaries featuring American and Irish stars Big Tom, Daniel O'Donnell, Margo, Brendan Shine, Bobby Bare, Patsy Cline, Hank Williams and Jim Reeves, among others. In later years he moved away from country music to concentrate on programmes about the Irish diaspora, including *The Irish Abroad* and *The Irish Experience*. In 2008 he presented a series for RTÉ called *Irish Music Legends*.

With the decrease in interest from the national broadcaster, pirate stations continued to provide a lifeline to Irish country performers. Then, in 2002, the Commission for Communications Regulation (ComReg) was founded by the Irish government to replace the Office of the Director of Telecommunications Regulation (ODTR). This well-resourced body set about dismantling the pirate radio industry. On Tuesday 20 May 2003 – a day which later became known as 'Black Tuesday' – the organisation, with the help of An Garda Síochána and the Electricity Supply Board, launched a major offensive against Dublin-based pirate stations. Subsequently they chased all other illegal operators off the airwaves, even carrying out raids at night in their thorough campaign. Not everyone in the industry appreciated their work, and some argued that only those stations which interfered with broadcast frequencies should have been eliminated and that some consideration should have been given to niche operators.

Paschal Mooney had mixed thoughts on current coverage of Irish country music on the national broadcaster when we spoke in September 2017:

> There is still a weekly country programme on RTÉ Radio but it features exclusively American artists. How can you have a country music programme on the national broadcaster and have no Irish country music on it? It's to be welcomed that RTÉ Television has bought into the current Irish country scene and is to be applauded for the high profile it has given and continues to give to the new generation of Irish country music talent. It's telling that the highest audience for *The Late Late Show* last season was the country music special. If you give your audience what they want, they respond.[8]

Today it is local radio stations that are the heartbeat of country music in Ireland. There are now twenty-five radio stations licensed on a regional basis in Ireland and more than twenty licensed community-radio stations; more are in the process of obtaining certification. The Joint National Listenership

Research (JNLR) survey, an industry research project conducted on behalf of the Irish radio sector, provides reliable estimates of audiences to national, regional and local radio. Its figures show that Ireland is a radio-friendly country: eighty-three per cent of adults – just over three million – listen on an average day, with fifty-eight per cent tuning in to their local or regional radio station. The average audience member listens to four hours of radio per day. The level of penetration of local markets by local and regional radio stations varies considerably, however – the nearer the local station is to an urban area, the lower the listenership. For example, local radio had just twenty-six per cent of the audience in Kildare, while the figure for north Donegal was sixty-three per cent.

When JNLR figures were released on 17 February 2017 there was great news for Midwest Radio. Its 'yesterday listenership' (the average daily listenership) had risen by six per cent from the previous year, to a remarkable sixty-one per cent of the total available listenership in its targeted area. The story of Midwest Radio and its owner, Paul Claffey, is well told by John Waters in *Jiving at the Crossroads*.

Claffey was a hero to a young Waters and his friends, and an example of how a local boy could make good in an area with limited employment opportunities. But his career started the hard way. He invested in the ballroom business just as the showband circuit was grinding to a halt. Legislation allowing hotels to have late-night bars finished the industry and he lost all his premises except one – the Midas nightclub in Ballyhaunis. From a small room at the back of that building, he began to broadcast a small pirate radio station – Midwest Radio. His initial musical tastes were for rock bands such as Thin Lizzy and Horslips, but he believed in giving the punters what they wanted to hear. Waters described the response of the local audience:

People who had become disconnected from what RTÉ was saying to them began to tune in and speak to each other through the medium of the station. Many of them were older people, whose children had left, and so found themselves alone all day in an empty house. They called up Claffey on the air and asked him to play their favourite come all ye's. Some would sing duets with him on the airwaves.[9]

One such was Kathleen Loftus from Ballyhaunis, who had an electric organ in her front room, and would call Claffey to sing her favourite songs, including 'Danny Boy', 'Amazing Grace' and 'South of the Border (Down Mexico Way)' live on air. Midwest Radio changed the local music scene; halls which a decade previously had played the music of Horslips or Thin Lizzy now jived to local country stars like Mick Cuffe, Kevin Prendergast and Mick Flavin. The station was, according to Waters, a 'pure and spontaneous explosion of a set of cultural values that had all but been wiped out by the optimism of the sixties'.[10]

In the summer of 1988 Midwest Radio had to close after the Irish government announced the forthcoming distribution of local radio franchises. If pirate stations wished to be considered, they had first to cease operating illegally and then complete a formal application. Claffey presided over the closing of Midwest Radio's original incarnation and was successful in his bid for one of the new licences. It is to his great credit that Midwest Radio is where it is today. His station and programme have never fallen outside the top three in popularity in the country. Since 2005 the station has run an online-only version called Midwest Irish Radio.

Waters concludes:

Claffey was the ultimate pragmatist, and his radio station, unencumbered by grandiose notions, began to provide the kind of service that he sensed his people wanted. There was no pop music: all the pop fans had left. There was country, country-and-Irish, traditional, and the mixture of all three, which, when played by oddly named local outfits, functioned as a sort of surrogate folk music. It was the kind of music which, years before, perched high on our platform shoes and thinking we could see for miles, we had pronounced to be as good as dead and good riddance. It was the maudlin music of a darker past which those of us who had left had come to associate with resignation and despair.[11]

Today, the west of Ireland is a more vibrant place, but the music remains the same; Irish country music has never been as popular.

Local stations often employ men and women who are living repositories of country music. Midwest Radio has one such man, Michael Commins, while another, Tom Gilmore, recently retired from Galway Bay FM.

Michael Commins has a huge following for his unique radio programme on Sunday and Wednesday nights. His personable and relaxed presentation style reinforces the sense of community that good local radio programmes can create. For him, country music listeners are one big family, and this sense of belonging is clear in his broadcasts. Commins constantly makes connections between people he has met and events in the community, an approach which has a huge appeal to his listenership.

Born near Kiltimagh, County Mayo, Commins spent his early working career in the bank, before turning to journalism. He got his first break with *Entertainment News*, which was based in Castleblaney, County Monaghan. He spent eight months there, writing on various aspects of the Irish music scene. Subsequently he moved back to his native Mayo to work for the short-lived *Western Journal* newspaper – it lasted from 1977 to 1983 – before writing for *The Connaught Telegraph* for thirteen years and the *Western People* for a further ten. In 2006 he joined *The Mayo News*, where he is still the entertainment correspondent, resident hurling reporter and contributor of stories of local interest. In 2006 and 2007 he wrote a country music column for the *Irish Mirror*, which, by his own admission, was not a natural fit, and in 2011 he began writing a weekly column for the *Irish Farmers Journal*. This, he says, is the perfect place for his writing, because it gets straight to rural Ireland, where Irish country music is most popular.

Louise Morrissey, the 'Bansha Lass'. *Courtesy of Louise Morrissey*

Sandy Kelly and George Hamilton IV in the Patsy Cline tribute show. *Courtesy of Sandy Kelly*

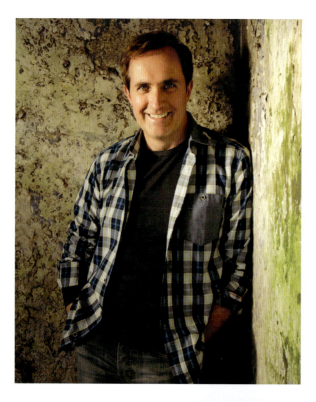

Marc Roberts, singer, songwriter, television presenter and DJ.
Courtesy of Marc Roberts

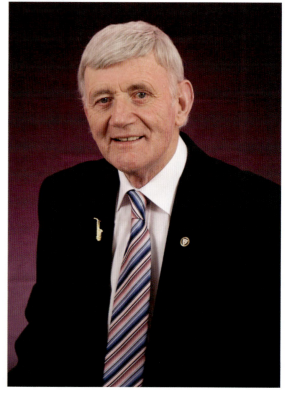

Henry McMahon, songwriter and original member of Big Tom and The Mainliners.
Courtesy of Henry McMahon

Right: James Kilbane, leading Irish country gospel singer. *Courtesy of James Kilbane*

Below: Robert Mizzell, Irish country music's best-known American star. *Courtesy of Sharon Kelly and Robert Mizzell*

Keelan Arbuckle, 'a young lad who sings the old songs'. *Courtesy of Keelan Arbuckle*

Michael English, the classical pianist who became a country star.
Courtesy of Tom Gilmore

Lee Matthews, who went from pop singer to country singer.
Courtesy of Lee Matthews

Johnny Brady, who was raised on rock but now lives on country.
Courtesy of Johnny Brady

From left: Willie Carty (Mike Denver's manager), Daniel O'Donnell, Mike Denver
and Kieran Kavanagh (Daniel O'Donnell's manager), all heavy hitters in the Irish
country music world. *Courtesy of Willie Carty*

Lisa Stanley, daughter of Maisie McDaniel and now a singing star in her own right.
Courtesy of Lisa Stanley

Lisa McHugh, the Scottish lass who has made it big in Ireland.
Courtesy of Lisa McHugh

Shauna McStravock from Ardboe, County Tyrone, a rising star in Irish country music. *Courtesy of Shauna McStravock*

Cliona Hagan and her manager Aidan Quinn. *Courtesy of Cliona Hagan*

Nathan Carter, the new superstar of Irish country music. *Courtesy of John Farry*

Declan Nerney, the man from Drumlish, County Longford. *Courtesy of Declan Nerney*

The column has become one of the pre-eminent sources of country music news in the Irish media.

Despite Commins' huge success in print, it is perhaps his radio programme on Midwest Radio – which has run since the launch of the official station in 1989 – that has most endeared him to the public. His homely presentation goes out twice weekly – on Sundays between 10 p.m. and 1 a.m. and Wednesdays between 11 p.m. and 2 a.m. While the show is scheduled to last for three hours, he regularly loses track of time in his efforts to mention all those who send in requests and often goes up to a half-hour over the indicated time slot. Commins reckons two nights a week is enough for any person on the radio: 'any more and they could get sick of you'.[12] The presenter has one of the highest profiles in the wider country music industry and, as well as organising his own country music weekends, he is a prolific and highly regarded songwriter. In finest country music tradition, Commins has been paid the ultimate compliment by Colman Cloran – a tribute song expressing the essence of what the presenter means to those who listen:

When the moon shines bright over Mayo
There's a sound nowhere else you will find
For at twenty past two in the morning
You will hear a voice that is gentle and kind.[13]

Like Michael Commins, Tom Gilmore has worked in both the broadcast and print media. Gilmore was the music-and-entertainment correspondent for *The Tuam Herald* for forty-two years, as well as working as a presenter on Galway Bay FM, where, until his recent retirement, he presented *Country Crossroads*, which delved 'into the diversity of sounds and styles that make up the chameleon musical collage that is the genre described as country' with a range of material from 'a Hungarian country band playing Johnny Cash songs to country music from Scandinavia, the Faroe Islands,

Namibia in Africa, Italy, Switzerland, Australia as well as that of Ireland and the USA'.[14] In his time, Gilmore has interviewed Garth Brooks, Johnny Cash and a whole host of luminaries in the industry. As well as writing for *The Tuam Herald*, Gilmore has produced pieces for *Country Music People* magazine (UK), *The Irish Scene* magazine (Western Australia) and *The Blackwell Guide to Recorded Country Music* (UK and USA). He also penned *Larry Cunningham: A Showband Legend* – a best-selling book in Ireland. Gilmore was given the high honour of putting the Irish case on record in *The Blackwell Guide*, which provides a summary of the world of country music up to 1993 and is an invaluable and singular document. No publication before or since has provided such a thorough 'state of the nation' analysis of the industry in Ireland and my hope is that he will one day get a chance to update it. Gilmore also co-presented radio programmes on a number of stations in Australia, where he lived for some time.

Tom Gilmore was relaxed in the foyer of the Ard Rí House Hotel in Tuam, County Galway, when we met to reminisce about his nearly fifty years working around the music industry.[15] From his varied career as a town clerk, Coca-Cola press officer, secondary-school teacher and journalist, he can look at the industry from all angles. He is annoyed at the narrow perceptions people have of the genre. 'The thing is you can like country music, but you don't have to like all of it. Country music is a broad church,' he says.

There is no aspect of or individual in Irish country music Gilmore does not seem to know. 'It goes all the way from bluegrass to your typical country and Irish. Some people dismiss country music without really knowing that much about it. I always tried to get across the breadth of the music on the radio show. I liked to play things people mightn't have expected to hear and I generally got a good response,' he says.

He continues, 'I understand that some people just don't like the old-style country and Irish music. That's fine, but there's a whole lot of other country music out there to be explored. I tried to show people that on my radio shows.'

I mentioned Michael Commin's view that there was musical apartheid in the national media when it came to country music in the past and Gilmore agreed: 'Michael is 100 per cent right. That's what it was. There were too many people in RTÉ that looked down their nose at country music.'

Like Commins, he is happy to see the expanded coverage of country music in the national media: 'It's great to see the awards on RTÉ Television. They ignored country music for long enough, but I think they've woken up to the fact that the people want to see it. That's certainly one good thing that I've seen in my lifetime.'

Tom Gilmore and Michael Commins are at the beating heart of the Irish country music industry and deserve every accolade that comes their way. But there are others forging the way ahead in the world of Internet radio. Howard Myers, originally from Wigan but long resident in Dublin, is an Internet-radio presenter and country-music disc jockey. He came to the profession by happenstance when asked to replace the famous cowboy-hat-wearing Tommy Flanagan, the long-time, colourful music maestro in Barry's Hotel – a bolt-hole for the country-music-loving crowd in Dublin. When I caught up with him he was tired from ongoing treatment for a chronic illness but was generous with his time. Along with his partner, Kathy Cullinan, Myers is the regular DJ at the Red Cow Inn (Dublin's premier – and only, at the time of writing – country-dancing venue) and he has also been a regular presenter for the last seven years on Internet-radio channel Irish Country Music Radio.

'My role as a DJ is basically to start the car, turn the ignition and get people warmed up for the main act of the evening,' he says. 'I have to play music that will get people up on their feet so the tempo is so important. I've learned that over the years.' He added a unique observation on the different music tempos popular in different parts of the country: 'The further south you go in Ireland, the faster you have to play the music. The further north you go, the slower they like the music.'[16]

Before joining Irish Country Music Radio Myers worked for Sunshine

Radio, originally called Country Sound. He presented a show in the small hours of the morning: 'It was the only programme dedicated to Irish country music on an FM station in Dublin.' His ambition to have a daytime programme dedicated to Irish country on the station foundered when the licence came up for renewal and the music schedule was reoriented.

While it continues to be a growing medium, there are restrictions with Internet radio, Howard notes. 'There is certainly an issue with access. Not all the demographic we are trying to reach are comfortable with technology. Internet radio sets are expensive. We are listed in the top ten listened-to Internet country-music stations in the world, but these things are hard to measure.' Regardless of the size of his listenership, Myers 'was overwhelmed by the enormous expression of goodwill' he received when he spoke of his illness on the radio.[17]

Unlike their national radio counterparts, television has recently shown itself to be more willing to publicise Irish country music. TG4, the national Irish-language television station, has done much to promote Irish country music from the time of its establishment in 1996. *Glór Tíre* – literally translating as country voice – is a talent show seeking to discover Ireland's next country star. Since it first went on air in 2002 it has consistently topped the station's charts, with an average viewership of more than 100,000. The show follows a format similar to that of many other reality series: contestants are ejected by public voting over a series of shows, until three are left to compete in the final show. Filmed in the Quays Bar in Galway, each participant in the show is mentored by an established Irish country music performer. Lisa McHugh, the runner-up in 2009, is now one of the most popular young female performers on the country scene.

With six seasons under its belt, *Opry an Iúir,* another TG4 show, is presented by Daniel O'Donnell. Each week it features a prominent country star performing both solo and in duets with O'Donnell. O'Donnell also sings a song or two in Irish, even though this is not his first language. On 23 December 2015 the show celebrated singer Brendan Shine's fifty years in the Irish country music business. TG4 has also screened individual programmes on the life and careers of various Irish country artists.

Galway woman Máire Ní Chonláin, the commissioning editor with TG4 and producer of long-running serial *Ros na Rún*, produced a number of successful country music programmes for the channel for the independent company Gael Media before she assumed her current role. Now occupying a central role in TG4, she holds trenchant views on the coverage of country music on the station. 'Country music is an important part of our culture,' she explains. 'It is as relevant as traditional music. We are about programming for the people. It is our job to give them what they want ... there will always be a slot on TG4 for country music.'[18]

There may be ideological opponents and those who look down on country music, but Ní Chonláin will always make sure it is included on the TG4 schedule. 'There is country music in the Outer Hebrides. It's a music form that is popular all over the world,' she goes on, before referring to the increasing coverage of country music on RTÉ: 'I think they saw what we were doing and how successful it is. Before that they wouldn't have realised that.'[19]

It is also, she points out, a two-way street. 'A lot of the country artists are making a genuine effort to learn some Irish, which is a great thing. Even Robert Mizzell has a "cúpla focail" now.'[20]

Despite all the criticism of RTÉ's promotion, or lack thereof, of Irish country music, of all the contributions to media outlets in recent years, many industry insiders particularly note that of Ryan Tubridy of RTÉ, presenter of the flagship *The Late Late Show* on RTÉ Television and his own daily show (Monday to Friday) on RTÉ Radio 1. Tubridy has presided over *The Late Late Show Country Music Special* in recent years and has made a point of promoting the genre by interviewing prominent artists on his show. He is widely regarded as one of the most intellectually able and gifted presenters in recent times. Henry McMahon, as key a figure in the industry as there is, cannot praise Tubridy highly enough. 'Ryan Tubridy is not a fair-weather guy,' he says. 'He believes it and likes it. He's done great things for Irish country music.'[21]

***

Not surprisingly, the first television channel entirely dedicated to country music was launched in North America. Country Music Television (CMT) was launched on 5 March 1983 by Glenn D. Daniels and was the first television channel to broadcast continuous country music in North America. The very first footage shown was a clip of Faron Young's 1971 'It's Four in the Morning'. Daniels subsequently sold the channel to Opryland USA and its owner, the Gaylord Entertainment Company.

CMT Europe was launched in 1992 but ceased broadcasting in 1998 due to continuous losses precipitated by British cable company Sky dropping it in 1996 because it believed the price was too high relative to the number of subscribers. CMT Europe hobbled on for two more years but ultimately became unsustainable after reported accumulated losses of ten million dollars. While it was available, it was a great way for Irish audiences who could afford cable television to see American country music artists. This was the golden age of music videos, and the images of artists such as Randy Travis, Garth Brooks and Billy Ray Cyrus lit up the screens of Ireland for its duration. Many viewers were bitterly disappointed when the channel departed the television world in Europe. However, a new phoenix has arisen from the ashes and is showing signs of becoming a remarkable success story.

Philip McLaughlin is the chief executive officer of Keep It Country TV – 'Europe's dedicated country music channel' – which was launched on 25 January 2016, the first such channel since the closure of CMT. McLaughlin, born in London to Donegal emigrant parents, developed an early love of the songs of Johnny McCauley and originally launched the *Phil Mack Country Show* in December 2010 as a standalone programme available on cable television. The very first show was recorded in Henehan's pub in Westport and featured performances by singers Frank McCaffrey and Bernadette Ruddy.

McLaughlin, who is based in London, spoke to me about the show from his Killala summer home in County Mayo – his wife is from nearby Ballina. 'Our second show was up in Tyrone with Philomena Begley. It was filmed in The Mill Wheel Bar, Kildress, County Tyrone, on a snowy, freezing day in December 2011,' he said. 'It was a gradual thing and we later branched out into the format where we mixed both American and Irish artists.'[22]

How he reached the point where he decided to launch a twenty-four-hour country music station is a remarkable story, which he recounted in his unmistakeable cockney accent. 'I played in a band called the Untouchables with a few mates when I was a young lad. We played all over North London. We had a residency in the Harp dance hall, a great place for the Irish, for a number of years and we played in the Amersham Arms in New Cross regularly.' Following this McLaughlin established a successful mini-cab business, which he sold in 2010. It was then he set about his ambition to establish a country music television channel.

'It's an expensive business. If you want to set up a television station you need to have a million quid sterling in the bank,' Phil notes. He explained in great detail the intricacies of the workings of cable television, but the bottom line seems simple: it can be a money pit if it is not properly orga-nised. 'It costs £40,000 per week to run a cable-television channel like ours. That's £160,000 per month. Nobody believed it could be done,' he says. Many indeed said it could not be done. How, then, did Philip McLaughlin do it?

'I'm an out and out gambler. I have been all my life, racehorses that sort of thing,' he says. 'I'm not afraid of taking chances. I don't spend my time looking over my shoulder. If it happens it happens. At the end of the day I don't give a toss.'

He tells a story about Donegal singer and songwriter Shunie Crampsey, to whom he is related: 'Shunie said I sail in, cause a storm and sail back out again.' McLaughlin laughs and emphasises that he believes this is only the beginning for his cable channel. 'We recently advertised for a presenter's job in London. We got 652 applications. I'm prepared to give anyone a chance, you know,' he explains. 'People say that some of the presenters don't have much to do with country music, but I'm looking for good personalities.'

The channel is becoming increasingly internationalised and consistently striving to gain footholds in new markets. McLaughlin sees room for expansion in country gospel, folk music and crossover acts. 'Of a hundred emails I get, forty of them offer new possibilities. It's a very exciting time for the industry.' Phil McLaughlin is a relentlessly upbeat character and is out to prove the doubters wrong. Programmes on the channel are constantly evolving, with a steady rotation of artists, and he is happy with the progress: 'The early response has been phenomenal. It has surpassed all expectations. In our first week of broadcasting we outdid our projections for where we should be in ten months. People in the television business were amazed and word got around.'

He adds, 'This is a very exciting time to be associated with the country scene.' The viewing figures for what is Europe's only dedicated country music channel are proof that the market was always there for such a venture. The Keep It Country TV website sings his praises: 'While the critics sat back dismissively Phil did what Phil does best – he defied all the odds and turned what seemed like an impossible dream into a reality.'[23]

McLaughlin was not the only one to see an opportunity in country music television. *Hot Country TV* is the brainchild of Hugh O'Brien from Cork. O'Brien – once the owner of the first video-rental shop in Cork city, a seller of industrial cleaning agents, the manager of Tony Stevens and T. R. Dallas, and founder and owner of the now-defunct *Personalities* monthly entertainment magazine – set up the cable television show *Hot Country TV* in 2009, when he perceived the lack of a platform for Irish country music artists. 'There was nowhere for people to see their work.

RTÉ wasn't interested. They've jumped on the bandwagon later of course,' he explained.[24]

His first show, *Hot Country*, went on air on 28 September 2009 and has gone from strength to strength. It is now broadcast as part of Keep It Country TV, but it is still independently owned by O'Brien. He has recently added an app to his business, whereby customers can download songs and videos on demand. At the moment it is free, but viewers will pay a small fee when the service develops further. 'Demand technology is here to stay,' he explains. 'I put up a concert yesterday and there have been 4,812 views already. Once people see what is on it they will buy it.'

He forecasts further success for Irish artists in the United States, Canada and New Zealand: 'Irish country music is different to anything else on the market and is no threat to anyone.' He tells a story to illustrate the ever-widening popularity of the music through his company's technological developments. 'I was parked in a garage a few weeks ago having a cup of tea inside. This woman saw the van and asked if I owned it. It turned out she was from New Orleans, and her son was a steel player in a band over there, a lad called Spitz. He had watched some of the stuff on the app and she took my photograph and autograph.' He adds, 'I was a bit embarrassed, but that's the way things are going.'

Hugh stresses the need to give new acts a chance but acknowledges the difficulties: 'Now an act has to be division one from the start, with all the lights and the technology and that. It's an expensive game to break into, but we need more acts for the future.' O'Brien is a man with major plans; he finished our interview by hinting at new developments to come with his app technology – 'things that even the BBC don't have'.

But factual shows on the various channels are no longer the only medium for country music on Irish television. The new country sound in the United States is perhaps best embodied by a fictional television drama series which has achieved huge popularity in Ireland. *Nashville* is a glossy tale of love and betrayal in the country music industry, the original soundtrack of which sold 150,000 copies in the UK alone. Since its debut the show has inspired seven 'Music of Nashville' soundtracks as well as a Christmas album, which have collectively sold more than a million copies. The first series won the 'Most Exciting New Series Award' at the Critics' Choice Television Awards in the United States. *Nashville* became so successful that some of the cast put together a live show and went on tour in 2014, repeating the venture in 2015. On 20 June 2016 cast members Clare Bowen, Chris Carmack, Charles Esten and Sam Palladio performed in Dublin. *Nashville* entered its sixth season in 2018.

***

One traditional medium which has seen increased coverage of Irish country music in the last few years is print. In recent years the regular columns of Michael Commins in the *Irish Farmers Journal* and Father Brian D'Arcy in the *Sunday World* have been widely read. In July 2016 Nathan Carter – by some distance the biggest country star for younger people in Ireland – began to write a column for the *Sunday World*, making it the biggest national Sunday paper for the promotion of Irish country music.

However, for many years professional print was not the only print medium where people could read about country music in Ireland. The story of eighty-one-year-old Roger Ryan, now resident in Ballinlough in Cork city, is one of true fandom and love of country music. In an era when media coverage was thin on the ground, Ryan, originally from Tallow, County Waterford, decided – with all the vim and vigour of youth on his side – to take things into his own hands and establish his own newsletter. He recalled his original inspiration in a telephone interview:

> I remember as a teenager passing the door of my neighbour John William McCarthy and hearing Hank Williams and Hank Thompson on the old 78s. I fell in love with the music there and then. I used to tune in the old radio in my bedroom to AFN from Frankfurt when I was going to bed. The

reception would get better the later the night went on, and the next thing I'd hear my father coming down the hall telling me to turn it off.[25]

Having moved to Cork to work in 1960, the young Ryan became an avid vinyl collector. The first album he purchased was *Johnny Cash with His Hot and Blue Guitar*, which he bought in Hennessey's of Oliver Plunkett Street for the princely sum of twenty-seven shillings and six old pence.

In 1968 Ryan took it upon himself to offer his services as a country music columnist to several Irish newspapers and magazines. He was met by indifference from all with the exception of Ken Stewart, Irish correspondent for *Billboard* magazine. Undaunted, and with the help of advice from Jo Walker-Meador of the Country Music Association (CMA) in Nashville, he set up a newsletter called *Country Cuts*, which went on to have 500 subscribers at its height. In addition to the magazine, Ryan established – with the help of Jim Hourihan, Mick Mooney, Maureen Hourihan, Gerald Fitzgerald and Pat Long – the Irish Country Music Association.

When the Irish media eventually began to take notice of country music, Ryan was invited to contribute a weekly column for the *Cork Evening Echo*, going on to write more than 1,200 columns, reviews and interviews. Over the years he has also worked on South Coast Radio, Cork City Local Radio and Hospital Radio, presented a series of programmes on Multi-Channel TV and appeared on *Hot Country TV*, and he regularly puts on shows featuring country and bluegrass at his local GAA club in Blackrock.

In 2008 the American Country Music Association in Nashville presented Ryan with the prestigious Wesley Rose International Media Achievement Award for 'outstanding contribution to the advancement and promotion of country music internationally'. In 2015 *Hot Country TV* honoured him for his contribution to country music in Ireland.

'Over the years I have built up a large list of friends and contacts throughout the world, and am always willing to act as a conduit between artists and promoters and give them a helping hand in their career,' Ryan said. He has also built up an extensive collection of vinyl, and is now looking for a good home for it. Roger Ryan is a true fan of country music: 'For some people it might be a hobby, but for me country music is a type of passion.'

Whatever the future holds, the continued increase in media outlets for Irish country music is a reflection of a buoyant and successful industry. There is a huge demand for material, particularly on the younger stars coming through. It will be interesting to see how things develop in an age of ever-increasing technology and the development of social-media platforms. Students of the media refer to the replacement of broadcasting by 'narrowcasting', whereby particular media aim to target a selected audience. But whatever way the information is spread, it is likely the band will play on.

12

PORTRAITS FROM THE TRADE

Although it is the really successful singers like Daniel O'Donnell and, more recently, Nathan Carter who tend to get the most publicity and whose names are recognisable even outside the world of country music, these stars only represent a small part of the country music business. It takes a multitude of people, both in front of the audience and behind the scenes to keep the industry strong and in this chapter a few of these people have been profiled in an effort to show the scope of talent that exists in the Irish country music world.[1]

THE PRINCE OF IRISH COUNTRY MUSIC:
JOHN HOGAN

Saint Lucia – the only country in the world named after a woman – is a small volcanic island in the eastern Caribbean Sea with a population of under 200,000, of whom eighty-five per cent are black. It is roughly two-thirds the size of County Louth and one of the least likely places imaginable for an Irish country music singer to become a cult figure. However, John Hogan, the 'Prince of Irish Country Music', is credited with popularising the genre there, and if visitors mention their Irish nationality, the singer, it is said, will often be the first point of conversation. On 2 December 2017 Hogan was the headline act at the first Annual Saint Lucia Country Music Festival. In a country where the national dish is green banana and salt fish, and the national slogan is 'Simply Beautiful', his is a remarkable story.

Saint Lucia is best known for zouk music – a fast, jump-up carnival beat originating in the Caribbean islands of Guadeloupe and Martinique – but in recent times the people have developed an affinity with country music and John Hogan has played a significant part in that. The singer recounted his story to me as he was on his way to Máire Luke's Bar in Tourmakeady, County Mayo, to play at a 'big country dance':

> It started with the song 'Stepping Stone'. If you want to hide a song, put it on an album, and that's where it was. I got a call from some people in America who asked me would I like to come to Saint Lucia. They met me in New York. They looked important, but I didn't think a whole lot of it. When I got down there I was treated like royalty. It was unbelievable. The song was played on the radio all the time. It must have been something about the beat and the lyrics. It just struck a chord with the people. It's a simple song. It's just about helping people. The world must meet the people of Saint Lucia. They are the most open and kind people you will ever meet, so gracious and loving.[2]

Both 'Stepping Stone' and others of Hogan's songs are played daily on the radio stations in Saint Lucia and surrounding Caribbean islands. 'Stepping Stone' is about a childhood memory:

> Let me be your stepping stone
> Let me be your light in the dark
> Let me hold your hand when you need a friend
> Let me love you my Diane.

It is a simple but beguiling and addictive song. 'It's just a childhood memory, nothing more than that,' he says.

There is a startling video of Hogan performing 'Stepping Stone' at a concert in Saint Lucia available on YouTube. In a red jacket and black slacks, he sings to an entranced crowd. Many sing along, some are dancing, some reach up to shake hands with the singer while others just stare up adoringly at him. He allows some to sing a few words by reaching down with his microphone, while a few women come up on stage to hug him. It must be the nearest an Irish country singer has come to feeling like a rock star. Halfway through the song, Hogan stops to speak about a concert he will be having later in the year: 'I will be coming home to Saint Lucia. I love every one of you. Thank you so much for everything.'

Everything that matters is about simplicity, according to Hogan. 'Simplicity is at the heart of all great things. Just look at the music of George Jones or Jim Reeves. Simplicity in life and music are sometimes the hardest things to get right, but they are the most important,' he says. 'You have to teach yourself how to see, to really open your eyes and see how things really are. Everyone looks at things, but you have to learn how to see.' It is fitting that the people of an island which has as its motto 'Simply Beautiful' have come to embrace the Irish singer.

Hogan came to Ireland's attention when his first single, 'Brown Eyes', became a number-one hit in 1988. Amazingly he had never performed live before this song, but with the encouragement of his friends he left his secure job as a supervisor in a peat-briquette factory in Croghan, County Offaly, and embarked upon a career in music; he used the money he needed to service his next mortgage payment to make his first recording. The song, a favourite of his mother's when Hogan was a child, found immediate favour with listeners on the local radio station. Having only played on the local music scene for twenty-five weeks, he was invited to appear on *The Late Late Show* on RTÉ Television.

'I had always loved country music, stuff by Jim Reeves and Hank

Williams, and it was my dream to make it. It took perseverance,' he told me. Hogan put a band together and signed Gerry Walsh and Brian Finlay of the Mighty Avons as his managers. He performed his first gig to a packed house on 19 April 1987 and in 1990 he joined the Ritz label.

He is also a songwriter and his early compositions, 'My Feelings for You' and 'Turn Back the Years', found a willing listenership when they were included on his first album, *Humble Man*, released in 1992. The Slim Whitman classic 'China Doll' and the Davis Daniel song 'Still Got a Crush on You' also proved popular numbers on Hogan's debut recording. In 1993 he got a chance to record in Nashville, where he had the privilege of working with top session musicians, including drummer Milton Sledge, piano player Hargus 'Pig' Robbins and steel-guitar player Sonny Garrish.

However, things have not been all plain sailing. Having invested heavily in the music business, Hogan lost his voice in 1996. He was unable to sing but continued appearing in concert from 1996 to 2002, taking the unusual approach of hiring a stand-in to help him through this difficult time. The logistics of the business exacted a toll on the singer:

I suppose I had a pretty sheltered existence until I went on the road playing music, so it took me some time to adjust. When I started in the music industry there was a big band and I was thrust into the middle of all this … I was never really ready for the business as it was. As far as I'm concerned, now you would need to have a degree in business before you go into the music industry to keep up with all that goes on in it. I never really wanted this big-band thing because it just wasn't for me. Music for me is probably different than what it is for other people. I just love simplicity.

There were also financial and managerial difficulties:

In the latter days of when I had the big band I used to struggle so much how to know at the end of the week where am I going to get the money for these guys? It's a difficult business. I got into all sorts of debt. In the end I had to cut my cloth to my own measure, but it was something I wanted to do anyway.

He was glad to leave the big-band scene and the intricacies of the business behind:

I love the music, but I was never enthusiastic about the business. I never liked the disingenuous nature of some of the people involved. Too much of it is tied up in greed. I always believed you should never let greed eat you up. Some of the treatment artists got was criminal. These people couldn't see reality and some of them suffered the consequences. It comes back to simplicity again.

John Hogan has established his own belief system based on his experiences. 'If I knew then what I know now, as they say. I never sing the blues, ever. I always have that man above in my corner,' he says. 'I'm no longer afraid to say no when I think I should. It's all about keeping it simple. I'm not a man who's afraid to say what he believes.' He is not shy about giving his opinion on the lack of support from the national media for country music either: 'I'm not afraid to say, RTÉ Radio 1 are a disaster for doing anything for the Irish music industry … we depend very much on local radio.'

Hogan now has a 'small band with a big sound'. He is expanding his boundaries with acoustic theatre performances allowing him to play material he could not at dances. His many songs – including 'Candle and Wine', 'My Guitar', 'My Feelings for You', 'I Loved Her So', 'Maria', 'My Christmas' and 'Love You More' – are proving as popular as ever.

In 2017 Hogan released 'The Three of Us' with fellow Irish country singers Mick Flavin and Paddy O'Brien. It tells the story of their musical journey as they each celebrate thirty years in the country music business. Hogan spoke about the recovery of his voice:

I don't look back. I always look forward. As someone once said there's not a minute gone out of tomorrow. I've been blessed in so many ways. There's no point in singing the blues about the past. I'm blessed to have that gift. I realise it is a gift and I am grateful for it. I have a lot of blessings, thank God. No matter where I go I give it a hundred per cent. Thank God my voice recovered and I can give it everything.

THE BOY FROM BALLINAMUCK:
MICK FLAVIN

Mick Flavin from Ballinamuck, County Longford – frequently referred to as 'Gentleman Mick' – has been a consistently successful performer on the Irish country scene for nearly three decades. In 2005 he was nominated for the Country Music Association Global Artist Award, the first time an Irish artist was considered for the famous prize. Such is the quality of his voice that many commentators and music insiders believe Flavin would have been a country music star had he been born American.

Flavin was one of six children – three boys and three girls – raised on a modest sixteen-acre holding. It was, he has frequently said, a time of little money but a lot of happiness:

> There was always music in our house. My father was from Listowel in County Kerry and was a *sean-nós* [traditional Irish] singer. We had an old record player and there was always something playing on it, including American singers like Buddy Holly, Eddie Cochran, Hank Williams and Tex Ritter.[3]

Flavin's first exposure to an audience came early. 'I was only ten when I took part in a talent show at McFadden's Roadshow over in Drumlish. It was part of the summer carnival.' He sang the Doctor Hook song 'She Was

Only Sixteen'. 'I won it and remember cycling home with the small silver cup. It was like winning the Sam Maguire [the cup given to the All-Ireland Gaelic Football Championship winners each year]. I was that delighted,' he said.

After completing his education in Ballinamuck Vocational School he became an apprentice carpenter and also joined local country band The Bright Lights. By this time he had taught himself to play the guitar, and remembers his first gig was in McGuire's hall in Leitrim. After qualifying as a carpenter Flavin moved to Dublin for work, but in the mid-1970s he returned to Longford to work for the local council. Like so many other performers in the Irish country music world he then started singing in the local pub scene with a band called The Country Travellers. He continued with this part time until 1986, when, encouraged by Declan Nerney, he recorded his first album. 'Declan was a great help to me. He encouraged me to give it a go, fair play to him.' Flavin sold copies of this record, *My Kind of Country*, at concerts. The album *I'm Gonna Make It After All*, released in 1987, provided his first big success in the Irish charts and allowed him to leave his day job. In 1989 he played at the Wembley festival in front of 80,000 people and got to meet his long-time hero, Buck Owens.

Flavin has toured relentlessly, achieving a loyal following across the British Isles, and he was voted the number one Male Country Singer in Britain in 1995, 1996 and 1997 by the British Country Music Association. 'The Old School Yard', written by Patsy Kavanagh from County Donegal, is one of his signature songs. In 2001 he founded his own record label, School Yard Records. In 2012 he toured Australia for a month to celebrate his twenty-fifth year in the music business. He is particularly popular in Tamworth, the country music capital of Australia.

Almost as famous as Flavin himself in his local area, was his dog Duke, who could take clothes out of the washing machine, collect the milk from the bottom of his driveway, bring Mick his socks and boots in the morning and, after dinner each evening, bring his lead to Mick, or his wife, Mary, indicating it was time for a walk. When Duke died, Michael Commins brought the sad news to the readers of his column in *The Mayo News* of 16 February 2016. Flavin told Commins: 'We had Duke for fourteen years and he was truly part of the family. … It's a shocking sad feeling to lose a dog. You grieve for them and it takes a long time to get over it.'

Mick Flavin has now released over twenty albums and on 19 May 2016 he was the first singer inducted into the Irish Country Music Hall of Fame at the Irish Country Music Awards. He posted on Facebook about the award:

> Not often that I am speechless but tonight I am. I cannot believe I won the Irish Country Music Hall of Fame award and that I am the first person in Ireland to be inducted into the Irish Hall of Fame. It's a privilege and an honour but I could not have done it without the help of each and every one of you that voted for me and who have supported me in the last twenty-nine and a half years. Thank you so much. I would also like to thank the band who backed me and indeed my own band who have stuck with me through thick and thin and back me each time I go on stage. Please Keep Travellin' To Flavin.

THE ANGLO-INDIAN COWBOY:
ROLY DANIELS

Roly Daniels is the only well-known Anglo-Indian on the country music circuit in Ireland. Born in Jubbulpore (now Jabalpur) in the centre of India, his is an intriguing story:

> I first heard country music when I was a boarder in secondary school. There was a Scottish boy in my class called Jock Jordan who used to sing Jimmie Rodgers songs for everyone. I was intrigued by the words. We called them

cowboy songs. After that my mother bought me a guitar and I started to learn the songs of Eddy Arnold and Hank Williams.[4]

He remembers his first success as a country performer. 'I was staying at my aunt's house and she entered me in a talent competition. I sang "Mother, the Queen of My Heart" by Jimmie Rodgers and I won. I had country music in my heart after that.'

Hal Monty, a touring comedian and actor with Granada Pantomimes, heard Daniels sing in an open mic session in Bombay and asked his mother if she would consider sending him to England to perform. 'He came up to me and said he would like to make me a star. I didn't know what to do and spoke to my mother. We knew India was to become independent in 1947 and that things might be more difficult for Anglo-Indians after that. She told me I should go.' Monty sent the young Daniels to the Oberoi Grand Hotel in Calcutta to practise his act for two months before departing for Europe. Daniels remembers stopping in Paris on his way to London:

I played for a few weeks on the US military bases around Paris. I remember when I first got to the hotel where I was staying and Hal Monty hadn't got there yet. I sat in the lobby because I didn't want to go up to my room. I was too afraid. I had just finished secondary school. I noticed people were laughing and I thought they were laughing at me. I looked beside me and saw a box with a picture. It was the first time I ever saw a television.

After his short sojourn in France he travelled to London: 'Things went very well for me at first. I was even on television with Burt Weedon, a famous guitar tutor. But after a while things began to get a bit tighter because groups like The Beatles and Freddie and the Dreamers came along. Opportunities for solo singers dried up.'

While in London Daniels was invited to Dublin by impresario Louis Rogers to fulfil a short engagement with the Jim Farley Band. He made more friends in Ireland in a short space of time than he had in England in four years. After his return to London things were still quiet, but Daniels got a lucky break:

> I met Louis Rogers on the street one day and he asked me what I was up to. I told him not much and he invited me up to a place called the 32 County Club in Harlesden to audition for the resident band because the lead singer had left. It was an Irish place. I remember thinking I needed to sing a song with a good range in it to show off my voice and what I could do. I sang 'You Don't Have to Be a Baby to Cry' by Tennessee Ernie Ford and got the job.

He worked in the resident showband for a few months before fate and love intervened. 'I met the lovely lady who is now my wife in the club. She was going back to Ireland because she had a very good job. I didn't want to let her go so I followed her and I'm here ever since.'

He took to the showband circuit, playing first with the Memphis Showband and later reuniting with Jim Farley and the Nevada Showband. After finishing with the latter in 1971, he pursued a solo career. While he had successes, by his own admission he found the music business tough. His solo hits include 'Sunny Tennessee' (1971), 'Hello Darling' (1972), which reached number two in the charts, and 'Mr Jones' (1980). In the spring of 1974 he again reached the number two position in the Irish charts, this time with an impressive cover of the Charlie Rich song 'The Most Beautiful Girl'. He was also an accomplished duet singer and achieved minor success with Ann Williamson when they released 'Like Strangers' in 1983.

In the mid-1980s Roly Daniels decided it was time to stop:

> I was burned out by that time. I had a bad experience. I had a tour set up to go to Britain. I went on a short holiday and when I got back to Ireland

someone had pinched my band. That person could pay a lot more money than I could so I just left it at that. I spent a lot of my time breeding horses after that.

He owes his comeback to Paul Claffey, CEO of Midwest Radio, and band manager Willie Carty:

Paul Claffey rang me up and asked me if I would be interested in going on a musical tour to Portugal. I wasn't sure at first, but I loved it. Around the same time Willie Carty organised an Irish tour for me with Butch Moore and Brendan Bowyer and that went well. I had gotten the bug again. I've gone on trips all over the place with Paul since and he has been great to me.

These days he's taking it easy. 'I did some work last year and I will do some this year. I had open heart surgery earlier in the year so I have to take it fairly easy.'

Roly Daniels has travelled a long way and has one of the most distinctive voices on the Irish country music circuit. He finishes our telephone conversation with an Indian valediction: 'Thank you. May all your children be fat ones.'

THE SHOW-BUSINESS LEGEND:
SANDY KELLY

When we spoke, Sandy Kelly was packing her bags for a trip to Glasgow where she would once again perform her phenomenally successful tribute show *The Patsy Cline Story* to full houses. The Sligo-based singer's background is unique in the world of Irish country music. Kelly's family were travelling entertainers and she has known no life outside show business since appearing as an assistant to a magician at three years of age. Her grandfather founded the Dusky Dan Variety Show, a business which was carried on by Kelly's father. Such 'fit up' groups were popular before television and cinema became available in Ireland. Kelly explained:

> I sometimes wonder what it would have been like to have been what I call a real person, a normal person. We didn't have much materially, but looking back now it was a wonderful life. Seeing all the happy faces smiling up at me when I was on stage was a great experience. It was a tough life, but we were a close family and we were always together. It was a great education and I got a real sense of music. I'm very appreciative of the experiences I've had.[5]

Her father moved the family to Wales when the show's appeal began to wane following the advent of television in Ireland. There, Kelly had the tough experience of singing in working-men's clubs, while her home life also provided challenges. Her mother had a brain haemorrhage at thirty-nine, and Kelly, just sixteen at the time, became her mother's full-time caregiver, putting aside her own ambition to be a teacher. In 1974, at the age of nineteen, she returned to Ireland and joined the Fairways showband and subsequently the Duskey Sisters, achieving considerable success – including representing Ireland in the Eurovision Song Contest in 1982 with 'Here Today, Gone Tomorrow'. It was only in the mid-1980s that she began to focus on country music full time:

> I get cross when people say that I came late to country music. In the roadshow we used to have a section where we sang western songs. My grandmother Maggie O'Dea was a great yodeller, and they would dress up in cowboy clothes with this fabric on the colours that would light up when the lights went off. The travelling roadshows were like a version of Hollywood, so country music was a part of my life even then. I sang everything from Shirley Temple songs to cowboy songs. I'm very proud to be a country singer. I was always into singing country, but people just don't

know that. I was country when it wasn't cool to be country. I've never done anything to be cool, sometimes to my cost.

In 1983 Kelly won the European Gold Star Award, a country music version of the Eurovision Song Contest, and the following year her recording of 'If I Needed You' with Big Tom reached number ten in the Irish charts. She had the honour of representing Ireland at the world-famous Fan Fair in Nashville in 1985 and 1987, but her biggest break came in 1988 when Johnny Cash was on tour in Ireland and heard Kelly's version of the Patsy Cline standard 'Crazy'. Cash invited her to come and see his show, and brought her on stage. Impressed by her performance, he invited her to Nashville, where – with the help of producer Harold Bradley and Patsy Cline's husband, Charlie Dick – they recorded a duet called 'Woodcarver' at the world famous Bradley's Barn studio. The song went on to become Kelly's second gold record in Ireland. She also recorded 'Ring of Fire' with Cash in 1990. She subsequently toured the United States, including holding a ten-month contract with Johnny Cash in Branson, Missouri, in 1992, and had her own show on RTÉ Television for three years in the early 1990s. At the height of its success, *Sandy* was only second in the ratings to *The Late Late Show*. In 1993 she recorded and toured with American icon Willie Nelson, and in the following year, having already toured her own Patsy Cline show, she was asked to star in West End production *Patsy Cline: A Musical Tribute* with George Hamilton IV. She went on to tour with that show for seven years.

During the course of her long career, Sandy Kelly has toured with Slim Whitman, Glen Campbell, Waylon Jennings, Merle Haggard, Loretta Williams and a host of other American stars. In more recent times she worked as a disc jockey on Sligo's Ocean FM. She is still recording and performing and is an enduring feature of the Irish entertainment landscape, the embodiment of the resilience and long-lived popularity of many performers in the Irish country music industry.

Kelly frequently travels with her daughter Barbara, who was born with a brain injury. 'She's my road manager when she comes with me. She wears the T-shirt and everything. It's important to me that there is public awareness of such conditions,' explains Kelly. 'When I'm away she goes to her dad and sometimes into respite. I think that's important too because there will be a time when I won't be around. She can get a break from my music too,' she says laughingly.

Kelly believes country music is interpreted in a very narrow way in Ireland: 'If you look at the States and the Country Music Awards, they will give Garth Brooks an award, but they will also give an award to Ricky Skaggs. You don't see that in country music here.' Her son, William, is in band Rackhouse Pilfer, and is also aware of the limitations of the genre in Ireland.

Kelly has frequently spoken about the difficulties women face in the music industry. 'I always say you should never throw out the grandparents with the water,' she said. 'We have something unique here in Ireland. It won't work for girls just copying what happens in Nashville. We need to keep our own traditions alive too. That can be difficult, but I think it is important.'

Sandy Kelly is refreshingly honest in her approach and calls everything as she sees it: 'I haven't played on the social-dance circuit for twenty-six years. It just isn't my type of thing. I do like going to hear other people play though.' However, she continues to perform. As she says herself, it is all she has ever known.

THE 'BANSHA LASS':
LOUISE MORRISSEY

Louise Morrissey is busy at home when I call – 'I live on a farm and there's always something going on, but that's the best way to have it' – but is generous with her time.⁶ The 'Bansha Lass' (Bansha being her home village in County Tipperary) started her musical career surrounded by members of her own family in the Morrissey Folk Group and, in keeping with Irish country music, hers was a rural upbringing. Morrissey was 'immersed in music' from the time she was born. 'There was an awful lot of music going back the years in the family and in the area around me at home,' she explained, 'so I didn't have any excuse, but I loved it from the start. It hasn't changed. There's still great music in that part of the country. They really love the dancing.'

Those of a certain vintage in Ireland may remember Morrissey's performance at Croke Park during the half-time interval at the 1988 All-Ireland Hurling Championship final between her native Tipperary and Galway, when she sang 'Slievenamon'. 'Yeah, it's still a highlight of my career, but unfortunately the match didn't go our way on the day. I was there to sing for the boys when they got back with the cup last year [2016] though,' she said, laughing.

The last time I had seen Louise Morrissey, she was performing at a local heritage day in Westport on an afternoon when the rain had not stopped pouring. She had sped up in a high-powered car, given a great performance and then sped away again. I noticed on the day that she wasn't driving. She laughs when I mention this: 'I always bring a driver with me and I like the cars all right. I had a bad crash years ago and I prefer someone else to drive if it's a good way away,' she said. 'I don't mind driving locally. There's a lot of driving in this business, a lot of time spent on the road.' On 26 September 1993 Morrissey survived a head-on crash when travelling to a concert. She was scheduled to fly to Nashville the following day to record and make concert appearances, but her injuries were so severe that it was six months before she was able to perform again. 'I was very lucky, thank God. I survived and things have gone great ever since,' she said.

The Morrisseys – Louise along with her brothers Billy and Norman –

released their first single, 'Farewell to Carlingford', in 1978 and achieved considerable success singing Irish folk and ballad songs, including 'Galtee Mountain Boy', 'The Old Rustic Bridge by the Mill', 'Bansha Peeler' and 'Rose of Allendale'. After going their separate ways for a year, in 1987 they reformed as the country-oriented Louise Morrissey Band, with Norman as the bass guitarist and Billy as manager, and quickly found success with 'The Night Daniel O'Donnell Came to Town', her second single in an Irish country style. It was a version of the old Johnny Cash song 'The Night Hank Williams Came to Town', rewritten by Tipperary songwriter Nick McCarthy, and became a hugely popular number at her performances.

'I was always comfortable with the country material. "The Night Daniel O'Donnell" is a great old song and I always enjoy singing it,' she says. 'It gave me a good shot in the arm. It was huge when it came out and really got things going for me. I have a lot to thank Daniel O'Donnell for.'

In 1990 Louise Morrissey won the prestigious European Gold Star Award in Zurich with 'Tipperary on My Mind', another Nick McCarthy composition. After surviving the trauma of the life-threatening car crash, her career went from strength to strength. She received a tremendous response when she toured Britain with American singer Charley Pride in 1995.

These days she usually plays with the Ryan Turner Band and has developed a special relationship with the people of Newfoundland, where her folk-oriented singing has a profound resonance. 'The Newfies are great,' she enthuses. 'It's such an interesting aspect of Irish history. I find it amazing the way some of them speak with an Irish accent, but they haven't even been here. It's given me a whole new lease of life.' She predicts continued success for the live country music scene: 'Things are flying down this direction anyway. I haven't seen any let up, thank God.'

'THE MAN WITH THE MAGIC WORDS' FROM 'THE BAND WITH THE MAGIC BEAT': HENRY McMAHON

Henry McMahon, as well as being the long-time saxophone player with Big Tom and The Mainliners, is Ireland's most venerable country music songwriter and has been instrumental in launching the career of a number of contemporary artists. The genial McMahon explains his writing methods to me: 'I don't get up in the morning and say that I'm going to write a song. It's whenever inspiration hits. I might be in the car and an idea would come to me. I suppose it's sort of a gift.'[7] He recalls how his first song 'The Little Hills of Monaghan' came about:

Liam Clancy and Tommy Makem were on tour in Canada and were telling me about people they met in Prince Edward Island who still spoke with Monaghan accents even though none of them had been there for generations back. That got me thinking about Monaghan emigrants all over the world and the attachment they had to back here. That's a very strong theme in Irish country music of course.

Inspiration can come from anywhere, he says, going on to recount the genesis of his second song 'The GNR Steam Train':

I was listening to the American singer Boxcar Willie one day in the car. He was singing a medley of train songs on an old cassette and I thought to myself that we had no train songs here in Ireland, even though they're a huge part of country music. The Great Northern Line is only up the road from me here in Castleblaney, so that's how that one came about.

McMahon wrote one of the most emotive songs in the entire Irish country music canon when he composed 'An Irish Nurse' for Big Tom. 'We were over in Romford in Essex and I saw all the Irish nurses. It struck me how important a job they were doing and how many of them were there,' he says. 'It was incredible the amount of girls that were over there keeping the whole thing going back then. They were a credit to the nation.'

It is a song that has held profound resonance for Irish generations over the years:

She was just a girl of nineteen years when she set out on her own
She left a brother and four sisters and her parents back at home.
The reason she was leaving, she saw no future here
To fulfil her one ambition, to make nursing her career.

To the Oldchurch in Romford that's where she went to train
And it would be a long long time before she'd be home again.
She said goodbye to all her friends and the ones that she loved dear
As she left her home for London to make nursing her career.

She was just a nineteen-year-old girl who loved her parents dear
But she left her home in Ireland to make nursing her career.

Many hours of work and study, oh how time passed away
Soon with her fellow students on graduation day.
Before she graduated, for weeks she saved the fare
To bring her mam and dad from Ireland for her special day to share.

But a drunk man in a speeding car stole her dream away
And her parents never seen the girl on her special day.
She never did return to Ireland and sometimes she shed a tear
As she recalls the day she left home to make nursing her career.

She was just a nineteen-year-old girl who loved her parents dear
She left her home in Ireland to make nursing her career.
She left her home in Ireland to make nursing her career.

McMahon's song 'Your Wedding Day' was instrumental in launching contemporary singer Jimmy Buckley's career. McMahon also managed Buckley for a period. When Buckley asked him to take on the role, the young singer told McMahon that he'd had 'more managers than Elizabeth Taylor had husbands'. The song is a personal favourite of Henry's: 'I like all my songs to tell a story. That one was about my daughter getting married, so it meant a lot. She's an only child so that's a special song for me.' The clever structuring and emotive narrative twists of McMahon's work are well demonstrated in the song about a father handing his daughter over on her wedding day. The opening points to a song of heartbreak:

> The first time I saw you I loved you with all of my heart
> The first time I held you I knew someday we would part.

The story then changes:

> Next Saturday morning in church I'll give you away
> In my eyes heavy tears I can't hide on your wedding day
> It's hard to imagine a baby so tiny and small
> Is now a young lady of beauty so pretty and tall.

It is a story of family, and a song praising the strong Irish mother and wife:

> Your mother she nursed you through many a heartache and pain
> And if you were to ask her she would do it all over again
> She's watched you grow into the woman you are today
> She's so happy and proud of her daughter on her wedding day.

McMahon, who also wrote the Robert Mizzell hit 'Mama Courtney' after the American had told him his life story, reckons he has written close to one hundred songs during his career. He explains: 'I left school at fourteen. Of course we all did then, but I always liked to write.' McMahon takes great pains to point out that there are 'many other great songwriters' at work in Ireland, including Derek Ryan, Shunie Crampsey, John Farry, Brendan Graham, Eugene Cunningham, Marc Roberts and Michael Commins.

It is clear McMahon has the interests of the music at heart and is delighted it is still alive. 'I think the social dancing and all that is great,' he says. 'I'm delighted it got all the young ones out of the disco.' He is always encouraging new acts to try to break through but sees the difficulties. 'The way it is, a lot of people follow the winning ticket the whole time,' he explains. 'I always like to see new talent break through, and if I can get them a good song to start them off I get great satisfaction in that.' Gerry Guthrie from Ballina, County Mayo – for whom he wrote 'The Lucky Horseshoe' and 'The Old Guitar' – is McMahon's sole present managerial responsibility.

McMahon has reservations about the way country music has developed in recent years but believes the best will come to the top in the end. Among his many other successes are Margo's 'Footsteps Through the Rosses', Philomena Begley's 'The Song From Way Back Then' and the iconic Declan Nerney's 'Marquee in Drumlish'. When Michael English told the songwriter of his overwhelming desire to make it in the Irish country music business, McMahon also wrote 'The Nearest to Perfect'. Henry McMahon is as near to the perfect gentleman as it is possible to meet.

THE TRIBUTE ARTIST AND RENAISSANCE MAN:
MARC ROBERTS

Although tribute acts are not a significant part of the Irish country music landscape, Marc Roberts has acquired a stellar reputation for his John Denver tribute act. But that is only part of the armoury of this Renaissance man of Irish country music. Roberts, who was the Irish entrant into the

Eurovision Song Contest in 1997 with 'Mysterious Woman', is a presenter on country music programmes on TG4 and is a prolific songwriter. He is also a DJ on Galway Bay FM, where he presents *The Feel Good Factor* on Saturdays and Sundays, and was one of the six finalists in Eurosong 2008, where he performed his own composition 'Chances', losing out to the regrettable 'Irelande Douze Pointe' by television puppet Dustin the Turkey. His tribute show to Denver is highly regarded, and he has been invited to play in Aspen, Colorado, the great man's home town. So why did the music of Denver have particular appeal?

> I think my attraction to John Denver's music was always down to the fact that he wrote about important things like family, friends, nature and simple things that we can all identify with. Also, when you perform a John Denver song there is such a feel-good element, and Irish people and, indeed, people all over the world love it.[8]

Songwriting has always been a huge part of Roberts' career: 'One of my favourite things is a sheet of blank paper. I just love the process of sitting down and writing. I always did.' All five of his albums to date have included his own material, and he has co-written with Charlie McGettigan, Derek Ryan, Grammy nominee Billy Yates and Daniel O'Donnell.

The affable Mayo man also spoke about the contemporary scene when we met in a hotel overlooking the promenade in Salthill in Galway city. 'I think things are great here in Ireland at the moment in the country music scene,' he said. 'There is new talent coming through in writing and performing all the time. There's a very positive vibe in the industry. Maybe the social-dancing thing will change, but all musical genres evolve over time.'

Roberts is relentlessly positive and is a prime example of an individual whose talents stretch across various areas of enterprise in the music industry. Only a few are given the array of talents bestowed on him. It is clear that he has consistently challenged himself to reach new goals. For example, I noted the greater fluency of his Irish since earlier days. 'Yeah. I've worked hard on it over the years. I've gone on courses to the Gaeltacht and that. I had to improve it for TG4,' he said. When we parted, he was going to get ready for his appearance in *Trad on the Prom*, a musical showcase which runs three nights a week from May to September at the promenade in Salthill.

THE CLUB KING:
FRANK McCAFFREY

'He had the best voice of all of them. It was a privilege to play with him when he came to Ireland. God rest him. George Jones was the man, all right,' says Frank McCaffrey in his music studio adjacent to his house in Westport, County Mayo.[9] The walls are covered in photographs and various coloured records representing sales targets reached. Pride of place goes to a large, autographed picture of American singer George Jones, for whom McCaffrey played support when Jones toured Ireland. 'He was something else,' McCaffrey says, as he drinks his coffee and looks around the studio to see if everything is in its proper place. He has just finished playing the club circuit in Great Britain following a career of twenty-seven years and has decided to focus solely on concert performances:

> The clubs in England have been great to me. When I say clubs it's not just the Irish clubs – all sorts of places. I played my last gig in Roy's Country Club in Bramley last week. I'd played there twice a year for the whole time I was at it, fifty-four times all together. I did more or less the same in Tony Best's place in Shrewsbury, The Lazyacre. That's what we had to do when the scene went flat here with the discos and nightclubs.

The closures of the dance halls were particularly felt in the west of Ireland, McCaffrey explains: 'Mayo was the best county in the country for dancing.

Every village nearly had one. We had to do something. I taught music for a while, and then I tried a one-man show in London and I was lucky.' Now his time on the road is drawing to a close and he is looking forward to a quieter life. Tonight he is playing in Westport Town Hall as part of a fundraiser for Irish emigrants in Great Britain. 'It's a cause that is very close to my heart. The people over there have been very good to me and I have a lot to thank them for.'

After leaving school, Frank McCaffrey joined local band the Beat-minstrels – then owned by Basil Morahan, who went on to perform as Dan the Street Singer – and later joined Pat Friel and The Frielmen. In 1970 he got a big break when he was invited to join Margo and the Country Folk as bass guitarist, his first professional engagement. When she was hospitalised as a result of a car crash, McCaffrey assumed lead singer duties. During this time the band had hit singles with 'I'll Forgive and I'll Try to Forget' (1970), 'Don't Read the Letter' (1971) and 'Shamrock from Glenore' (1973). While fulfilling this role, McCaffrey released his debut album *Introducing Frank McCaffrey*. In 1973 he formed Band of Gold and started recording with Ritz records. During the course of his long career, he has recorded enduring songs like 'It's Our Anniversary', 'More Than Yesterday' and 'When I Was a Lad'.

Frank McCaffrey is a contented man. 'I've had a great career,' he says. 'I worked with Margo, Tom Jones, George Jones and a whole load more. I've been lucky. I'll keep doing the concerts and the corporate work. Music has been good to me.'

THE PRODUCER:
GERALD O'DONOGHUE

Gerald O'Donoghue owns Greenfields Recording Studios in Claran, outside Headford in County Galway. Located three miles or so from the town, down a narrow road, it is easy to miss. The building looks like a larger-than-average domestic garage behind an ordinary white bungalow, but stepping inside makes the wealth of valuable equipment clear. O'Donoghue brings me around, pointing out various bits of technical paraphernalia and explaining their purpose. The cost of much of it is staggering. He recalls the early days of the studios:

> I started this place with my wife, Carmel, in 1979. I was always interested in messing around with speakers and stereos and overdubbing. I imported an eight-track system from England. It was the first in the west of Ireland. Before that most people had to go to Dublin to record. The first recording I did here was 'Rockabilly Rebel' by Johnny Carroll and his Magic Band. It took off very quickly after that. The following year I bought a sixteen-track system and after that it was a who's who of artists in the Irish music world.[10]

The list of those who have recorded at Gerald O'Donoghue's studio is staggering. Among other famous Irish country music standards, 'Say You Love Me' by Robert Mizzell, 'Stop the World and Let Me Off' by Declan Nerney, and 'Your Wedding Day' by Jimmy Buckley were recorded in Greenfields. It is clear that O'Donoghue is master of his own domain:

> What I bring to the recording is what people want. They are buying the studio time, but I can offer them a lot more than that. For that reason I don't employ anyone else to do production or engineering work. In the last five years we have got into video production as well, and my son helps me with that when he's at home, but he's on the road a lot with his band.

Until 1998 O'Donoghue worked as a bank manager in nearby Headford, confining his recording work to the evenings and weekends, but since then he has been at it full time, recording a variety of musicians, bands and singers. While he is best known for his work in the Irish country music industry, he also records and produces the music of traditional and classical artists.

The biggest problem he identifies is the lack of development in the music. 'It's an expensive business and unless money is invested the music cannot develop. People cannot afford to take risks so we are getting more of the same,' he explains. 'Essentially it's not about what the market wants but about what they are given. Technology is a large amount of the problem. Recorded music simply doesn't sell the way it used to. Recordings are now money that is gone.' O'Donoghue, like many others, points out that it is a vicious circle:

> The industry needs new talent, but it is very difficult to break through. There is really only a living in it for a certain number of bands. It takes a lot of money to get established. A new artist really needs to have four singles recorded to get up and running and that doesn't come cheap. They also need to be good singles. Realistically it takes forty to fifty thousand to set up properly to give yourself a chance.

While the costs vary, depending on what an artist is trying to achieve, the figures he mentions are sobering. 'You can get someone to make a recording for €300,' he said, 'but that will be reflected in the quality of the product. You get what you pay for in this business.' Technology is killing off old-style, high-end production values and the future for studios like his might be difficult. 'What you have to remember is recordings are now a form of marketing,' he pointed out. 'It's not like the old days when a band could sell loads of records to make the cost of the recording back quickly. At the same time the work needs to be of a good enough quality to get noticed.'

Does everyone who turns up with the money get recorded? 'You have to tailor the product to the ability of the individual and try to give them the right advice,' he said. 'Not everyone who comes to me has the ability and sometimes I advise people to go off and cut a demo recording first before they invest their money here.' O'Donoghue estimates that maybe two per cent of those who record will make a breakthrough. 'That's the nature of the game. It's a tough industry,' he says.

What about recording contracts? 'They're largely gone now. Records don't sell, so artists aren't contracted the way they used to be, with the exception of someone like Daniel O'Donnell or Nathan Carter,' he said.

Leaving Gerald O'Donoghue, it is impossible not to have an admiration for those artists who have made successful careers in the music industry. From all that he says, it is an expensive and competitive business and those who ultimately achieve success have often travelled a long road.

13

BORN IN THE USA: THE ROBERT MIZZELL STORY

Robert Mizzell is far and away the best-known American artist plying the Irish country music circuit, working with both his backing band the Country Kings and occasionally as part of the trio The Three Amigos with fellow country singers Patrick Feeney and Jimmy Buckley. As an American, he provides a direct link from Ireland to the home of country music and has also made a small business out of bringing Irish people over to Nashville.

A surefire indicator of Mizzell's popularity in Ireland is the fact that RTÉ Radio 1 saw fit to give him his own radio show on Saturday evenings called *Simply Country*. The show began broadcasting in August 2017 and plays the best in American and Irish country music. How Mizzell came to be where he is today is one of the great stories of Irish country music and deserves, in time-honoured style, to become the subject of a tribute song in due course.

The honesty and self-disclosure of Mizzell is a breath of fresh air in Ireland, and all the more enthralling when heard in his beautiful, drawling Louisiana burr. He was born prematurely on the shores of Lake Bistineau near Shreveport and, by his own admission, things were not easy in his home life. His parents' marriage was troubled and he was removed from the family home for the first time when only six months of age, with a broken arm. He was put into the care of the Courtney family, who fostered him on and off over the following years:

> Mama Courtney and her husband, Drafton, were Baptists and they were very strict … we had to do well in school and have manners, but it was a humble place and a peaceful and loving environment. I almost looked forward to the beatings at home, just to get out of the house and go back to Mama Courtney. She saved me from the trauma of my own home and gave me love.'[1]

Mizzell's foster parents are now both deceased. During their lifetime they helped bring up thirty-two children, but Mizzell believes he formed more of an emotional connection with them than many of the other children. When he considered the difference between his birth mother and Mama Courtney he put it down to 'craic': 'Me and Mama Courtney clicked together … with my own mother I never had the craic, but with Mama Courtney you could just sit and laugh with her.' He is at pains to explain the value of the Courtneys to his upbringing. 'They knew how to parent,' he said. 'They were strict and they were not my friends like you see now, but they knew how to parent and sadly my own did not.'

At the age of seventeen Mizzell moved to Connecticut to work with his father in the painting-and-decorating business and later joined the United States military. At twenty he was discharged from the army after suffering from regular blackouts, probably brought on, he now believes, by stress. He first learned about Ireland when he met Elaine from Naas, County Kildare, who was working on a student holiday visa in Connecticut. She was the first Irish person he had ever met; before meeting her all he knew about Ireland, he claims, was that if you did not wear something green on St Patrick's Day in Shreveport you got pinched.

In 1991 the couple moved to Ireland to start a new life. They got married four days after arriving in the country, but the marriage did not survive.

Mizzell is as eloquent as he is forthcoming about the failure. 'We had money troubles because I stopped working as my past was coming back to haunt me. If I had been more stable and able to deal with things, Elaine and I could have worked it out,' he said. 'The marriage only lasted for about seven years, and while we had marriage counselling, I never had personal counselling. I'm sure if I did, my life would have gone a lot more smoothly.'

Garth Brooks' appearance in Ireland was a revelation to Mizzell. He went to see the American country superstar perform in the Point Depot, Dublin, not for the music but because Brooks was American and he had not seen a fellow American in a long time. The response of the Irish audience shocked him, but it was also a motivating factor. 'I knew I could sing, but I had never tried it at home except to myself. I did know I had a good voice,' he confided, 'and when I saw the way the audience responded to Garth Brooks, I decided to give it a go.' He added with a chuckle, 'Not that I ever thought I was going to be as big as Garth or anything.'

Mizzell saw country music performance as a viable future, but success did not come immediately. He recounted holding the microphone in the middle of the dance floor in The Well pub in Moate and playing to four people. It was not as easy as it had looked when Brooks interacted effortlessly with the crowds in Dublin. 'I found it very invasive, initially, but I got over myself,' he explained. 'I started opening myself up to people, and found that if you do that, you will have great times and good craic. Some of the people who come to my gigs have now become close friends.'

'Say You Love Me' was Mizzell's first significant Irish success and was followed by a string of hits including 'Mama Courtney', 'Louisiana Saturday Night', 'Cajun Dance', 'Papa Loved Mama' and 'Wham Bam!'. 'Mama Courtney', written for him by Henry McMahon, is an emotional telling of the story of his upbringing:

I remember as a baby barely one year old
When I first met Mama Courtney with her heart of gold

I didn't know it way back then how she influenced me
But I thank Mama Courtney for the man I grew to be.

When my mother lost her way in life, Mama Courtney took me in
She became my foster mother and my best friend
She'd drive us kids around the town in her old black Oldsmobile
Till this day I remember how good she made us feel.

There are many children in this world that suffered hurt and shame
I thank all Mama Courtneys that took away their pain
God works in mysterious ways, I believe this is true
Though she had no children of her own she fostered thirty-two.

Blackie was her husband, he drove a pickup truck
He worked at the power station to earn an honest buck
At weekends he'd go hunting squirrels up in Arkansas
And every night when he tucked us in we would call him Pa

Us kids are all now grown up and gone our separate ways
I look back on my childhood, many happy days
And when I go back to Shreveport I place flowers on her grave
And I thank Mama Courtney for all those kids that she saved.

In time-honoured country music style there is a coda at the end:

Though she had no children of her own she fostered thirty-two
God rest you Mama Courtney, I will always love you.

The song has a level of self-disclosure rarely heard in Irish country music and is an evocative expression of Mizzell's love for his foster family – a lasting testament to the care Mama Courtney and Drafton lavished on the young Robert.

In an interview with Andrea Smith in the *Irish Independent*, Mizzell spoke movingly about his birth mother:

My mother lives in a care home and I visit her every year. I can't say I look forward to it, but I do it out of respect and a sense of duty because she's my mother. The day she dies will be a happy day for her, because this life wasn't good to her, and it made her the way she was. I believe that there is an afterlife, and I hope that the next time around, she will get better opportunities.[2]

Mizzell also spoke to Marian Finucane on RTÉ Radio 1 about his mother, in January 2015: 'My mother is still alive and well in Louisiana. She's doing well now. She has come to that time in her life when she's put a lot of the ghosts in her life behind her.'[3]

In 2010 'Murder on Music Row', a duet with fellow American singer Collin Raye, reached number one on the European country music chart, staying there for twenty weeks. It was an important song because it bemoaned the death of traditional country music; the gradual exclusion from the airwaves of hard-core artists, such as Merle Haggard, George Jones and Hank Williams; and the increasing dominance of crossover acts. Ironically, Raye is largely considered a crossover act.

On Saturday 29 October 2011 Robert Mizzell was inducted into the Shreveport Walk of Stars in recognition of his achievements in country music. It is the highest award his home city can bestow on an individual; Robert, appropriately, followed in the footsteps of singers Elvis Presley, Hank Williams Senior and Hank Williams Junior.

Despite a self-administered ban on dating fans, Mizzell married Adele Speer in 2013. He had met her through the music business; her father, Gordon, was a promoter based in Castlederg, County Tyrone. There has been nothing simple and nothing uninteresting in Mizzell's life. She was much younger than the American, who explained:

When I first met Adele, she was seventeen and I was in my thirties, so while I thought she was beautiful, I would never have put us together because she was so much younger. She told me she was in college and I told her, jokingly, that when she graduated, I would marry her. She came to all of the gigs, and when I got engaged to a girl from Donegal, I didn't want to tell her.[4]

His engagement broke up and he started dating Adele when she was twenty-three. Now married with a child and a dog and living in Mullingar, Mizzell is a happy man. 'Adele is so soft … she hasn't got a bad word to say about anyone … she enjoys the simple things and doesn't want a fancy life,' he said. 'We have a great relationship and I love coming home to her, whereas in my younger days, I would stay out drinking to avoid going home.'

Mizzell is thankful for what Ireland has brought to his life:

I came through my childhood not knowing what lay ahead, so I owe a debt of loyalty to Ireland for giving me this opportunity. I am in a great place, and the most important thing for me is that my daughter is happy, my ex-wife is happy with a family of her own, and I have a wonderful relationship with Adele and we are starting a family. The only thing that would improve my life now would be if I won the lottery and could pay off the taxman!

This last statement refers to his financial woes from 2012, when he had to make a €60,000 settlement with the Irish Revenue Commissioners.

In a concert in August 2017 at the McWilliam Park Hotel Mizzell was in great form and interacted brilliantly with the audience. There is no doubt that his southern drawl brings an authenticity to his singing that is not otherwise seen on Irish stages. Following the concert, he talked to me about the difficulty of breaking through: 'You can put a purple hat on with yellow polka dots on it, but if you don't have a good voice you don't stand a chance. I always knew I had a good voice.' He mentioned exceptions to the rule who have prospered in the United States, but he cannot see the same thing happening in Ireland. 'There are people like Willie Nelson and Kris Kristofferson who aren't technically great singers, but they have something unique,' he said. 'But Irish audiences are not generally interested in very different voices. They know what they want, that's for sure.'

Mizzell is critical of some contemporary recording methods. 'You can take someone into a studio and airbrush their voice and they will sound fine,' he said. 'Then, when you go to see them play in a concert they don't sound half as good, but that's the price to be paid for technology, I suppose.' He mused further on this point; one which seems to tax him: 'A live concert is a whole different animal. You've got to be able to stand up there and do it in front of a live audience and there is no escaping it.'[5]

I mentioned this to Gerald O'Donoghue when I went to visit him at his recording studios in Headford, where Mizzell has recorded extensively. He was unsurprised:

I'm not surprised he said that. Robert is a fantastic singer, one of the best you will ever hear. There are very few people who can do what he does. He can come in and lay down an album in no time. He is technically excellent. There aren't too many like him around. I think it helps that he's from Louisiana. He's a great man to work with.[6]

At the end of the night's dancing in the McWilliam Park Hotel, Robert Mizzell comes out to the foyer to his merchandising stand, where he joins his manager, Sharon Kelly, to sell his CDs and DVDs, talk to people and allow those who would like to take photographs to do so. Some of the audience walk by with their heads down, while others stop to talk and buy something. Most of those who stop are women and many ask for a photograph. Robert tells them about a forthcoming trip – it is clear that he is an excellent communicator and totally at ease with all comers: 'It'll be great craic, the first ever Irish country music skiing trip. It's going to be in Andorra, a beautiful place. We'll be staying in a top hotel and you'll have a ski pass every day.'

'We'll think about it,' many say and laugh.

'You'll have plenty of time to save,' he says, smiling and tipping his Stetson. He looks tired but happy and, after another half hour of photographs and chat, heads off to his room. It has been, by Sharon's account, a successful night for a Tuesday.

14

'THE LONE RANGER OF IRISH COUNTRY MUSIC': JAMES KILBANE AND COUNTRY GOSPEL

James Kilbane from Achill Island, County Mayo, is travelling a definite path – one guided by his Christian faith and his belief in the ability of country gospel music to spread the word of God and bring comfort to his listeners. Such is Kilbane's singular focus, the American country singer George Hamilton IV saw fit to name him the 'Lone Ranger of Irish Country Music' when they met on the American's final Irish tour. A quiet, unassuming man, Kilbane is a big name in the growing world of Irish Christian country music.

Christian country music – also called 'country gospel' or 'inspirational country' – can be considered a subgenre of both gospel and country music. It is as old as country music itself; the genre has always been historically intertwined with conservative Christianity. From The Carter Family's 'Can the Circle Be Unbroken' (1927) to Vince Gill's 'Go Rest High on That Mountain' (1995), religious-themed songs form a large part of the American country music canon. Christian country acts like Jeff and Sheri

Easter, Diamond Rio and Point of Grace consistently perform to sold-out stadia in North America, while mainstream country music artists such as Carrie Underwood, Randy Travis and The Oak Ridge Boys have released hugely successful Christian albums.

While much of earlier Christian country centred on the wrath of God and the need to obey the Ten Commandments, more recent material has been more upbeat; the term 'positive Christian country' is becoming increasingly popular. While it has not been particularly prominent in Ireland historically, this has started to change and James Kilbane is leading the charge.

In 2004 Kilbane entered the RTÉ Television talent-search competition *You're a Star*, entertaining the nation with a set of performances of country, folk and gospel standards. His hybrid repertoire and soaring voice proved hugely popular with the viewing public, who voted for him in huge numbers to return week after week. The seasoned judges admitted that they had never seen an artist like Kilbane before and seemed bewildered by his popularity. During the course of the competition, he sang songs as diverse as 'Losing You' by Sinead McNally, 'Save Your Kisses for Me' by Brotherhood of Man, 'Cracklin' Rosie' by Neil Diamond and 'King of the Road' by Roger Miller; he sang the last of these in the final, in which he was narrowly beaten by Chris Doran from Waterford. The 'priest', as the other competitors had dubbed Kilbane, had outdone all the critics.

Not all were kind in the media. The *Wicklow People* featured a review of the show:

James Kilbane and the way he might look at you, eh? There's nothing quite as creepy as a bloke with knitted eyebrows, a maniacal glare, and the hint of the Daniel O'Donnell's about him. Yes, 'You're A Star' should have been renamed 'You've A Stare' for the Achille [*sic*] crooner – who proved over the last 10 weeks that the blue rinse brigade have come to terms with texting technology … For legions of fans – the majority from the 'wesht' of

Ireland, boy – James Kilbane was the brilliant white hope for Eurovision, only to be thwarted in the final shake up …[1]

Shortly after appearing on *You're a Star*, Kilbane set up independent label Gold Eagle Music and released his first album, *King of the Road*. Among the diverse collection of material, several tracks stand out: Alan Jackson's 'Here in the Real World', Randy VanWarmer's classic tear-jerker 'Just When I Needed You Most' and Roger Miller's classic homage to the life of the hobo, 'King of the Road'. It was a remarkable demonstration of the depth and range of Kilbane's unique voice. There is no other performer in the world of Irish country music with a similar vocal skill set; he has frequently been compared to Elvis Presley, particularly in his interpretation of gospel standards.

In March 2012 Kilbane released his tenth album, *Gravel & Grace: Songs of Faith, Life & Hope*. It was appropriately launched at Lorain Correctional Institution and Grafton Prison, in Grafton, Ohio, in the United States, following an invitation extended from the institution's inmates to Kilbane to give a special concert at the prison during St Patrick's week. Two brothers – Owen and Martin Kilbane (no relation) – were inmates at the time, and wrote to James to tell him that his music had come to their attention and had helped them come to terms with prison life. They wondered if James would see his way to coming to see them; the 'Lone Ranger' duly obliged.

There is a long and close relationship between the people of Achill Island and Cleveland, Ohio, which Grafton is just outside, forged from a long history of emigration across the Atlantic Ocean. For James Kilbane, going to see the inmates in Grafton was a sort of homecoming. 'Walking into the prison after all the high security checks,' he said, 'just as one of the prisoners was about to open the door, there on the mat was the word "Welcome". I thought, "Thank you, God. I'm meant to be here. I will go to wherever there is a genuine welcome."'[2]

There is a mantra running through Kilbane's thoughts and utterances, one he repeated a number of times when we talked:

I know that I am just the messenger. I am only human, however I know that so much of the music I have recorded has reached and helped many in prisons, people suffering with health problems, addictions, family-life issues, marriage problems, and other situations. I know because so many have told me and written to me and I believe I am being called to do this work for God ... the music is not about James Kilbane. It's about the message.

Kilbane is at pains to get across the point that he works outside the mainstream of Irish country music. By his own admission he is 'not invited to all their parties'. Some in the industry have 'blackballed' him for this reason: 'Sometimes your face doesn't fit and the doors don't open.' In the end he believes this will not hold him back: 'I have one of the finest voices in the country and the cream always rises to the top.' His music is about 'helping people overcome the adversities of everyday life'. He would prefer his words to be listened to in quiet contemplation rather than in the frenzied atmosphere of social dancing.

Kilbane stresses his independence as an artist:

I work for myself. I am independent and not contracted to anyone. That's the way I like to operate. Not everyone in the industry might like that but that's the way it will stay. I'm not a yes man. Don't get me wrong. I value mentorship and I'll take advice if I think it is constructive. In the end of the day I am my own man. I'm always willing to negotiate and work with people but I appreciate being respected.

He continues:

In many ways I'm like a wild horse coming out of nowhere, and that's the response you get from some people in the industry. Who's backing you? How are you getting all the media attention? I just don't fit the picture for some. Some of them wish I would go away, no doubt, but I'm here to get the message across.

The singer has strongly held religious beliefs:

James Kilbane loves Jesus. I'm no angel or saint. I'm not perfect. I've a lot of failings. I'm just human. God exists. It's a fact. It's reality. Everything is true. We cannot walk away from fact. I have a responsibility to do what I believe. It might seem nuts to some people … but not in my world.

He points out that not all within the Christian tradition appreciate what he does. He explains:

There's religious snobbery wherever you go. Some might think there's no role for country music in the development of the faith but I don't believe that … I'm equally interested in the person who goes to mass every day of the week as I am in the person who has problems with the way things are run and hasn't been in a church for fifty years. My music is for anyone and I have found listeners in all sort of places.

Kilbane's beliefs are unwavering. 'I have been attacked for my views. I take a pro-life position, and I have contributed to groups who take that view. I take the Christian view of marriage equality. I've been laughed at for my views on blasphemy,' he said.

As well as making albums, Kilbane runs 'Spirit and Soul of Mayo Holiday' weekends in Westport. The three-, four- and five-day packages involve a nightly gathering with James for fellowship, songs and prayer, in addition to a plethora of activity choices during the day, including energising sessions, reflexology, meditation, cooking demonstrations, 'reflecting on the Christian ethos' and heritage, and Christian-based tours of the local area. He referred me to one of his regular attenders to discuss the attraction of his work.

Mary from Mullingar is a quietly spoken retired teacher with deep Christian and religious beliefs who has found comfort in Kilbane's music. She had seen him on television and first heard his music in Emmanuel House of Providence in Clonfert, County Galway, a retreat centre run by Eddie and Lucy Stones. The music, she said, 'opened a different window to God. It speaks to me in a different way than other religious ceremonies do. It's just a different type of prayer. I get what he is trying to do in spreading the Christian message.' She feels so strongly about the importance and power of the work Kilbane does in spreading the Christian message that she wants others to 'have their faith rekindled or find the Lord'. In order to help spread the 'word' she has given away many of Kilbane's CDs to friends, relatives and 'complete strangers' who were struggling with health, family or personal issues. Copies, she said, have gone to England, Paris and as far afield as Ethiopia and Madagascar. It is 'the message of overcoming life's obstacles through belief in God' that resonates through Kilbane's music with her. She went on:

> During difficult times in my life over the past decade Jesus has spoken very clearly to my heart through James' songs and helped strengthen my wavering faith and renew my hope. James is a very special person and bears witness in a very special way. He is a great example to all of us. He is prepared to stand up for his beliefs and that's not easy in today's society with the backlash against organised religion.[3]

On a beautiful day in Westport in early June 2017, James Kilbane is sitting with his 'great friend' John Morrison in the restaurant of the Castlecourt Hotel. Morrison, a Derry man, travels the country bringing his country gospel CDs to radios stations with the intention of promoting God's word. Each CD contains a segment in which he discusses a specific idea imparting what he terms 'a lighthouse message', along with a selection of country gospel music, all recorded in a full professional studio. Throughout

Ireland roughly 2,000 of Morrison's recordings, varying in length from ten minutes to an hour, make it onto the radio waves each year. He uses local and regional newspapers to advertise upcoming broadcasts.

Through the dissemination of the CDs, Morrison hopes 'the country gospel message will lead the nation of Ireland to the promised land' and provide listeners with 'a personal encounter with God'. He does not charge the radio stations any money; his ventures are funded by his own resources and donations from those who want to help him spread the message. Following each broadcast, Morrison likes to go somewhere peaceful and 'pray three times that God will bless the people who hear my message'. He said there is 'a vast difference between doing things for God and being employed by God to do what he wants done'; only a few are chosen to pass the message on. It is evident that the two men have a deep bond. 'There is more to James than meets the eye,' Morrison says of his friend, calling him 'one of God's men', echoing the words of Mary.[4]

John Morrison has worked with eighteen radio stations during his career and on that day he was in Mayo to deliver his CDs to Castlebar Community Radio and Midwest Radio, both of which, he says, have been very receptive to his message. He praises many Irish country artists who have included gospel and sacred numbers in their repertoire, including Brendan Shine, Mary Duff, Big Tom McBride, Hugo Duncan and, of course, James Kilbane. Through once being sent a five-song mini-CD by Kilbane, Morrison has come to know the singer's music and now uses it frequently in his broadcasts. His is a message of hope and understanding; people can go off track but can be rescued by receiving the message and establishing a personal relationship with God.

The world of James Kilbane and his country gospel fan base may have a low profile, but there is no doubting their fervour and belief in the music. It will be interesting to see how the genre develops in the future.

15

A NEW COUNTRY

But someone killed country music, cut out its heart and soul.
They got away with murder down on music row.

From 'Murder on Music Row'[1]

In 2000 the song 'Murder on Music Row', recorded by artists George Strait
and Alan Jackson, was selected by the Country Music Association as the
Vocal Event of the Year, while the International Bluegrass Music Associa-
tion voted it Song of the Year. The song decried the death of traditional
American country music and these sentiments have been echoed by writer
Bill C. Malone:

> Some musicians have attached themselves to country music because it is in
> vogue or because they were advised to do so, mainly as a marketing decision by
> promoters or recording executives who believed their client could 'fit' the mar-
> ket niche and profit from country music's popularity with a 'target' audience.[2]

Malone points to the fact that these new artists who were offending the
traditionalists grew up in an age when things were different from the experiences of the older generation:

Most were easily lured by the crossover success and were therefore more and more prone to dabble in the lucrative world of pop. All of these artists played the game of being country ... but they had also grown up in an era dominated by pop and rock and, to a degree unprecedented in country music history, their performances revealed these non country styles.[3]

The 1980s had witnessed a 'neo-traditionalist' revival in country music circles in the United States, with artists like Randy Travis, Dwight Yoakam, Patty Loveless, Brad Paisley and Alan Jackson, who played their music in the way purists thought it should be played, with a lot of 'twang'. In early 2001 the soundtrack from popular movie *O Brother, Where Art Thou?*, which included old-time singing from artists such as Alison Krauss, Emmylou Harris, Gillian Welch and Ralph Stanley, quickly sold a million copies and acquired platinum status. Despite its popularity, radio stations were initially reluctant to play the material because of its dated, 'hillbilly' sound, until fans made the media aware that they were not best pleased. With the resulting radio play, Dan Tyminski's version of 'I Am a Man of Constant Sorrow' entered the *Billboard* charts; by mid-April the album had sold more than three million copies and won five Grammy awards. But this resurgence in the older style of music failed to halt the progress of crossover acts.

Since the early 1990s, an avalanche of young, good-looking entertainers – sometimes called 'new country' or 'young country' – have come to dominate country music in the United States, for better or worse. Malone and others point to the introduction of SoundScan in the United States as a crucial turning point. Up to May 1991 *Billboard* used information from sales clerks to ascertain the popularity of particular music. SoundScan instead read the CD barcodes and could provide accurate statistics on sales. When the industry discovered that seventeen per cent of all sales were in the country genre, this finding set in train an explosion of the music, bringing the world of Garth Brooks and all that followed. Once a winning formula was discovered, imitation became rife and critics have argued that a significant number of acts are now virtually indecipherable from each other. The battle between old and new, what is country and what is not country, continues to rage to this day.

It has often been said that when America sneezes the world gets a cold. There is much to suggest that the developments in the United States country music industry are now dominating the way the music is produced and manufactured in Ireland, and the likelihood is high that artists of the calibre of Big Tom, Margo and Philomena Begley may never again come to prominence. The move towards a more hybrid performer appears to be a tide that is not for turning, for better or worse. Many of these acts have come to prominence on the back of the huge rise in social dancing in recent years, although increasingly many divide their time between the dancing circuit and concert performance. But while some older hands might look askance at the way the music has developed – particularly in respect of its similarity – most are quick to acknowledge the fact that there is talent coming through in Ireland and, encouragingly, not all of it is going down the crossover route.

**

The unusually named village of Burnfoot lies at the southern end of the Inishowen Peninsula in County Donegal and is home to one of Ireland's newest and youngest country stars. Local teenager Keelan Arbuckle – from the only family so named in the phone directory in the Republic of Ireland – is facing the challenge of the Leaving Certificate examination in June 2018 and, despite a burgeoning musical career, is attending secondary school every Monday to Friday at Crana College in the neighbouring town of Buncrana just like his peers.

Brought up in an environment surrounded by music, Keelan made an early break into the Irish country music world, having played the guitar from the age of nine. 'My grandfather used to play in the John Kerr Band around here. I used to go down to the room where he was playing the accordion when I was three or four and learn a new song every day. I was always into the music, particularly the country songs,' he said in his beautifully measured Donegal drawl.[4] When producer Steve Bloor from Roscommon first saw Arbuckle perform he was so impressed that, having consulted Keelan's parents, he signed him immediately. Under the guidance of Bloor, Arbuckle released his debut album, *That's Important to Me*, in February 2015. It was a cover of the George Strait song 'Amarillo by Morning' from that album which first brought the young Donegal singer to wider public attention.[5]

One of the highlights of Arbuckle's career to date is an appearance he made on 'A Night with the Stars' in Cookstown, County Armagh, where the words of superstar Philomena Begley inspired him. 'Philomena Begley said that nine years ago she had heard a young lad perform and she predicted he would be a star,' he said. 'It turned out to be Nathan Carter, and she said on stage she predicted the same for me. I couldn't believe it. I hope she's right.' Another highlight was playing for Big Tom in the superstar's sitting room:

That was a day I will never forget. Margo had told him I had written a song or two and he wanted to hear them. He said, 'Keelan, have you the guitar with you?' I had it in the boot. I take it everywhere I go. It was a dream to be in his home … to sing a song I wrote myself was unreal. He said, 'Keelan, it is one thing to be a singer and a musician, but to write your own material is brilliant.' Mum and Dad said while I was singing it Big Tom had tears in his eyes. It was a song I wrote about my late grandparents who had a big influence on my music.

He adds:

I love music and my dream is to be out on the road performing through the country and Europe. My big dream is to play in America. As my late grandparents, Big Tom, Margo, Mike Denver, Michael English, Robert Mizzell, Declan Nerney, Louise Morrissey and Trudi Lawlor have all said to me: 'never give up'.

Arbuckle is adamant that he will stick to traditional country music in the style of his heroes. 'I'm known as a young lad that sings old songs. Real country music is my thing. My all-time hero is Merle Haggard,' he explained, before continuing: 'A young lad singing old country music goes down fierce well down in the south. The new pop stuff is only taking away from country music.'

Does he ever get teased by his contemporaries for his preference for country music? 'Aye surely,' he said, 'there'd be the odd boy with something smart to say, but I just say, "Is that so?" I don't get involved. I get great support from the teachers and the school.' When reminded that the American crooner Liberace used to tell his detractors that he was crying all the way to the bank, Arbuckle laughed: 'They say the same thing about Daniel O'Donnell. I'd be happy enough with that myself.'

Recently Arbuckle was offered the chance to be part of a final selection for a boy band in Los Angeles, with an all-expenses paid trip over there, but he declined the offer. 'I thought about it but it's not my dream to be in a boy band. They were asking me would I be the one that would always be early or the one that would always be late,' he explained. 'They were trying to make me a certain image. If I had gone I would only be taking away someone else's dream. That wasn't my dream. Mine is to be a successful country singer.'

For now he is concentrating on his school exams and is considering taking a year out after that to see how far his country music dreams can take him, before going to college. If Keelan Arbuckle does go on to huge success, it could not happen to a nicer lad.

***

Keelan Arbuckle is not the only young Irish male country artist striving to keep true to the roots of American country music. Gerry Guthrie from Ballina, County Mayo, got his first guitar at eight and claims never to have gone a day in his life since without picking it up for at least an hour. In 2010 he launched his own band following a chance meeting with Henry McMahon. This proved a lucky break when the songwriter provided him with his first two big hits: 'Shut Up Heart' and 'The Lucky Horseshoe'. Guthrie is known for his dedication to the roots of true American country; there are few other artists on the Irish scene who would release a tribute song to renowned honky-tonk American star Lefty Frizzell.

Frizzell's music also influenced Jordan Mogey, whose music is an interesting proposition in a marketplace dominated by artists who largely shape their repertoire to suit the dancing circuit. Another country purist, from Ballymoney, County Antrim, he likes the music of the late Merle Haggard and George Jones, both of whose phrasing and style are audible in his recordings and live performances. Mogey's uncle, Johnnie, contributed to the wide range of his musical influences, introducing him to Bob Wills and his Texas Playboys – pioneers of a style of country music that later became known as 'western swing'. Johnnie also brought some of the great honky-tonk pioneers to the young singer's attention – among them Webb Pierce, Faron Young and Lefty Frizzell. Mogey expresses a love for 'real country music with the grit still on' on his impressive website. Not too many contemporary Irish country music artists would choose Tompall & the Glaser Brothers as their all-time favourite performers. He also lists Johnny Cash, Vern Gosdin and Hank Williams – 'one of the cleverest heart poets of all time' – as further influences on his work.[6]

***

Ireland also has its share of country artists who started off in other musical backgrounds before breaking into the country scene. When asked about new, up-and-coming artists, Henry McMahon, like a number of other songwriters, mentioned Derek Ryan as someone to be reckoned with. Ryan is the epitome of the contemporary Irish country music star: good-looking, sharply dressed, multi-talented, and even, once, big in Japan – as a member of D-Side, a manufactured boy band which released three albums and had a number one there, as well as three top-ten singles in the British charts. Following the demise of D-Side in 2006, Ryan, after a period playing as a solo artist in London, found his version of country. His pop sensibilities shine through in songs such as his 2016 number-one hit 'You're Only Young Once (#YOYO)'.

Ryan is far from the only prominent artist on the contemporary Irish scene to have crossed musical genres to country music. Lee Matthews, born Lee Mulhern in Omagh, County Tyrone, also made the transition from the world of pop to country music. Matthews has been a singing star since the age of eight, when he released an album of pop and country ballads called *Hey Good Looking*. In 2001, aged thirteen, he performed in a Las Vegas New Year's TV Special on a bill with megastars Barbra Streisand, Billy Joel and Neil Diamond. Having gone through different rock- and pop-band formations – his previous projects included working as an Irish 'electro pop dance duo' with Pete Doherty, and a stint with the boy band Access All Areas – he reinvented himself as a country artist in 2013. Matthews explained his decision to change musical direction to the *Strabane Chronicle*:

> In America I got a buzz from seeing the country scene explode with a new generation of young country artists making country cooler. When I got back to Ireland I was so excited to see that Derek Ryan and Nathan Carter were also making country cool again here. It's such a buzz to be back on stage again singing great songs that people love and enjoy dancing to. The people in Ireland appreciate good country music and they go out of their way to make you feel welcome. The first couple of gigs I did this year people were coming up and thanking me and shaking my hand and just talking country music, it's great.[7]

Matthews has had success with his albums *A Little Bitty Country* (2014) and *It's a Great Day to Be Alive* (2015). A remarkably productive artist, he continues to churn out new songs for online distribution and to tour extensively.

Unlike Matthews and Ryan, Michael English from Castledermot, County Kildare, came to country music from a musical genre that is its polar opposite. Although brought up in a household where his father played button accordion with a traditional music outfit and his mother was a traditional Irish dancer, Michael took an interest in formal piano and composed his first classical piece of music – 'Perestroika' – at the age of eleven, performing it on *The Late Late Show*. He continued his formal music studies at the Royal Irish Academy, and also holds five All-Ireland Ballroom Dancing Championship medals. When he expressed his strong desire to launch a country music career to venerable songwriter Henry McMahon, the Monaghan man provided him with the song 'The Nearest to Perfect'. It was to prove a significant hit for English and his career went from strength to strength afterwards. He has gone on to front one of the most successful dance bands in the country, singing a mixture of his own compositions, such as 'High Five' and 'Loughlin's Bar', and country standards. He also frequently showcases his virtuoso piano skills and is regarded as a superb technical vocalist.

Before Johnny Brady from Randalstown, County Antrim, started his venture into the world of country music at the age of thirty-eight, he fronted Raised on Rock, a tribute band specialising in covers of Bon Jovi, Guns N' Roses and AC/DC. But country music was in his blood – his grandfather was Big Tom McBride's uncle – and he frequently talks fondly of time spent in Castleblaney during his school holidays and days spent playing snooker in the famous singer's house. Johnny Brady says the return to country music is sentimental and also a reminder of his mother's musical tastes. A seasoned performer, having been in a band with his uncles since the age of fifteen, he has a phenomenal following in his native Northern

Ireland and is today well known for his high-energy performances, a legacy of his days on the rock-and-roll circuit. Brady's unique vocal style and emphasis on music conducive to dancing are hallmarks of his act. He has recorded four albums to date and continues to go from strength to strength.

Some members of the younger brigade have emerged from a background of traditional Irish music. Patrick Feeney from Culfada, County Sligo, is another hugely popular artist on the contemporary country music social-dancing circuit, but his background was as much in traditional as country music. Feeney's provenance as a traditional musician is not surprising: the area around Gurteen is famous for Irish traditional music and it is the birthplace of the renowned fiddler Michael Coleman. Feeney began performing traditional Irish music in public with his father when he was only fourteen, having played the piano, drums and accordion since the age of eight. At nineteen he went into the music business full time, and it was in the country music world that he would really make his mark. His striking tenor voice is demonstrated in his version of the old country favourite 'Bury Me Beneath the Willow', unrecognisable from The Carter Family's famous rendition. Feeney is an exceptional accordion player, something he frequently displays as part of his stage performance. He is also one of the Three Amigos along with fellow country singers Robert Mizzell and Jimmy Buckley, who get together when their individual schedules allow.

Other artists have immersed themselves in the world of Irish country music from the start of their careers. 'Galway Boy' Mike Denver – born Mike Fallon – is a hugely successful artist on the social-dancing circuit, and his band is widely regarded as one of the best in the business. Denver changed his name because it sounded too Irish and a little too close to fellow country singer Mick Flavin. He is managed by Willie Carty, formerly a member and now manager of popular covers band the Conquerors, who says of his client:

The way things are going Mike is doing more and more concerts. This is getting more and more popular. Not everyone wants to dance to the music. The social dancing thing might top out, but there is a big potential market for concerts and you're seeing a lot of artists going more in that direction. It gives them a chance to try out different music.[8]

Denver records much of his music at Greenfields Studios under the guidance of Gerald O'Donoghue, whom the singer has frequently cited as a major influence on his career. The respect between the two men is mutual. 'Mike is a great lad and I'm delighted he succeeded in the industry. He's a bit like Big Tom,' says Gerald. 'He is genuinely interested in his fans and often spends hours talking to them after the gigs. They really respect him for that.'[9]

***

It is not only the men who are making their way in the modern Irish country music business. More and more young women are attempting to forge a career in Irish country music, although they often find it even more of a struggle to succeed than their male counterparts do. In 2014 the well-established singer Sandy Kelly discussed the difficulties women face in launching careers in the country music business with Marian Finucane:

It's still hard for the ladies ... women will go to see cute, good-looking, sexy guys – so they go to the dances to see Mike Denver, Gerry Guthrie and all these people, and the guys follow the girls ... the ladies have never had the same following; the guys don't go unless the girls are there, and the girls are not particularly interested in following female singers.[10]

Eunice Moran is in a good position to see the industry from a gender perspective. She worked her way up through local community-radio stations and is now a full-time presenter on Midwest Radio, as well as being a leading dance teacher. Her view is:

There is no doubt it is tougher going in the industry for women. It seems to be more and more about appearance and image. If you don't look a certain way and don't wear a sparkly dress, the doors don't open for some people. People say it's about the antisocial hours, but it's more than that. It's ironic because if you look at the Irish country music industry it was women like Margo and Philomena Begley who have made it what it is.[11]

Shauna McStravock from Ardboe, County Tyrone – a young female singer who has come to prominence in recent times and who has shared the stage with Daniel O'Donnell, Philomena Begley, Susan McCann and Derek Ryan – spoke to Fiona O'Brien of *The Irish World* newspaper about the gender divide in country music:

Although males like country music, they tend to come along to shows with their girlfriends and I can't compete with the heartthrob status that Derek [Ryan] and Nathan [Carter] have. But I would like to be that person that they think 'oh, she's a lovely girl, I'd like to be her friend', and a few people have announced me as the girl next door. I do like that vibe and hopefully we can split the stage between male and female.[12]

But despite the challenges they face, a number of female artists have a growing following in the Irish country world. As with the men, they reflect a range of musical influences, from the more traditional to what is considered a more crossover style.

One of the biggest new female names in Irish country music is Lisa McHugh. She was born in the village of Carmunnock, near Glasgow, of Irish parentage; her mother is from Falcarragh in County Donegal and her father is from Castlederg, County Tyrone. At three years of age, McHugh came close to death from a lethal germ contracted from calves on her family farm – an infection which killed all the animals but one. The singer thankfully managed to surmount her illness, but it has made her family bonds very tight and must be a factor in the relentless determination she has exhibited in making her way to the top of the country music pile. Her career trajectory is worthy of analysis, as she has been in the vanguard of the rise of young female artists.

At home she was, like many children of Irish immigrant families, exposed to the music of Philomena Begley, Daniel O'Donnell and a host of Irish country music stars. While McHugh's tastes ran wider during her teenage years, to pop and rock music, she has frequently said that country was always her first love and the genre in which she wanted to make a career if the opportunity arose. McHugh was particularly drawn to American female artists and has frequently cited Dolly Parton, Loretta Lynn, the Dixie Chicks and Martina McBride as influences.

Following the release of her debut album, *Dreams Come to Life*, in 2012, McHugh went on to be voted Female Vocalist of the Year in the Irish Country Music Awards for the following five years in a row. Like so many of the new generation of acts, her music is far more upbeat than that of previous Irish female artists. Many of her songs have an American sensibility to them and her music is emblematic of the increasing internationalisation – some would say homogenisation – of the genre. However, the likes of 'Hillbilly Girl', 'Apple Jack' and 'Bring on the Good Times' are filling the dance floors of Ireland and further afield, and if things keep going the way they are it seems like her career will continue to go from strength to strength.

Like the men, some of the women have also come from a different musical background, including Cliona Hagan from Ballinderry, County Tyrone. Hagan first came to national attention when she reached the final of talent show *Ireland's Got Talent* on RTÉ Television. For that series her performances tended towards the operatic; not surprising, considering she is a trained classical singer. Her performance of 'You'll Never Walk Alone' did not win, but it helped her develop her musical career. If good looks and a bubbly image are prerequisites in the contemporary country music industry, then Hagan has been dealt a great hand. Many predict a bright future for the Tyrone singer, who is under the astute management of Aidan Quinn, a son of Philomena Begley and a country music singer in his own right. Her 2016 hit 'We're All Gonna Die Someday' is a good example of the relentlessly upbeat type of country that has become increasingly popular both here and in the United States in recent years. Hagan has also mastered the art of yodelling, which she uses to good effect in her song 'Cowboy Yodel'. Her popularity was reflected in her being awarded Newcomer of the Year at the inaugural RTÉ Irish Country Music Awards in May 2016.

Lisa Stanley, daughter of Maisie McDaniel, is an artist who has passed from the world of pop music to the country genre. Stanley's entry into the music scene was late by standards in the Irish country scene; she was nineteen before she began singing with the Treetops in her native County Sligo. After plying the local circuit for six years, she wrote the song 'Shine' and in 2000 entered it in the Irish National Song Contest, which was shown live on RTÉ Television. This gave her the opening she was hoping for. 'On the back of that exposure,' she explained, 'I did several festivals in Europe. It was more pop-orientated at the time, but ultimately I decided to go down the country music route; after all I knew that best from my mom.'[13] Promoter Willie Carty approached Lisa about putting a band on the road and she subsequently became lead vocalist with the Fender Band. Now resident in England, she divides her time between performing with her own band and with Nathan Carter in Ireland and the UK, and television work.

Contrary to a sometimes-expressed stereotype, not all new country singers are from the verdant countryside. Niamh Lynn is a country performer from an urban environment with a sophisticated delivery style. The Dublin-based singer's version of 'Sing Me an Old-Fashioned Song' released in 2015 was an immediate hit. Her second release – 'Got a Lotta Rhythm in My Soul', a cover of an old Patsy Cline number – also gained significant airplay and may indicate a successful avenue for others to follow.

In contrast, successful newcomer, Kathy Crinion from Trim, County Meath, has tended so far to stick to new material. As well as being a singer and songwriter, she also writes stories for children and is a qualified psychotherapist. Her voice is frequently compared to that of the American singer Karen Carpenter. Her debut single, the self-penned 'We Need More Time', released in 2015, made it to number fourteen on the US Indie Airplay chart, while her debut album *Ups, Downs and Merry-Go-Rounds* included songs co-written with well-known writers Charlie McGettigan and Don Baker.

Another up-and-comer to watch is Niamh McGlinchey, who received acclaim for her performance of the Irish folk classic 'Raglan Road' when she represented Northern Ireland in RTÉ's *All-Ireland Talent Show* in 2009. In 2013 she memorably sang an off-the-cuff version of 'Live Forever' on the BBC's *The Nolan Show*.[14] She is frequently in demand as a duet singer, and has worked with a number of big names from the world of Irish country music, including Nathan Carter, Daniel O'Donnell, Louise Morrissey and Derek Ryan. She is also forging a successful solo career, with her fourth album, *At Long Last*, released in December 2017.

***

Despite the many new faces in the world of Irish country music, both male and female, the range of music played in Ireland is still narrow given the breadth of the wider country music genre. The vast majority of the acts are aligned to the dance scene and the music is tailored to the market. William Kelly of Rackhouse Pilfer, a County Sligo outfit who range wide across country music, has noticed this. The six-piece outfit describe themselves as a 'bluegrass, folk, alternative country and Americana band'.

'It' a matter of branding,' says Kelly. 'A lot of what is a type of country music is not acknowledged as such. It's a pity because the music has so much more to offer. It has to be built slowly over time.' Having lived and worked in Nashville for a number of years, he is in a good position to judge. 'The culture here is different,' he continues. 'To get to a position where people will pay in to get to see your music is difficult. We don't have as much patronage as they do in Britain. It's very difficult for bands to get started.'[15]

Bluegrass remains a minority interest, although the scene continues to thrive, albeit largely away from the glare of the general public. We Banjo 3 (which, despite the name, has four members), while not bluegrass purists, are gaining a strong foothold in the market. The two sets of brothers – Enda and Fergal Scahill and Martin and David Howley – play 'Celtgrass' music, which they describe as a blend of traditional Irish, old-time and bluegrass. They play four-string banjos, whereas bluegrass artists generally use a five-string instrument. Martin is a seven-time All-Ireland Banjo Champion, while Enda has recorded with famous American bluegrass artist Ricky Skaggs and is considered an authority on Irish-banjo techniques. Siobhan Long, music critic for *The Irish Times*, wrote about We Banjo 3: 'The band are a musical Betty Ford Clinic, almost single-handedly rehabilitating the much maligned banjo in four short years.'[16]

The band are quickly developing a reputation and have garnered a number of awards, including the *Irish American News* Album of the Year 2015, the *Lonesome Highway* RTÉ Radio 1 Album of the Year 2015 and the *Celtic Connections* Radio Show Album of the Year 2015. Renowned music critic Lee Zimmerman of *Elmore Magazine* paid them a handsome tribute when he wrote that their music is like a combination of great bluegrass and The Chieftains. It is, he wrote, as if they 'got together for a battle of the bands but decided to pool their resources instead'.[17] He believes 'the future of world music' is theirs. Now with four albums under their belts – *Roots of the Banjo Tree* (2012), *Gather the Good* (2014), *Live in Galway* (2015) and *String Theory* (2016) – the band is going from strength to strength.

We Banjo 3 are not the only successful contemporary artists playing the bluegrass sound. Bluegrass authorities Niall Toner, Tim Rogers, Uri Kohen and Tony Friel (long-time bluegrass DJ on Finn Valley FM) all point to the same cohort of artists and groups plying their wares on the Irish circuit as worthy of attention. Prominent among them are Cup O'Joe, JigJam, Pine Marten, I Draw Slow, Land's End, Dublin Bluegrass Collective, the Bill Whelan Band, Lena Ullman, Woodbine and The Tennessee Hennessees. Toner also noted the talent on the 'alternative country' scene which, he wrote, 'is underground by its very nature', mentioning Nine Stone Cowboy, the Beverage Hillbillies, Pete Cummins' band, Custer's Last Stand and The Remedy Club. The alternative country scene in the United States has evolved into a bewildering number of subgenres and labels – cow-punk, psychobilly and gothabilly, among others – but Ireland has not witnessed any such fracturing of the music in any significant manner. The costs of recording outlined by Gerald O'Donoghue would suggest it would prove difficult for any such group to become established.

Those bluegrass groups mentioned here continue to do their best to promote an alternative country sound in Ireland. However, they could never hope to equal the impact that the subject of the next chapter has had on the Irish country market.

16

THE PAST IS A FOREIGN COUNTRY MUSIC: THE RISE OF NATHAN CARTER

The past is a foreign country; they do things differently there.

L. P. Hartley, *The Go-Between*[1]

In many ways, he is the 'everyman' musician … In conversation, he is polite, friendly, easygoing; on stage, he is the handsome rogue who regularly has knickers and bras flung at him with a recklessness that suggests his audience are there for more than just the music. In other words, Nathan Carter is a mix of Daniel O'Donnell's 'nice guy' demeanour and the sex appeal of a young Tom Jones. The combination causes both girls and their mammies to fall in love with him.[2]

John Farry, Carter's manager, is just back from the United States, where his young charge is recording and touring. 'Nathan has all the tools to succeed in America,' he says. 'Most importantly he has the likeability factor. He is a personable young man. The Nathan you see on stage is the same Nathan you meet in real life. I suppose he is the son-in-law every mother would like to have and the boyfriend a lot of girls would like to have too. He's the envy of plenty of boyfriends too. He's a great guy, a genuine all-around good lad, and his star is continuing to rise.'[3]

Farry himself has been a prolific songwriter for over three decades, penning fifteen songs for Daniel O'Donnell alone, including 'Summertime in Ireland' and 'Mother's Birthday Song'. He also wrote 'Mysterious Woman' for Marc Roberts, which finished second in the Eurovision Song Contest, a feat that has not been bettered since by a song penned by an Irish songwriter, and has recorded six albums of his own. He has been Carter's manager from the start of the rise of the young singer's career and enthusiastically recounts the first time he saw him sing:

I was playing a gig at the Inishowen Gateway Hotel in Donegal in April of 2009. Nathan was on the same bill, just a young man in a waistcoat. He was singing the old Del Shannon song 'The Answer to Everything' and, looking back now, in many ways he *was* the answer to everything. I knew straight away he had the talent to succeed. His voice was exceptional and his musical ability was extraordinary. From the very start we got on like a house on fire.[4]

At the time Carter was singing a mixture of different genres, but Farry recognised a specific sound in the singer's voice:

I thought his voice would be well suited to country, so I put a country feel to the Joe South song 'Games People Play' and it was a hit. It wasn't as easy as people might think, but things moved fairly quickly. I remember the first gig in the Greenvale Hotel in Cookstown, and even then it was obvious he would be successful. He had the audience in the palm of his hands. We went from there with some country songs – 'The Way That I Love You', 'One for the Road', 'Welcome to the Weekend' – that sort of thing. We've never looked back since.[5]

Nathan Kane Tyrone Carter has attracted a whole new audience to Irish country music – if his music can be called 'country' in the first instance. It may, in the not-so-distant future, be more appropriate to call it 'Nathan music', in a similar fashion to the work of Daniel O'Donnell. His ascent to fame has been extraordinary. He is the boy wonder, crown prince and leading heartthrob of the music combined in one smooth package.

Born in Liverpool, Carter moved to Ireland to pursue a career in the country music industry when he was only eighteen, following his meeting with John Farry. He had left school two years earlier because he was – in his own words – 'crap at it':

> I had no intention of studying or carrying that on anymore. Music was what I wanted to do; it's what I wanted to pursue. Mum didn't really want me to [leave school] because I couldn't even drive. So my Nan and Dad would drop me off to gigs and help me with the gear and stuff. When I started getting gigs, Mum said she didn't mind if I was earning money and wasn't just sitting on my arse all day, to put it bluntly. So that was what I did. I remember the fellas in the bars used to look at me a bit strangely when I was bringing the speakers in and setting up, because I was only a young kid. But it was great experience. It was like an apprenticeship, in a way.[6]

Although neither of his parents were musicians or singers, Carter was a child prodigy, mastering the accordion by four and becoming an All-Ireland Singing Champion by ten. He was also the head chorister at the Liverpool Boys' Choir for a short period, even getting to sing for Pope John Paul II in Rome. Like many British-born children of Irish extraction, he was brought up to the sounds of country music. American heavyweights like Johnny Cash and Tammy Wynette were popular in the Carter household, while Philomena Begley, Big Tom, Brendan Shine and other stars of the Irish country scene were also frequently heard on the family CD player. The young Carter was particularly influenced by the accordion skills of Brendan Shine.

He released seven albums in the first six years of his career, all to great acclaim. Carter recounted his story to *Irish Mirror* journalist Siobhan O'Connor in 2016. The article notes that at a gig in Ballymena, County Antrim, seven years earlier, just twenty-six people had attended; 2,000 had attended the same venue for a Carter concert shortly before the interview.[7]

Even those who have no interest in Irish country music are likely to have heard a specific song of Nathan Carter's, which seemed to play on every radio in the country for a period of time. 'Wagon Wheel', Carter's anthemic signature tune, is an up-tempo, country-rock number, originally written by Bob Dylan and subsequently modified by Ketch Secor of Old Crow Medicine Show. The chorus and melody of the song come from a demo recorded by Dylan during the *Pat Garrett and Billy the Kid* sessions, while Secor later added in the verses. Dylan's original work was called 'Rock Me Mama', but it became 'Wagon Wheel' after the addition of Secor's lyrics; they share the copyright evenly. The song describes a hitchhiking journey along the eastern coast of the United States, starting from New England in the north-east, passing through Roanoke, Virginia, and ending up in Raleigh, North Carolina. There the singer intends to meet his lover. At the end of the song we do not find out if the narrator makes it to see the woman, but we do get to hear the chorus a lot. The theme of the song is a world removed from the emigration and heartbreak sung of in much traditional Irish country music. Carter's version spent a total of fifty-two weeks in the Irish charts after it was released in 2012.

Despite the fact that Carter does not earn any royalties when his songs are played on the radio, as they are cover versions, his finances still seem to be in good health. In 2012 the singer established Nathan Carter Music Group – in which he owns all the shares – to deal with his business ventures. The vast bulk of his money comes from touring, album and merchandise sales.

On 30 December 2015 RTÉ Television broadcast the first *Nathan Carter Show* from Dublin's Mansion House. His guests included Mary Black, John Sheehan of The Dubliners, Paddy Casey and British country duo The Shires. The production values were high and the audience overwhelmingly female. Carter provided a virtuoso display of his accordion-playing and singing skills. He praised his fans as the best in the country and told the audience of all the gifts he is constantly sent, from 'cuddly toys to underwear – thankfully all clean'. He introduced some of his family who had come over from Liverpool for the show. His mother, Noreen, told the audience Carter 'came out singing': 'You were singing before you were talking. That's all you ever did.' He then introduced his seventy-five-year-old grandmother Ann, who still sells the merchandise at his concerts. Originally from Warrenpoint, County Down, her family had intended to emigrate to the United States but were robbed in Liverpool and got no further. When Carter asked his grandmother if he was a good singer as a child she told him he was rubbish: 'You used to charge people to come into our lounge … your cousins and aunties, and they'd ask for the money back because it was rubbish … you did try hard … you got better as you went along.' The audience appreciated her sharp humour. A home video showed Carter tearing the wrapping off a present on Christmas morning and discovering to his delight that he was the proud owner of a new accordion.

Carter turned to his father, Ian, and mentioned his time on the building sites working as a joiner and, again, inquired as to his ability. 'You cost me an arm and a leg in gloves … you brought four or five pairs a day,' his father responded, 'because you didn't want to get your hands dirty.' Carter junior explained that he needed to protect his hands; his father nodded and smiled: 'I can understand now why you did it, but not then.' His grandfather John was the last to be introduced – he was eighty-two on the night. He had also loved singing from an early age. John told a story behind the first song Nathan remembers him singing, the Elvis Presley standard 'Are You

Lonesome Tonight?'. He had entered and won a talent competition on his honeymoon in Jersey with his version. On the show he sang a couple of verses before being joined by his grandson. Carter finished up by singing his all-time favourite folk song, 'Caledonia', with the help of the Dublin Gospel Choir. It was clear from this first show that the young performer was determined to broaden his musical appeal.

Senator Marie Louise O'Donnell has discussed the appeal of Carter's music with Sean O'Rourke on RTÉ Radio 1: 'The women follow Nathan and the men follow the women. He is a phenomenon.'[8] She had gone to the McWilliam Park Hotel in Claremorris, County Mayo, to hear Carter, along with 1,100 others. She went on:

You could feel the rhythm of that music. It's just full of old story and verse and melody … there's brilliant instrumentation and you have a live audience … I think young people are sick of the disco where it's all electronic … you want to see the jiving couples, the twisting, dragging and pulling … it's just magic … and fellas up by the bar and pints and great music with great stories about love affairs and about meeting people and getting left.[9]

The cosmopolitan O'Donnell fell under the Carter spell: 'He's special; he's talented … a multi-instrumentalist, marvellous fun and he's extremely well mannered … a honey pie.' When asked to compare his future to the success of Daniel O'Donnell and Garth Brooks, she stated her belief that he would be bigger than both:

Nathan Carter is a wonderful new pop Celtic artist. I'm a great believer in energy and I'm a great believer in movement and in fun and enjoying yourself and he is that, as well as talent and musicianship … he sang his heart out for two hours and the people loved it … they were entirely involved; moving and twisting and bobbing.[10]

To date Carter's career has been laced with impressive achievements. He was the first country artist to reach number one on the Irish album charts since Garth Brooks in 2007, and he gave a remarkable 170 performances, live and on television, in 2015. On 29 April 2016 he released his fourth album, *Stayin' Up All Night*. The previous three had been released only in Ireland but this one was also given a UK release. He spoke to *Access All Areas Edinburgh* – an online guide to entertainment in the Scottish capital – about his musical popularity in Britain:

> People in the UK really seem to be embracing country music at the moment and it's amazing to see so many fans coming out to my shows, so hopefully they're going to like the album. I grew up in Liverpool and I've always played live across the UK, and I want to make all the people who have supported me here proud.[11]

Birmingham-based *The Harp* newspaper wrote of his performances in the United Kingdom:

> You won't find too many artists outside of the calibre of perhaps Elton John, who will allow his fabulous band go off on a break, calmly stroll to the piano, and accompany himself on a superb version of 'The Leaving of Liverpool' and a raft of other numbers. In addition, his totally relaxed and laid-back manner while being bombarded by iPhones right, left, and centre is to be lauded and admired.[12]

In May 2016 Carter's anthem 'Wagon Wheel' was the subject of a bizarre court case. Fifty-three-year-old Stephen Leighton of Coleraine, County Derry, received a suspended sentence for breaking the windows of his upstairs neighbour, Jason Kane, on the previous 10 January. Leighton described Kane's continual playing of 'Wagon Wheel' as 'some sort of psychological torture'. Kane provided an account of the episode in Derry

Magistrate's Court. He was playing his stereo in his bedroom when the accused came to his door and said that if he heard 'Wagon Wheel' one more time he would 'smash that stereo'.[13] Instead he broke two window panes and told the police to 'fuck off' when they were called to the scene. Such was his state of agitation, limb restraints had to be attached before he was taken away. Leighton shouted all the way to the police station and punched an officer in the face.[14] Kane admitted to playing the Nathan Carter album for an hour. It was not, he claimed, just 'Wagon Wheel'. His fiancée, Bronagh, was pregnant with twins at the time and they were worried the incident would affect her pregnancy. Leighton received a suspended sentence of four months and was ordered to pay £200 to repair the damage by the judge.[15]

When Carter was made aware of the case, it was reported that he offered four concert tickets to Kane:

I'd like to offer the person tickets to the Belfast gig, if they want to come after what they've been through. Obviously it's a serious matter but I couldn't help but laugh when I saw the story ... I can imagine it would be annoying over a certain amount of time, hearing the same song over and over again. I'm sure there are an awful lot of people out there that don't like it but fortunately enough there is [sic] enough people out there that do and they're the ones I'm worried about ... It's a song that I sing an awful lot, but it's been good to me and I'll say I'll be singing it for a long time to come.[16]

One of Carter's more unusual appearances was on the Irish-language soap opera Ros na Rún. In 2013 the singer appeared in an episode of the popular TG4 series in which the locals discussed the possibility of holding a Nathan Carter tribute night. John Joe, one of the village characters, assured the other organisers that he could get the famous artist to perform in the flesh. This was met with incredulity by the other characters, but on the night of the tribute show, John Joe walked into Gaudi's restaurant along with Carter, to the amazement of the assembled crowd.[17]

John Farry outlined the progression of Carter's career for me. 'He has moved away from the social-dancing circuit where he started,' he said. 'I suppose he has outgrown it, but concerts are where it's at now. It is a natural progression. If you look at other artists it's the same thing. Derek Ryan is moving more and more towards concerts as well.'[18]

On 4 July 2017, Independence Day in the United States, RTÉ Television appropriately broadcast a one-off special titled *Nathan Goes to Nashville*. Carter performed a self-penned number in the Bluebird Cafe, a venue that holds just ninety people and is known as the premier spot for those trying to break through in the industry. (It was where Garth Brooks was first spotted by a talent scout from Capitol Records.) The young Liverpudlian was well received by an enthusiastic audience. 'Nathan Carter is awesome. We love him,' said a radiant girl in her twenties following the gig. Carter was also brought for a short recording session in RCA Studios, where he was shown the particular historical Nashville code of country music production, where the same session musicians are consistently employed by studios. (The system originated during the era of the Nashville Sound, and musicians were often referred to as the 'Nashville A Team'.) The residual influences of this system make for highly accomplished musicians who are quick to adapt to varying demands and have the confidence to have an input into the creative process. The mixing editor was happy to turn Carter's voice high in the mix because of its quality – an excellent recommendation given the stellar standards that pertain in Nashville. The show ended with Carter's expression of hope that one day he might make a breakthrough in the toughest place of them all for country music singers. If anyone from Ireland's country scene can do it, there is no doubt that person is Nathan Carter.

Over the last weekend of August 2017 the Harvest Country Music Festival took place. The two-day event was held simultaneously in Ennis-

killen, County Fermanagh, and Westport, County Mayo. The line-up performed on alternate days at each venue. Nathan Carter was the headline act
on the Saturday night in the magnificent grounds of Westport House. Due
to an unfortunate clash with a football match involving Mayo, and very wet
weather during the preceding week, the attendance at the festival was poor,
although the day itself was bright and clear. An impressive range of food
stalls were open on the verdant grounds, but business was slack. Thirteen
people staffed a lengthy outdoor bar, which never had a queue of more than
three or four people. But when Nathan Carter finally took to the stage at
just after 8 p.m., the field immediately came to life. Suddenly it seemed like
there were five times as many punters as half an hour earlier. It was evident
many of the audience, particularly the younger female demographic, had
come solely to see Carter. The impressively built Kilkenny senior hurlers
were in attendance and endlessly jumped up and down and cheered,
fuelled by alcohol and youth, dressed in their best cowboy duds. Carter
was relentlessly upbeat and had the audience clapping their hands in the
air to his up-tempo music in a matter of minutes. When he sat down at
the piano and launched into 'Caledonia', the field, now bathed in semi-
darkness, was a sea of lights from mobile phones and cigarette lighters.
Despite the small attendance, the singer never relented in his upbeat and
cheerful demeanour. But an interesting comment from a country outsider
at the concert reflects the change that Carter has brought to the style of
country music in Ireland. Egbert Polski from Germany had never been to
a country music festival, yet he could not reconcile Carter's music with his
conception of country music: 'If this is country and western music, I think
I am an opera singer.'[19]

I thought about what John Farry had said about his artist earlier in the
week when he compared him with Big Tom:

In time I hope Nathan will become the king of the music world here in
Ireland. You have to put a bit of mileage up on the clock to get there. As

his career progresses his music is expanding too. It's up to other people to put a name on it. Other people can be a judge of the music. He is an artist who likes to stretch the boundaries, but you have to be careful how far you stretch it too. It has a bit of everything in it. He is a multitalented guy, incredibly talented. There will never be another Big Tom. He was a one-off, unique, but I do think Nathan will stay on top of the pile for a long time.[20]

There is little doubt that the arrival of Nathan Carter at the pinnacle of the Irish country music world represents a changing of the guard. This is most definitely not the music of Big Tom, Margo, Philomena Begley and a host of other traditional Irish country music acts. Carter himself reflects this in an interview he gave to Claire McCormack of the *Irish Independent* in which he said that one of the main factors giving country music such an appeal to the younger audience is what he calls the 'easygoing style … a mixture of pop, rock, country and folk'. He is aware of the changes in the themes as well: 'Years ago, country music was very sad. Musicians mostly wrote about their wife dying or getting divorced. But now it's a lot happier and more upbeat.'[21]

Carter has helped bring the genre into a new country and he might not be the only one of his family to make a job in show business. His sister, Ciara, also sings and his brother, Jake, plays the fiddle and guitar as well as singing, but, for now, their elder sibling is as far ahead of the posse as can be.

17

FOREVER AND EVER: THE ENDURING POPULARITY OF IRISH COUNTRY MUSIC

I think there are a lot of people on the periphery of it all that don't really understand exactly what the whole country-and-Irish music culture really means and how important it is. Looking back down the road I think it will become part of a bigger picture of our inheritance of what our culture was all about.

Declan Nerney on *A little Bit Country*, TG4[1]

Irish country music is as valid a folk art as traditional singing and dancing. I will make no apology for having it on television.

Máire Ní Chonláin, Commissioning Editor of TG4[2]

On Friday 24 June 2016 the inaugural RTÉ Irish Country Music Awards were broadcast live on RTÉ Television, hosted by Daniel O'Donnell and Nathan Carter and run in conjunction with the *Irish Farmers Journal* and the Irish Country Music Association.

Singer Mike Denver spoke in the build-up to the event:

Everywhere I go people say how much they are looking forward to the big night. They are thrilled that country music is being put on the pedestal that it should have been on ages ago. I am delighted that it is happening now for country music and that it is at long last getting the recognition that it truly deserves. I would like to compliment those in RTÉ and the *Journal* [the *Irish Farmers Journal*] and behind the scenes who are putting together what should be a massive show and one that simply has to be a major advantage to the entire scene in the times ahead.[3]

In many respects it was a breakthrough for Irish country music. The national broadcaster had long been criticised for ignoring the genre, but this was a fully fledged extravaganza with high-end production values and a prime-time slot. It attracted an audience of more than 550,000. As well as the standard awards given at such events, the show included the selection of the country's all-time favourite country song from a shortlist of four: 'Pretty Little Girl from Omagh', made famous by Brian Coll; Gloria's iconic gospel anthem 'One Day at a Time'; the Big Tom super hit 'Four Country Roads'; and Nathan Carter's 'Wagon Wheel'.

From the start it was a night of huge celebration. Two-thirds of the audience were on the floor dancing throughout the proceedings. During the show Shay Healy presented the Songwriter of the Year Award to Derek Ryan. It was a poignant moment. Healy, a prolific songwriter, is suffering from Parkinson's disease and spoke with difficulty. Album of the Year was presented to Mike Denver, who, in his acceptance speech, paid specific tribute to the DJs on local radio stations for keeping the flame of country music burning. It was then time for the greatest of them all, Big Tom McBride, to take the stage. Michael Commins was duly appreciative in his column in the *Irish Farmers Journal* the following week:

Possibly the most humbling moment of all was Big Tom McBride's induction into the Hall of Fame. His performance of 'The Same Way You Came In' very nearly took the roof off RTÉ. It was an emotional moment and you could clearly get a sense of how great his influence is on the country music scene.[4]

At the end of the night the award for the 'All-Time Favourite Irish Country Song' was given to Nathan Carter's 'Wagon Wheel', an indication of the huge growth in country music among younger audiences.

Michael Commins pointed to the changes in the industry that this ceremony reflected:

In the end, you got the feeling that the results of the awards ceremony almost came secondary to the success of the event. The perception that country music is an 'old man's game' was all but shattered. As the young fresh faces of the industry such as Derek Ryan, Mike Denver and, of course, Nathan Carter, and their female counterparts Lisa McHugh, Cliona Hagan and Niamh Lynn, to name a few, dashed across our TV screens last Friday night, you got the sense of a revolution of sorts within Ireland's music circles.[5]

Critics of Irish country music sometimes assume that Ireland is one of only a few places outside the United States where country music has attained such popularity. However, there are country music followings in countries which nobody would associate with twang and cowboy hats. The soundtrack of the Belgian film *The Broken Circle Breakdown* – dominated by bluegrass and American folk music, with cover versions by the Broken Circle Breakdown Band of 'Sister Rosetta Goes Before Us', 'Country in My Genes' and the ever-popular Carter Family song 'Will the Circle Be Unbroken' – became the biggest-selling soundtrack in the history of Belgian music.[6] Prague in the Czech Republic lays claim to Europe's first all-country radio station, while The Ritakado Saloon and the Amerika Country Saloon, both decorated in western style, are two of the most popular nightspots in the city.[7]

Iran is perhaps the least likely country in the world to have a country music scene, given its long history of political turmoil and oppression. Yet Iranian country, a mixture of American country sounds and native Iranian music, has been popularised by bands like Dream Rovers, Shahryar Masrour and Thunder. In fact, Thunder was the first band in contemporary Iranian history to be given permission to play music in English, and promptly sold out their first four shows. Also significant is the fact that it is composed of male and female members in a country which over the last four decades has had a history of oppressing women. The female members of Thunder wear headscarves to honour their religion. The band has toured Europe and always makes a point of asking the audiences to support musical freedom in their home country.

Argentina, long associated with cowboys and the open range, is a more plausible home for a booming country music industry. In a land of cattle and *gauchos* it is no surprise that the San Pedro Country Music Festival attracts huge numbers each autumn and that line dancing and cowboy paraphernalia are to be seen on the streets of Buenos Aires.

The first Indian person to record in Nashville was the appropriately named Bobby Cash, whose popularity inspired a wave of country-music-infused Bollywood films, a hugely popular art form in India and beyond. Known as 'The Indian Cowboy, One in a Billion', Cash's interest in country music was sparked by an aunt living in Nashville who sent records to his family. He imitated the sounds and developed a unique guitar style. A chance meeting in New Delhi with Australian film producer Colin Bromley resulted in an invitation to the Tamworth Country Music Festival in 2003, and from there Cash's career took off. Cash enjoys tremendous popularity in Australia as well as in his home country.

Australia is a unique case because its country music grew up independently of the American scene, although it draws on the same influences of Scottish, Irish and British folk ballads and instrumentation. The Tamworth Country Music Festival, one of the biggest in the world, began in 1973 in New South Wales; it now regularly attracts more than 100,000 people and frequently features Irish country artists on its roster.

Tex Morton, the pioneer of country music in Australia, established his name by moving around from one outback station to another, singing his American-infused western songs. After attaining national popularity in the 1930s, Morton formed and toured with his 'Rodeo and Wild West Show' in the 1940s before setting sail for the United States in 1949. There he carved out a substantial career as a stage hypnotist and in film, before returning to Australia in the 1960s.

Slim Dusty, who died at the age of seventy-six in 2003 after a career which spanned almost six decades, was widely known as the 'King of Australian Country Music'. His 1958 hit 'A Pub With No Beer' was the first Australian single to go gold and is still the biggest-selling country single of all time there. Such was Dusty's popularity that he was invited to sing 'Waltzing Matilda' at the closing ceremony of the 2000 Olympic Games in Sydney and was given a state funeral on his death. In more recent times Australian Keith Urban – an unlikely name for a 'singing hat' of the modern generation – has had more than ten number one hit singles on the American country music chart.

However, not all has run smoothly for Australian artists in the country music genre. When Olivia Newton-John was awarded the gong for best female vocalist in 1974 at the American Country Music Awards there were complaints from purists, who considered her more pop than traditional country, despite the fact that she had hits with standards 'Banks of the Ohio' and 'Take Me Home, Country Roads'. It was around this time that the greats of hard-core country music had begun their gradual slide off many American radio stations. The Australian singer still did not find favour with some when she was invited to present the prize to the best female vocalist at the 2016 CMA awards ceremony at the Bridgestone Arena in Nashville. Her leather outfit resulted in her being voted as one of the worst-dressed women at the event by the *ENews* website.[8]

Outside America, it is a close-run thing whether Canada or Australia has the greatest number of country music fans. Unsurprisingly, Canada has a huge constituency for country music and has contributed artists such as Hank Snow and Anne Murray to the genre, as well as modern-day superstar Shania Twain. The jury may be out on her country music pedigree and purists may not like her crossover style, but there is no denying her worldwide popularity.

Nearer to home, the 'C2C: Country 2 Country' concerts in March 2013 drew nearly 30,000 fans to London. The festival, promoted by AEG in conjunction with the Nashville-based CMA, brought a selection of American artists, including Tim McGraw and Carrie Underwood, to the city. It was such a success that in 2014 the festival expanded to include shows in Dublin, and in 2015 Glasgow became the third venue for the three-day celebration of country music. Another sign of the popularity of country in England came at the 2015 Glastonbury Festival, where Dolly Parton played to an estimated 150,000 people on 29 June. The headliners were heavy-metal superstars Metallica.

This should not come as a surprise, however, as country has a history of popularity in Britain. Between 1971 and 1988 *The Old Grey Whistle Test*, which was regarded as BBC Television's 'serious' music show, showcased some timeless performances by American country artists, including Bonnie Raitt and Emmylou Harris. One of the show's presenters, Bob Harris, still champions country music on his BBC Radio 2 programme *Bob Harris Country*. There is a thriving tradition of country music in Scotland, not surprisingly, given the origins of much of the sound and instrumentation which formed the basis of the genre in the United States. Glasgow even has its own Grand Ole Opry venue, while the country has been a happy hunting ground for many Irish artists, such as Mick Flavin and Philomena Begley.

As well as performing in international festivals, another opportunity for Irish artists to perform abroad, albeit to a home-grown crowd, has come into fashion in recent years. Organised country music tours, all-in holidays with full board and nightly music in far-flung locations have now become increasingly big business. Some are organised by entrepreneurs such as Paul Claffey, CEO of Midwest Radio; others by artists or groups of artists. Declan Nerney has his hugely popular 'Hooley in the Sun', while Robert Mizzell frequently takes groups to the United States.

Twenty-five years ago Paul Claffey limited his excursions to places like Westport and Galway, but these days South Africa and Las Vegas feature on the itinerary. He explained the origin of his tours to *Mature Living* magazine. He was on a golfing holiday with singer Joe Dolan and Joe's brother Ben. While the golfing was great, there was only bingo in the hotel at night and they were bored. The combination of good weather, golf and music appealed to Claffey:

> I figured if we could fill a flight it would be worth trying it, so straight away I booked the Conquerors from Portumna and Joe said he would sing a few songs as well. I arranged the charter flight on a Tuesday, advertised it on Midwest Radio on Wednesday and Thursday and by Friday the whole thing was sold out. That was two decades ago and it's still going strong.[9]

The main attraction of these holidays is the live music, and even Irish-based holidays of this type are popular. One of Claffey's favoured locations is Westport. The town is a jewel in the crown of the Irish tourism industry and is particularly popular with domestic tourists. There is a direct train to Dublin, which makes access a lot easier than to other tourist destinations in the west of Ireland. It is a planned town, which makes it pleasingly symmetrical, an unusual feature in Ireland. It is also beside the sea and only eight kilometres from Croagh Patrick, Ireland's holy mountain, where the national saint is said to have spent forty days and nights praying. Westport has much to offer the tourist.

A typical example of one of these holidays is taking place on a wet, cold, mid-April Sunday night. Paul Claffey Music Tours has a group staying in the Castlecourt Hotel as part of a three-day residential country music festival in the town. Each night the customers get to hear two of Ireland's best-known country performers as part of the package. This is the first night, and some extra tickets to attend the concert only are available. The subsequent two nights are completely occupied by those on the full package. In addition to the musical performances, the full-time ticket holders get their breakfast and evening meal and have the opportunity to go on optional tours.

Tonight Patrick Feeney and Stuart Moyles are the main attraction. The excitement is obvious and the audience are mature. The Ashleigh Suite is a conference room in the extensive Castlecourt Hotel complex and is used for large weddings and meetings; tonight it is wedged. There is limited consumption of alcohol. The music starts with a one-man-band warm-up act, and a large number of couples immediately take to the floor; in no time it is full. From sitting sedately, they are flying around the dance floor moments later. There are a lot of older female couples and a group of female line dancers from Scotland. Later, when Paul Claffey asks the audience to cheer for their home country, the number of Scottish people is striking – so too the number of English.

After the one-man band stops playing, Claffey takes to the stage. He welcomes all the people on the tour and tells them about the special extension to breakfast time in the morning; normally it would finish at ten but the hotel will take into account the needs of these late-night revellers and serve until eleven. This raises a huge cheer. Claffey gently warns them not to turn up in droves at five to eleven like the previous year's group, when it was 'bloody bedlam'. He is good at frying eggs, he tells them, but not that good. Claffey is an excellent communicator and the audience follows his every word like an obedient group of schoolchildren listening to a competent teacher. He tells them about the entertainment options for the next two days, which include a tour of Westport itself and a bus tour to Cong and Kylemore Abbey. Then comes the bit the audience have been waiting for. 'It is now time for music,' he announces, to a final, great cheer.

Claffey introduces 'the man from Gurteen, County Sligo, one of Ireland's greatest singers'. Patrick Feeney strides up to the stage, moving through the audience wearing a fashionably snug-fitting, navy suit with a light-blue, open-necked shirt and brown shoes. He looks like a young man who has just left an office job and taken his tie off for comfort. After asking the audience whether they are having a good time, and receiving a positive response, he launches into a set of upbeat tunes. Claffey thinks that the music is too loud and goes to the mixing engineer to turn it down. He is happy then and thumbs go up and a broad grin comes to his face. He moves around the room with ease, hugging and greeting people. Everything runs like clockwork. Fast sets are mixed with slow tunes. Feeney takes out his accordion half an hour into his set and plays excellently. The band is top quality. There is an excellent fiddle player, and the two guitarists and drummer ease through the routine with Feeney out front. A light shines on Feeney for the duration of his set, except when he asks his bass player to sing a song to give him a rest. Claffey stands at the bar with his arms folded, talking to the owner of the hotel. He is a content man, looking over his country kingdom. All is well in Claffey country.

Irish country music in the live setting is first and foremost about dancing. However, that is not the be all and end all of the country music story. It also has an enduring appeal in recorded and broadcast formats and the reason for this, more than anything else, is because the songs tell a story and Irish culture has always embraced storytelling. In ancient Irish culture, stories, poems and songs were passed from generation to generation. Poets and bards were revered and allowed privileges denied to others; their ability to entertain and record events was valued. Stories are central to human existence; we explain the world to ourselves by stories. Country music songs get to the essence of the subject with direct and accessible language and simple stories; there is a beginning, middle and end. Even the titles of country songs aim to tell a story in a phrase: 'Today I Started Loving You Again' or 'Tonight the Bottle Let Me Down'.

Praise for the storytelling ability of country music songs comes from many sources. In April 1995 the CMA held their spring board meeting in Dublin as part of the organisation's focus on the global development of the music.[10] The CMA, founded in Nashville in 1958, was the first organisation dedicated to championing the cause of a specific type of music. It aims to guide and advance country music worldwide, and is best known for its annual music awards. 'Nashville Comes to Ireland' was the name given to the three-day festival organised in Dublin to commemorate the meeting. It included concerts and free performances and was launched by Taoiseach John Bruton in the state apartments at Dublin Castle. He praised the music: 'Country has more followers in Ireland than in any other country outside the U.S. You can actually hear the words. The words do matter.'[11] That was high praise from an unlikely source.

Singer Declan Nerney put it well on the TG4 television series *A Little Bit Country* when he discussed the connection between the 'ordinary people of Ireland' and country music:

> One thing about country songs is that you'll always hear the tune someone is singing and say 'that's my life he's singing about'. If you reach forty years of age or fifty years of age or sixty years of age for that matter, there's some country tune out there that will sum it all up for you.[12]

Country music is predominantly an adult music form. The great American singer Emmylou Harris famously observed that 'you have to grow up, start paying the rent and have your heart broken before you understand country'.[13] Sandy Kelly outlined her views to Marian Finucane on RTÉ

Radio: 'Country music is music of the people. It's very simple to understand. The sound and the songs and the lyrics are about their everyday lives … they can go about their kitchen singing the songs.'[14] It tells the stories of lives lived, warts and all. It is not music of fantasy: it reflects real life.

In *The Swingin' Sixties Book*, Paschal Mooney discussed the attraction of the nature of the stories which populate country music:

> The Irish are a sentimental race who like their songs to fit their moods and country music and its lyrics fit very easily into that image. Songs of mothers, leaving home, affairs of the heart are all part and parcel of Irish life.[15]

The sentiments of Bill Malone echo this when he writes of the themes of the music of the early settlers in Appalachia:

> Their songs were about rural nostalgia, love (often broken) and pastoral retreats … songs that reaffirmed the values of home, family, mother and God, and they took to their hearts songs about dying orphans, neglected mothers, blind children, maidens who died of broken hearts …[16]

On *A Little Bit Country*, Big Tom McBride explained his thoughts behind the emotion these songs inspire: 'There's a story in every song and a lot of times there's a tear in it. You have to feel country music. You just don't sing the song.'[17] Big Tom referred to himself as a 'singer of sad songs' and echoed Mooney when he said, 'we're a sentimental race of people … we've had a lot of trouble down the years so maybe we have reason for it … but it's a happy kind of sadness'.[18]

When John Waters first saw Big Tom he was shocked by the contrast between the heartbreaking sentiments expressed in so many of the songs and the wild enjoyment in the dance hall. While McBride sang of lost love and dying mothers, the crowd danced themselves into an ever-greater reverie.[19]

Gail Walker of the *Belfast Telegraph* put it well:

> [I]t says something about the people we are. Sentimental, deeply imbued
> with traditional values, family-orientated (how many songs about mothers
> mending and making do and fathers who died before the crops came in?)
> and happy to listen to a foottappin' tune rather than some rock juggernaut.
> Everyone knows a Queen of the Silver Dollar, a man who has had a wheel
> come off the wagon.[20]

Father Brian D'Arcy is a significant presence in Irish country music circles.
The Passionist priest, journalist, writer and broadcaster has long been the
unofficial chaplain to many in show business and counted Gene Stuart
among his long-time friends. He described country music at the 1994
tribute night to singer Shay Hutchinson:

> It was about life, about family … it was about our emotions, it was about
> reality, it was about the sad things in life, it was about broken love, it was
> about drinking, it was about being out of work, it was about the joys of
> birth, it was about the lovely beautiful things life is about and sometimes
> the sad things that life is about … but if you can sing about them it's even
> better than praying about them.[21]

The hardships endured by pioneers in the United States were similar to the
tough life many people lived in early and mid-twentieth-century Ireland. It
was not simply that these American stories found a home in Ireland – they
were Irish: they had gone and come back.

Michael Commins calls it 'heart music'.[22] It is, he says, both about
loneliness and aloneness on the one hand, but family and community on
the other. It is about striking out for new lands as well as remembering and
sentimentalising the old. It is about pushing out the frontier, and it is about
self-reliance. It echoes the Ulster Scots and the cowboys' discovery of the

unknown and the taming of inhospitable territory. It often speaks of the hardship and the difficulties that nature places in the way of the pioneer.

The image of the cowboy is an enduring one, not least in the continuing popularity of the clothes associated with the lifestyle. Behind the clothes, the psychological make-up of the imagined cowboy continues to hold a fascination for the common person. He lives a life of freedom, free to roam on the prairie and move around according to his fancy. He is everything that modern life is not for the vast majority of people. He is, unlike his horse, unfettered and is free to walk away from relationships whenever he wants. His freedom is worth more than anything else to him; not for him are the tied-down rhythms of the city or domestic life. There is more to it than this though. At heart the cowboy is a good person, well intentioned, at one with nature and the landscape.

The music reflects the individualism of the explorer and the sense of community that all humanity ultimately seeks to achieve. It is, as Tom Gilmore says, 'music for real people'.[23] It is perhaps because of the sense of community that country music is overwhelmingly more popular in rural areas than in urban places everywhere in the world. Moreover, songs in American country music have always championed the open countryside and life on the range. The city is frequently portrayed as a corrupting influence on the 'good old boy' from the more innocent and appealing countryside. A return to the rural is a return to a purer existence and better people. Combined with the welcoming bosom of the family, the rural life is the ultimate safe haven.

In early 2015 'Hit the Diff' was a huge hit for Monaghan singer Marty Mone and his band The Mad Ass Mules. A YouTube video featuring Mone working with his tractor attracted over half a million hits in two months. He performed the song at the All-Ireland Football Senior Championship quarter-final between Monaghan and Tyrone and at the National Ploughing Championships in Ratheniska, County Laois, for which the *Irish Farmers Journal* published a guide to the terminology used in the song.

The article explained that being 'flat to the mat' means being 'really busy', while requesting 'a yoke with plenty of poke' meant looking for something with 'plenty of power'.[24]

There is a profound sense of place in Irish country music. From Larry Cunningham's 'Lovely Leitrim' to Declan Nerney's 'Marquee in Drumlish', the local is celebrated in the music. Irish country music – and Irish music in general – has always celebrated the local culture, geography, history and beauty. It is a way of binding communities together. Remembrances of local beauty spots or songs of allegiance to counties are particularly popular. Country songs may lament the decline of rural areas, but they will never criticise any aspect of the way of life in the countryside, villages and small-town Ireland.

Local festivals based around the music are a cohesive force in communities. No one knows this better than Declan Nerney, who is from Drumlish, County Longford, where The Marquee in Drumlish festival still takes place every summer. Ronan Casey went to see it in 2011 and wrote about it in his blog:

> Erected in the local school playground, the mythical Marquee in Drumlish stood surrounded by festoon lighting, a beacon in the darkness calling the locals from the village below. The village itself was packed; cars parked in every nook, cranny and ghost estate, local committee members in hi-viz vests directing traffic and punter alike. Walking towards the marquee it was like an All-Ireland Final – at night. Buskers, charity collections, chip vans and omni-present committee members in hi-viz vests directing us toward the ticket office … Inside the gates, a pair of chip vans manned by spotty teenagers did a roaring trade … Men in hi-viz vests ringed the snow-white marquee itself. These were the lucky committee members, the chosen ones, given access to the marquee, and the first big show of the weekend.[25]

Casey chose a historic occasion to attend the festival, as Big Tom McBride appeared on the opening night for the first time in more than forty years. The audience of 1,500 plus sang along with every word:

> All walks of human life were in the audience. Immaculately-dressed rural couples mixed with lads straight from the fields, young travellers mixed at the bar with bright young things, pensioners sat patiently along the side of the marquee, mineral in one hand, son or daughter who never left home in the other, gangs of friends out for the craic, locals in awe that the festival is still running, young lads out for their first drink …[26]

There were two busy bars in the tent – 'a beast of a yoke', according to Casey. The Wee Amigos and Declan Nerney also played, and Casey described the action:

> [The music brings] the audience back to simpler, happier times. Behind the 'pit' at the front, married couples twirl and waltz, single men patrol the marquee searching for a dance partner, available women crane their necks whilst the nervous prop up the bar serving only cans of stout, ale and lager, mini airplane bottles of spirits and minerals. To my left, a priest stands on a chair filming the entire marquee, whilst in the side bar, lairy locals sing along …
>
> It's a slice of an Ireland the rest of Ireland thought had disappeared, but it's alive and kicking in the village of Drumlish and long may it last.[27]

In July 2016 RTÉ Television broadcast *Ireland's Ancient East*, a travelogue series in which journalist and broadcaster John Creedon introduced some of the cultural highlights of the east and midlands of Ireland.[28] In the first episode the presenter went to see Nerney in Drumlish to discuss the popularity of country music. Nerney turned up to meet Creedon on a 1954 vintage tractor – one of his collection of six; it did not have sufficient horsepower to take the two men to see the local sights, so Creedon brought Nerney around in his vintage Volkswagen van. They first went to the site of the famous carnival where the marquee was erected each summer. As they sat in the van, Nerney recalled: 'I can still feel that great excitement there was and the build up towards it for weeks and weeks.'

When Creedon asked him about the essence of country music songs, he said, 'They were the songs of the people. I think they were songs that helped people in their lives … you know they were goin' along doin' their chores and they were singin' … "I love you because you understand dear" [sings] … and sure the wife was probably after beating the head off him with a brush that morning, but he still loves her anyway.' Creedon told Nerney that the first thing people think of when they hear of Drumlish is his song about the marquee. The singer nodded in agreement. 'That's what country music is and that's what gives the emigrants some sort of a stance in life when they go abroad … that they have a place of belonging,' he said, 'and they feel that no matter where they go they still fly the flag for their rural area that they grew up in and the people and everything that it stands for.'

They moved on to a bar in Longford town, where Nerney joined his friend and fellow country singer Mick Flavin in a sing-song. At the end of the piece, Creedon summarised what he had seen:

> Now that's what I call country music. Driving through Ireland's country music heartland I'm reminded again of how important the music is because it speaks not only to, but also for the people of small villages … like when your home village is put on the map with a song like Declan did it means so much to people … thanks to Declan the marquee is up again and not unlike Nathan Carter's 'Wagon Wheel', country music has come around again.[29]

That is not to say there is no support for Irish country music in urban areas.

One of the biggest venues for live country music is the Red Cow Inn on the outskirts of Dublin city. The biggest names in the business play here regularly, and every Thursday night is dedicated to social dancing – first to music played by prominent country music DJ Howard Myers, followed by the main live act of the night.

Nathan Carter, Lisa McHugh and other young artists have noted their increasing popularity in urban areas, bringing Irish country music to an ever-widening audience. Some artists are filling dance halls and concert venues in the city as well as in their traditional rural heartland. Carter told Deirdre Reynolds of the *Irish Independent* of his belief that country music no longer solely appeals to rural dwellers:

> I think there was a slightly rural-urban divide [in country music in the past], but I think that's being addressed now … I've noticed it changing a lot in Dublin in the last year and I think TV and radio are helping towards that. The more country is on TV, the more it's accepted.[30]

But as with everything, country music must move with the times and Bob Harris of *The Guardian* has written about the changing themes of modern country music:

> The themes of the songs from contemporary artists reflect the lives of people their age now. There's been one very specific change in terms of lyric-writing in country. If you go back to the 50s, there are a lot of songs about the consequence of bad behaviour – like hanging out with women and then coming back to your wife – there's a cause and effect that the song sees through. Eventually you have to repent for your sins. Now that doesn't apply. The general rule is there's no consequence, let's just party.[31]

It is unlikely that any modern Irish country music star would come up with a song like Big Tom's 'Gentle Mother'.

Perhaps it is appropriate to leave the last word on the subject of the enduring popularity of country music, not just in Ireland but throughout the world, to the great Hank Williams:

> For what he [a country music performer] is singing is the hopes and prayers and dreams and experiences of what some call the 'common people'. I call them 'the best people', because they are the ones that the world is made up most of. They're really the ones who make things tick, wherever they are in this country or in any country. They're the ones who understand what we're singing about, and that's why our kind of music is sweeping the world. There ain't nothing strange about our popularity these days. It's just that there are more people who are like us than there are the educated cultured kind. There ain't nothing at all queer about them Europeans liking our kind of singing.[32]

ENDNOTES

PREFACE: 'BIG TOM' WAS THE KING

1   'Big Tom Is Still The King' (1999) sung by Susan McCann, set to the tune of 'Bob Wills Is Still The King' written by Waylon Jennings. The words were modified by Michael Commins.

2   www.rte.ie/entertainment/2015/1027/737783-late-late-country-special-scores-huge-ratings

3   *The Ryan Tubridy Radio Show*, RTÉ Radio 1, 26 August 2015.

4   Commins, M., 'Stars shine on big night for country music', *Irish Farmers Journal*, 3 June 2016.

1   JIM REEVES HAD TO GO BUT LARRY CUNNINGHAM SAVED THE NIGHT

1   'Adios Amigo' (1959) written by Jerry Livingston and Ralph Freed.

2   *Kimberley Jim*, directed by Emil Nofal, Emil Nofal Productions, 1963.

3   www.jim-reeves.com/memoriam.html

4   Jordan, L., *Jim Reeves: His Untold Story. The Life and Times of Country Music's Greatest Singer* (USA, Page Turner Books International, 2011), p. 486.

5   Commins, M., 'Country singer Jim Reeves remembered', *The Mayo News*, 10 October 2010.

6   Power, V., *Send 'Em Home Sweatin'* (Dublin, Mercier Press, 2000), p. 119.

7   *Ibid.*, p. 120.

8   Martin, K., telephone interview with Marie Barnes, 21 October 2017.

9   Cushnan, J., 'The summer Gentleman Jim Reeves just had to go to Ulster', *Belfast Telegraph*, 24 August 2013.

10   Reynolds, A., *My Autobiography* (Dublin, Transworld International, 2010), p. 127.

11   Power, *Send 'Em Home Sweatin'*, pp. 121–22.

12   Jordan, *Jim Reeves: His Untold Story*, p. 235.

13   *Ibid.*

14   *Ibid.*

15   Streissguth, M., *Like a Moth to a Flame: The Jim Reeves Story* (Nashville, Rutledge Hill Press, 1998), p. 190.

16   Quoted in Gilmore, T., *Larry Cunningham: A Showband Legend* (Dublin, Mentor Books, 2009), p. 45.

17   *Ibid.*

18   *Ibid.*, p. 59.

19   *A Little Bit Country*, RTÉ Television, 29 October 2006.

20   Gilmore, *Larry Cunningham*, p. 11.

21   *Ibid.*, p. 17.

22   *Ibid.*, p. 25.

23   Kelly, T., 'Tribute to Country legend Larry Cunningham', *The Anglo-Celt*, 2 October 2012.

24   'Showband legend whose "Lovely Leitrim" made him 1960s star', *The Irish Times*, 6 October 2012; www.irishtimes.com/life-and-style/people/showband-legend-whose-lovely-leitrim-made-him-1960s-star-1.549030

25   http://bocktherobber.com/2012/10/larry-cunningham-father-of-country-n-irish/

26   McGreevy, R., 'End of an era for Irish in London as iconic Galtymore dance hall to close its doors', *The Irish Times*, 28 April 2008.

27   Gilmore, *Larry Cunningham*, p. 183.

28   *Ibid.*, p. 188.

29   *Ibid.*

30   *Ibid.*, p. 183.

31   *Ibid.*

32   *The Frankie Kilbride Show*, Shannonside Radio, 30 September 2012.

33   *Ibid.*

34   *Ibid.*

35   www.larrycunningham.ie/?Itemid=211

36   Carthy, B., *The A–Z of Country and Irish Stars* (Dublin, Gill & Macmillan, 1991), p. 21.

2   'THE CIRCLE IS UNBROKEN': A VERY SHORT HISTORY OF AMERICAN COUNTRY MUSIC

1   Malone, B. C., *Country Music, U.S.A.* (Austin, University of Texas Press, 2002), p. 1.

2   *Ibid.*, p. 17.

3   Sandburg, C., *The American Songbag* (New York, Harcourt, Brace & Company, 1927), p. v.

4   *Ibid.*, pp. vii–viii.

5   Malone, *Country Music, U.S.A.*, p. 75.

6   *Ibid.*

7   Wolff, K., *Country Music: The Rough Guide* (London, Rough Guides, 2000), p. 18.

8   www.billmonroe.com/bill-monroe-bio

9   Quoted in Tosches, N., *Country: The Twisted Roots of Rock and Roll* (Boston, Da Capo Press, 2000), p. 26.

10   Malone, *Country Music, U.S.A.*, p. 154.

11   *Ibid.*

12   *Ibid.*, p. 242.

13   Hinton, B., *Country Roads: How Country Came to Nashville* (London, Sanctuary Publishing, 2000), p. 136.

14   Malone, *Country Music, U.S.A.*, p. 1.

15   'Garth Brooks press conference', *RTÉ News*, 29 January 2014.

3   'BRINGING IT ALL BACK HOME': COUNTRY COMES TO IRELAND

1   Smyth, J., 'Dancing, Depravity and All That Jazz: The Public Dance Halls Act of 1935', *History Ireland*, Volume 1, Issue 2 (1993), p. 51.

2   *Ibid.*, p. 52.

3   *Ibid.*

4   *Ibid.*, p. 54.

5   *Ibid.*

6   *Ibid.*

7   *Ibid.*

8   Carson, C., 'In Praise of the Ceili Band', http://journalofmusic.com/focus/praise-ceili-band

9   Martin, K., interview with Michael Commins, Knock, 22 June 2017.

10   Martin, K., telephone interview with Henry McMahon, 10 May 2017.

11   *Ibid.*

12   'More Country Music Fills AFN Air', *Billboard Music Week* (25 September 1961), p. 3.

13   *Ibid.*

14   Forecast, K. G., 'Radio Éireann listener research inquiries, 1953–1955', *Journal of the Statistical and Social Inquiry Society of Ireland*, Volume XVIX (1955/1956), pp. 1–28.

15   Martin, interview with Michael Commins.

16   Smyth, S., 'On Your Feet Lads', in Coughlan, J. (ed.), *The Swingin' Sixties Book* (Dublin, Carrick Communications, 1999), p. 140.

17   McEntee, J., 'Imagining Ireland in a Ballroom of Romance', *Irish Independent*, 11 November 2012.

18   Brophy, E., 'The Ballrooms of Romance', in Coughlan, *The Swingin' Sixties Book*, p. 10.

19   www.irish-showbands.com/history1.htm

20   Martin, interview with Michael Commins.

21   Gilmore, T., 'Irish Country: 1963–1993', in Allen, B. (ed.), *The Blackwell Guide to Recorded Country Music* (Oxford, Blackwell, 1994), p. 288.

22   Gilmore, *Larry Cunningham*, p. 207.

23   Martin, K., telephone interview with Susan McCann, 17 September 2017.

24   Smyth in Coughlan, *The Swingin' Sixties Book*, p. 146.

4   SEARCHING FOR THE PIONEERS

1   Michael Commins, 'Ace Performer; Shay blazed a trail for Irish Country', www.thefreelibrary.com/ACE+PERFORMER%3b+Shay+blazed+a+trail+for+Irish+Country.-a0141032008

2   Commins, M., 'Melody Aces stars bring touch of class to Roscommon showband nostalgia night', *Western People*, 12 February 2003.

3   *A Man and His Music – A Tribute to Shay Hutchinson*, filmed at Cappagh Parish Community Centre, Killyclogher, County Tyrone, 13 February 1994 (available on YouTube).

4   *Ibid.*

5   *Ibid.*

6   Hutchinson, J. M., 'Shay Hutchinson: The Making and Breaking of the Mould' (unpublished).

7   *Ibid.*

8   *Ibid.*

9   Martin, interview with Henry McMahon.

10   Hutchinson, *Shay Hutchinson*.

11   Clifford, G., 'Songsmith who put Big Tom and Daniel on the map', *Irish Independent*, 16 January 2008.

12   *Ibid.*

13   Martin, interview with Henry McMahon.

14   Quoted in McLaughlin, S., 'Songwriting legend Johnny dies', *Derry Journal*, 29 March 2012.

15   Martin, K., telephone interview with Lisa Stanley, 12 August 2017.

16   *Ibid.*

17   *Ibid.*

18   *Ibid.*

19   *Ibid.*

20   *Ibid.*

21   Collins, L., 'Maisie McDaniel: Singing legend who livened up rural Ireland in the sixties', *Sunday Independent*, 6 July 2008.

22   Commins, M., 'Farewell Maisie', *The Mayo News*, 10 July 2008.

23   'Tributes as country legend Gene Stewart passes away', *Ulster Herald*, 12 February 2016.

24   Quoted in Young, D., 'Country music in mourning for Gene Stuart', *Belfast Telegraph*, 12 February 2016.

25   Commins, M., 'Remembering the great Gene Stuart', *Irish Farmers Journal*, 3 March 2016.

26   McHugh, W., 'Gone to the Grand Ole Opry', *The Mayo News*, 16 February 2016.

27   *Ibid.*

28   Martin, K., interview with Willie McHugh, 25 January 2018.

29   *Ibid.*

30   Commins, 'Remembering the great Gene Stuart'.

31   Martin, interview with Michael Commins.

5   HOW 'BIG TOM' BECAME THE KING

1   Carthy, *The A–Z of Country and Irish Stars*, p. 12.

2   Gilmore in Allen, *The Blackwell Guide to Recorded Country Music*, p. 303.

3   Martin, interview with Henry McMahon.

4   www.irish-showbands.com/Bands/mainliners.htm

5   Waters, J., *Jiving at the Crossroads* (Belfast, Blackstaff Press, 1991), p. 91.

6   Mooney, P., 'Jim Reeves had a lot to answer for', in Coughlan, *The Swingin' Sixties Book*, p. 91.

7   *Secret Languages: Folk Art*, RTÉ Television, 1982.

8   Article quoted in Waters, *Jiving at the Crossroads*, p. 91.

9   Commins, M., 'Big Tom's huge reception in London and Birmingham', *Western People*, 24 November 2004.

10   *Ibid.*

11   McGreevy, 'End of an era for Irish in London as iconic Galtymore dance hall to close its doors'.

12   *Ibid.*

13   *Nationwide*, RTÉ Television, 9 October 2017.

14   http://ronancasey.ie/2011/08/off-to-the-marquee-in-drumlish/

15   Martin, K., telephone interview with Paschal Mooney, 25 September 2017.

16   Martin, K., telephone interview with Charlie McGettigan, 24 September 2017.

17   Martin, K., interview with Gerald O'Donoghue, Claran, 5 October 2017.

18   *Nationwide*, RTÉ Television, 9 October 2017.

6   THREE QUEENS OF IRISH COUNTRY MUSIC

1   'It Wasn't God Who Made Honky Tonk Angels' (1952) sung by Kitty Wells, written by J. D. 'Jay' Miller.

2   *The Late Late Show Country Music Special*, RTÉ Television, 14 April 2017.

3   'The Wild Side of Life' (1952) sung and written by Hank Thompson.

4   Martin, interview with Susan McCann.

5   *Ibid.*

6   *Ibid.*

7   *On the Road with Lisa*, Irish TV, 2 November 2015.

8   Martin, interview with Susan McCann.

9   Paddy Kehoe, *RTÉ Guide*, 12 March 2006.

10   Carthy, *The A–Z of Country and Irish Stars*, p. 42.

11   Martin, interview with Susan McCann.

12   Carthy, *The A–Z of Country and Irish Stars*, p. 41.

13   Jackson, J., 'The Liberation of Margo', *Irish Independent*, 17 December 2006.

14   O'Donnell, M., *Margo, Queen of Country & Irish: The Promise and the Dream* (Dublin, O'Brien Press, 2014), p. 114.

15   *Ibid.*, p. 89.

16   *The Late Late Show*, RTÉ Television, 26 September 2014.

17   O'Shea, G., 'I'm Dan's sister … not mother', *The Irish Sun*, 27 September 2015.

18   'End of an era as the Galtymore closes its door', *Derry Journal*, 29 May 2008.

19   O'Donnell, *Margo, Queen of Country & Irish*, p. 158.

20   *Ibid.*, p. 161.

21   *Ibid.*, p. 160.

22   *Ibid.*

23   *Ibid.*, p. 161.

24   *Ibid.*, p. 120.

25   Carthy, *The A–Z of Country and Irish Stars*, p. 40.

26   *The Times*, 11 March 2009.

27   'A Pair of Brown Eyes' (1985) from the album *Rum, Sodomy and the Lash* by The Pogues, written by Shane MacGowan.

28   *Evening Extra*, RTÉ Television, 13 April 1987.

29   *Ibid.*

30   Gilmore, T., '"Old Friends" with a difference for Philomena Begley', *The Tuam Herald*, 22 June 2006.

31   *Ibid.*

7   THE RISE AND RISE OF 'WEE' DANIEL O'DONNELL

1   'The Night Daniel O'Donnell Came to Town' (1990) by Louise Morrissey, from the album *When I Was Yours*.

2   Egan, B., 'Viva La Espana: Daniel O'Donnell and Majella', *Sunday Independent*, 30 November 2015.

3   O'Donnell, D. with Rowley, E., *Daniel O'Donnell, My Story: The Official Book* (Dublin, O'Brien Press, 2003), p. 43.

4   Egan, 'Viva La Espana: Daniel O'Donnell and Majella'.

5   Carthy, *The A–Z of Country and Irish Stars*, p. 42.

6   Stewart, K., 'International Global Country Pulse: Dublin', *Billboard*, 7 October 1995, p. 52.

7   *RTÉ News*, 14 October 1994.

8   *Ibid.*, 3 August 2000.

9   *Ibid.*

10   *The Late Late Show*, RTÉ Television, 28 July 2014.

11   *RTÉ News*, 23 June 2012.

12   *Ibid.*

13   *The Ryan Tubridy Show*, RTÉ Radio 1, 16 February 2016.

14   *Ibid.*

15   Walker, G., 'Why it's time for the begrudgers to leave Daniel O'Donnell alone', *Belfast Telegraph*, 14 November 2012.

16   *Ibid.*

17   Freyne, P., 'Daniel O'Donnell: "I'm cleverer than people think"', *The Irish Times*, 22 April 2017.

8   IN THE COUNTRY OF 'REAL' COUNTRY

1   Martin, K., email from Niall Toner, 29 September 2017.

2   *Ibid.*

3   *Ibid.*

4   *Ibid.*

5   Martin, K., email from Gerry Madigan, 16 September 2017.

6   *Ibid.*

7   *Ibid.*

8   *Ibid.*

9   *Ibid.*

10   *Ibid.*

11   *Ibid.*

12   Martin, K., telephone interview with George Kaye, 15 September 2017.

13   *Ibid.*

14   *Ibid.*

15   Martin, K., interview with Uri Kohen, Westport, 14 September 2017.

16   *Ibid.*

17   *Ibid.*

18   Martin, K., interview with Hubie McEvilly, Westport, 21 September 2017.

19   *Ibid.*

20   *Ibid.*

21   Martin, K., interview with Tim Rogers, Westport, 23 September 2017.

22   Quoted on www.irish-showbands.com/Bands/hillbilliesp.htm

23   Gilmore in Allen, *The Blackwell Guide to Recorded Country Music*, p. 178.

9   GARTH BROOKS' HAT CAN SING: GARTH BROOKS AND IRELAND

1   McCormick, N., 'Garth Brooks interview: Croke Park cancellations "broke my heart"', *The Telegraph*, 13 November 2014.

2   Dawidoff, N., *In the Country of Country: A Journey to the Roots of American Music* (London, Faber and Faber, 1997), p. 193.

3   Quoted in Hinton, *Country Roads*, p. 402.

4   *Ibid.*, p. 403.

5   Quoted in Dawidoff, *In the Country of Country*, p. 193.

6   *Ibid.*

7   Wolff, *Country Music*, p. 515.

8   *The Big Breakfast*, Channel 4, April 1994.

9   *London Tonight*, ITV, April 1994.

10   'Ireland' (1995) sung by Garth Brooks, co-written by Garth Brooks, Jenny Yates and Stephanie Davis, from the album *Fresh Horses*.

11   McCormick, N., '"One of a kind": the Garth Brooks interview', *Hot Press*, 15 June 1997.

12   *Ibid.*

13   *Ibid.*

14   *Ibid.*

15   *Ibid.*

16   *Ibid.*

17   *Ibid.*

18   *Ibid.*

19   *RTÉ News*, 15 May 1997.

20   *Ibid.*, 23 January 2014.

21   *Ireland AM*, TV3, 23 January 2015.

22   *Ibid.*

23   O'Toole, E., 'Dublin residents had the right to turn a deaf ear to Garth Brooks' racket', *The Guardian*, 11 July 2014.

24   *Ibid.*

25   *Ibid.*

26   *Ibid.*

27   'Enda got 1,000 emails about the Garth Brooks concerts. Here's what some of them said …', http://www.thejournal.ie/enda-kenny-garth-brooks-emails-1616499-Aug2014/

28   Quoted in Smyth, P., 'Garth Brooks says concerts cannot proceed', *The Irish Times*, 14 July 2014.

29   *TV3 News*, 10 July 2014.

30   *Ibid.*

31   *Six One News*, RTÉ Television, 10 July 2014.

32   *Ibid.*

33   'Here's how many times Garth Brooks was mentioned in Leinster House last month …' http://www.thejournal.ie/garth-brooks-dail-july-1597106-Aug2014/

10   'YOUR NEXT DANCE PLEASE': TRIPPING THROUGH THE WORLD OF COUNTRY MUSIC DANCING

1   www.quotes.net/quote/10621

2   Brady, C., *Viceroy's Vindication? Sir Henry Sidney's Memoir of Service in Ireland 1583* (Cork, Cork University Press (Irish Narrative Series), 2002).

3   Brennan, H., 'Reinventing Tradition: The Boundaries of Irish Dance' in *History Ireland*, Volume 2, Issue 2 (Summer 1994).

4   *Ibid.*

5   *Ibid.*

6   Cowan, R., 'Dancers fall in line for damnation, says Paisley', *The Guardian*, 18 May 2001.

7   *Talkback*, BBC Radio Ulster, 17 May 2001.

8   Cowan, 'Dancers fall in line for damnation, says Paisley'.

9   'Burnside kicks out at Paisley line dancing comments', BreakingNews.ie, 19 May 2001, www.breakingnews.ie/ireland/burnside-kicks-out-at-paisley-line-dancing-comments-13074.html

10   *Ibid.*

11   *Talkback*, BBC Radio Ulster, 17 May 2001.

12   Cowan, 'Dancers fall in line for damnation, says Paisley'.

13   O'Connor, J., *Sweet Liberty: Travels in Irish America* (New York, Roberts Rinehart, 1996), p. 78.

14   *Ibid.*

15   *Ibid.*

16   Wolff, *Country Music*, p. 523.

17   *RTÉ News*, 17 March 1995.

18   *Ibid.*

19   Fay, L., 'I walked the line and the line won', *Hot Press*, 25 January 1995.

20   *Ibid.*

21   *Ibid.*

22   *Ibid.*

23   Martin, K., telephone interview with Howard Dee, 23 September 2017.

24   *Ibid.*

25   Martin, K., interview with Robert Padden, Crossmolina, 12 September 2017.

26   *Ibid.*

27   *A Little Bit Country*, TG4, 13 March 2013.

28   Martin, K., telephone interview with Eunice Moran, 2 October 2017.

29   Waters, *Jiving at the Crossroads*, p. 90.

30   *Ibid.*

31   Martin, telephone interview with Eunice Moran.

32   Martin, K., telephone interview with Gerard Butler, 5 March 2017.

33   Martin, K., telephone interview with Sean Joyce, 8 March 2017.

34   Martin, K., interview with Robert Mizzell, Claremorris, 27 June 2017.

35   Oldenburg, R., *The Great Good Place: Cafés, Coffee Shops, Bookstores, Bars, Hair Salons, and Other Hangouts at the Heart of a Community* (New York, Marlowe, 1999).

36   Martin, interview with Robert Mizzell.

37   Martin, K., telephone interview with Mick Flavin, 29 January 2018.

38   Lavin, R., 'Jive talkin' – how the oldest dance in town is swinging back into action', *Sunday Independent*, 14 February 2016.

11   TRYING TO KEEP IT COUNTRY: THE MEDIA AND COUNTRY MUSIC IN IRELAND

1   Martin, interview with Michael Commins.

2   Martin, interview with Mick Flavin.

3   'Ireland Capitalizes on Country', *Billboard*, 22 February 1975, p. 49.

4   *Ibid.*

5   Coughlan, *The Swingin' Sixties Book*, p. 93.

6   Martin, interview with Paschal Mooney.

7   *Ibid.*

8   *Ibid.*

9   Waters, *Jiving at the Crossroads*, p. 163.

10   *Ibid.*, p. 163.

11   *Ibid.*, p. 162.

12   Martin, interview with Michael Commins.

13   'When the Moon Shines Bright Over Mayo' sung by Colman Cloran, YouTube (uploaded 3 December 2014 by Star Trax Music Venue).

14   www.galwaybayfm.ie (accessed 2017; since the programme is no longer broadcast, this description is no longer on the website).

15   Martin, K., interview with Tom Gilmore, Tuam, 11 August 2017.

16   Martin, K., telephone interview with Howard Myers, 11 September 2017.

17   *Ibid.*

18   Martin, K., telephone interview with Máire Ní Chonláin, 4 September 2017.

19   *Ibid.*

20   *Ibid.*

21   Martin, interview with Henry McMahon.

22   Martin, K., telephone interview with Phil McLaughlin, 16 September 2017.

23   www.philmackcountry.com

24   Martin, K., telephone interview with Hugh O'Brien, 26 September 2017.

25   Martin, K., telephone interview with Roger Ryan, 19 September 2017.

12   PORTRAITS FROM THE TRADE

1   The information in this chapter is largely based on interviews that the author carried out with the subjects.

2   Martin, K., telephone interview with John Hogan, 2 September 2017.

3   Martin, interview with Mick Flavin.

4   Martin, K., telephone interview with Roly Daniels, 31 January 2018.

5   Martin, K., telephone interview with Sandy Kelly, 8 October 2017.

6   Martin, K., telephone interview with Louise Morrissey, 25 September 2017.

7   Martin, interview with Henry McMahon.

8   Martin, K., interview with Marc Roberts, Salthill, 12 August 2017.

9   Martin, K., interview with Frank McCaffrey, Westport, 2 August 2017.

10   Martin, interview with Gerald O'Donoghue.

13   BORN IN THE USA: THE ROBERT MIZZELL STORY

1   Martin, K., telephone interview with Robert Mizzell, 6 August 2017.

2   Smith, A., 'Keeping it all country', *Irish Independent*, 8 December 2014.

3   *The Marian Finucane Show*, RTÉ Radio 1, 24 January 2015.

4   Martin, telephone interview with Robert Mizzell.

5   Martin, interview with Robert Mizzell, Claremorris.

6   Martin, interview with Gerald O'Donoghue.

14   'THE LONE RANGER OF IRISH COUNTRY MUSIC':
     JAMES KILBANE AND COUNTRY GOSPEL

1   'You're not really much of a star', *Wicklow People*, 11 March 2004.

2   Martin, K., interview with James Kilbane, Westport, 5 June 2017.

3   Martin, K., telephone interview with Mary from Mullingar, 8 June 2017.

4   Martin, K., interview with John Morrison, Westport, 5 June 2017.

15   A NEW COUNTRY

1   'Murder on Music Row' (1999) written by Larry Cordle and Larry Shell and
     first released by Larry Cordle and Lonesome Standard Time.

2   Malone, *Country Music, U.S.A.*, p. 346.

3   *Ibid.*, p. 426.

4   Martin, K., telephone interview with Keelan Arbuckle, 17 October 2017.

5   'Amarillo by Morning' was first recorded by Strait in 1982 and later released
     as a single off his album *Strait from the Heart*. The song went on to become a
     massive hit, reaching number four on *Billboard*'s Hot Country Songs.

6   www.jordanmogeymusic.com

7   'Lee's new Major', *Strabane Chronicle*, 31 October 2013.

8   Martin, K., telephone interview with Willie Carty, 10 October 2017.

9   Martin, interview with Gerald O'Donoghue.

10   *The Marian Finucane Show*, RTÉ Radio 1, 13 July 2014.

11   Martin, interview with Eunice Moran.

12   O'Brien, F., 'Phil Mack gives rising country star her own TV show', *The Irish World*, 13 April 2016.

13   Martin, interview with Lisa Stanley.

14   *The Nolan Show*, BBC Radio Ulster, 5 June 2013.

15   Martin, K., telephone interview with Michael Kelly, 23 October 2017.

16   Long, S., 'On the Beat', *Cara* magazine, April/May 2014, p. 46.

17   Zimmerman, L., '*String Theory*: album review', *Elmore Magazine*, 23 August 2016.

16   THE PAST IS A FOREIGN COUNTRY MUSIC: THE RISE OF NATHAN CARTER

1   Hartley, L. P., *The Go-Between* (London, Hamish Hamilton, 1963), p. 1.

2   Murphy, L., 'Irish country music's big wheel keeps on turning on', *The Irish Times*, 10 January 2014.

3   Martin, K., telephone interview with John Farry, 23 October 2017.

4   *Ibid.*

5   *Ibid.*

6   Murphy, 'Irish country music's big wheel keeps on turning on'.

7   O'Connor, S., 'Country star Nathan Carter on fame, family and finding love', *Irish Mirror*, 26 December 2016.

8   *Today with Sean O'Rourke*, RTÉ Radio 1, 14 February 2014.

9   *Ibid.*

10   *Ibid.*

11   Quoted in 'Nathan Carter announces new album', *Irish Examiner*, 18 March 2016.

12   'Spotlight: Nathan Carter – Making Country Music "cool" again', *The Harp*, 19 August 2015.

13   Farrell, N., 'My terror after neighbour "lost it" over repeated playing of Nathan Carter's music', *Irish Independent*, 19 May 2016.

14   Farrell, N., '"Torture" of hearing Nathan Carter's hit Wagon Wheel cause man to attack neighbour's home', *The Irish Sun*, 16 May 2016.

15   Farrell, 'My terror after neighbour "lost it" over repeated playing of Nathan Carter's music'.

16   Ryan, K., 'Nathan Carter offers gig tickets to fan who had windows smashed after he didn't stop playing Wagon Wheel', *Irish Mirror*, 18 May 2016.

17   *Ros na Rún*, TG4, 30 September 2013.

18   Martin, interview with John Farry.

19   Martin, K., interview with Egbert Polski, Westport, 26 August 2017.

20   Martin, interview with John Farry.

21   McCormack, C., 'Country legend Nathan Carter makes women swoon but he's still looking for love', *Irish Independent*, 20 December 2015.

17   FOREVER AND EVER: THE ENDURING POPULARITY OF IRISH COUNTRY MUSIC

1   *A Little Bit Country*, TG4, 13 March 2013.

2   Martin, interview with Máire Ní Chonláin.

3   Hennessey, Á., 'Mike Denver: Irish Country Music Awards is the talk of the country', *Irish Farmers Journal*, 21 June 2016.

4   Commins, 'Stars shine on big night for country music'.

5   *Ibid.*

6   *The Broken Circle Breakdown*, directed by Felix Van Groeningen, 2012.

7   Mack, E., '9 Foreign Countries with Country Music Culture', www.wideopencountry.com/9-foreign-countries-country-music-culture/

8   www.eonline.com/photos/19691/cma-awards-2016-worst-dressed-stars/726373

9   King, T., 'Paul Claffey – Master of the Airways', *Mature Living*, 21 July 2015, p. 11.

10   Stewart, K., 'Country Music Gets Irish Welcome', *Billboard*, 22 April 1995, p. 61.

11   *Ibid.*

12   *A Little Bit Country*, TG4, 13 March 2013.

13   Dawidoff, *In the Country of Country*, p. 288.

14   *The Marian Finucane Show*, RTÉ Radio 1, 13 July 2014.

15   Mooney in Coughlan, *The Swingin' Sixties Book*, p. 88.

16   Malone, *Country Music, U.S.A.*, p. 16.

17   *A Little Bit Country*, TG4, 13 March 2013.

18   *Ibid.*

19   Waters, *Jiving at the Crossroads*, p. 61.

20   Walker, 'Why it's time for the begrudgers to leave Daniel O'Donnell alone'.

21   *A Man and His Music – A Tribute to Shay Hutchinson*.

22   Martin, interview with Michael Commins.

23   Martin, interview with Tom Gilmore.

24   Hussey, A., 'A guide to understanding Hit the Diff', *Irish Farmers Journal*, 26 February 2015.

25   http://ronancasey.ie/2011/08/off-to-the-marquee-in-drumlish/

26   *Ibid.*

27   *Ibid.*

28   *Ireland's Ancient East*, RTÉ Television, July 2016.

29   *Ibid.*

30   Reynolds, D., 'Country to Country: How Country and Western will take over Dublin next weekend', *Irish Independent*, 6 March 2016.

31   Quoted in Crummy, C., 'Detwanging country music: how Nashville took the UK', *The Guardian*, 13 March 2014.

32   Williams, R. M., *Sing a Sad Song: The Life of Hank Williams* (Champaign, Illinois University Press, 1981), p. 149.

BIBLIOGRAPHY

BOOKS AND ARTICLES

Allen, B. (ed.), *The Blackwell Guide to Recorded Country Music* (Oxford, Blackwell, 1994)

Brady, C., *Viceroy's Vindication? Sir Henry Sidney's Memoir of Service in Ireland 1583* (Cork, Cork University Press (Irish Narrative Series), 2002)

Brennan, H., 'Reinventing Tradition: The Boundaries of Irish Dance' in *History Ireland*, Volume 2, Issue 2 (Summer 1994)

Carthy, B., *The A–Z of Country and Irish Stars* (Dublin, Gill & Macmillan, 1991)

Chesterton, G. K., *The Ballad of the White Horse* (London, Methuen, 1911)

Clifford, G., 'Songsmith who put Big Tom and Daniel on the map', *Irish Independent*, 16 January 2008

Collins, L., 'Maisie McDaniel: Singing legend who livened up rural Ireland in the sixties', *Sunday Independent*, 6 July 2008

Commins, M., 'Melody Aces stars bring touch of class to Roscommon showband nostalgia night', *Western People*, 12 February 2003

Commins, M., 'Big Tom's huge reception in London and Birmingham', *Western People*, 24 November 2004

Commins, M., 'Farewell Maisie', *The Mayo News*, 10 July 2008

Commins, M., 'Country singer Jim Reeves remembered', *The Mayo News*, 10 October 2010

Commins, M., 'Remembering the great Gene Stuart', *Irish Farmers Journal*, 3 March 2016

Commins, M., 'Stars shine on big night for country music', *Irish Farmers Journal*, 3 June 2016

Coughlan, J. (ed.), *The Swingin' Sixties Book* (Dublin, Carrick Communications, 1999)

Cowan, R., 'Dancers fall in line for damnation, says Paisley', *The Guardian*, 18 May 2001

Crummy, C., 'Detwanging country music: how Nashville took the UK', *The Guardian*, 13 March 2014

Cushnan, J., 'The summer Gentleman Jim Reeves just had to go to Ulster', *Belfast Telegraph*, 24 August 2013

Dawidoff, N., *In the Country of Country: A Journey to the Roots of American Music* (London, Faber and Faber, 1997)

Egan, B., 'Viva La Espana: Daniel O'Donnell and Majella', *Sunday Independent*, 30 November 2015

'End of an era as the Galtymore closes its door', *Derry Journal*, 29 May 2008

Farrell, N., '"Torture" of hearing Nathan Carter's hit Wagon Wheel cause man to attack neighbour's home', *The Irish Sun*, 16 May 2016

Farrell, N., 'My terror after neighbour "lost it" over repeated playing of Nathan Carter's music', *Irish Independent*, 19 May 2016

Fay, L., 'I walked the line and the line won', *Hot Press*, 25 January 1995

Forecast, K. G., 'Radio Éireann listener research inquiries, 1953–1955', *Journal of the Statistical and Social Inquiry Society of Ireland*, Volume XVIX (1955/1956), pp. 1–28

Freyne, P., 'Daniel O'Donnell: "I'm cleverer than people think"', *The Irish Times*, 22 April 2017

Gilmore, T., '"Old Friends" with a difference for Philomena Begley', *The Tuam Herald*, 22 June 2006

Gilmore, T., *Larry Cunningham: A Showband Legend* (Dublin, Mentor Books, 2009)

Hartley, L. P., *The Go-Between* (London, Hamish Hamilton, 1963)

Hennessey, Á., 'Mike Denver: Irish Country Music Awards is the talk of the country', *Irish Farmers Journal*, 21 June 2016

Hinton, B., *Country Roads: How Country Came to Nashville* (London, Sanctuary Publishing, 2000)

Hussey, A., 'A guide to understanding Hit the Diff', *Irish Farmers Journal*, 26 February 2015

Hutchinson, J. M., 'Shay Hutchinson: The Making and Breaking of the Mould' (unpublished)

'Ireland capitalizes on Country', *Billboard*, 22 February 1975

Jackson, J., 'The Liberation of Margo', *Irish Independent*, 17 December 2006

Jordan, L., *Jim Reeves: His Untold Story. The Life and Times of Country Music's Greatest Singer* (USA, Page Turner Books International, 2011)

Kelly, T., 'Tribute to Country legend Larry Cunningham', *The Anglo-Celt*, 2 October 2012

King, T., 'Paul Claffey – Master of the Airways', *Mature Living*, 21 July 2015, p. 11

Lavin, R., 'Jive talkin' – how the oldest dance in town is swinging back into action', *Sunday Independent*, 14 February 2016

'Lee's new Major', *Strabane Chronicle*, 31 October 2013

Lomax, J. A., *Cowboy Songs and Other Frontier Ballads* (New York, Macmillan, 1920)

Long, S., 'On the Beat', *Cara* magazine, April/May 2014

Malone, B. C., *Country Music, U.S.A.* (Austin, University of Texas Press, 2002)

McCormack, C., 'Country legend Nathan Carter makes women swoon but he's still looking for love', *Irish Independent*, 20 December 2015

McCormick, N., '"One of a kind": the Garth Brooks interview', *Hot Press*, 15 June 1997

McCormick, N., 'Garth Brooks interview: Croke Park cancellations "broke my heart"', *The Telegraph*, 13 November 2014

McEntee, J., 'Imagining Ireland in a Ballroom of Romance', *Irish Independent*, 11 November 2012

McGreevy, R., 'End of an era for Irish in London as iconic Galtymore dance hall to close its doors', *The Irish Times*, 28 April 2008

McHugh, W., 'Gone to the Grand Ole Opry', *The Mayo News*, 16 February 2016

McLaughlin, S., 'Songwriting legend Johnny dies', *Derry Journal*, 29 March 2012

'More Country Music Fills AFN Air', *Billboard Music Week*, 25 September 1961

Murphy, L., 'Irish country music's big wheel keeps on turning on', *The Irish Times*, 10 January 2014

'Nathan Carter announces new album', *Irish Examiner*, 18 March 2016

O'Brien, F., 'Phil Mack gives rising country star her own TV show', *The Irish World*, 13 April 2016

O'Connor, J., *Sweet Liberty: Travels in Irish America* (New York, Roberts Rinehart, 1996)

O'Connor, S., 'Country star Nathan Carter on fame, family and finding love', *Irish Mirror*, 26 December 2016

O'Donnell, D. with Rowley, E., *Daniel O'Donnell, My Story: The Official Book* (Dublin, O'Brien Press, 2003)

O'Donnell, M., *Margo, Queen of Country & Irish: The Promise and the Dream* (Dublin, O'Brien Press, 2014)

O'Shea, G., 'I'm Dan's sister … not mother', *The Irish Sun*, 27 September 2015

O'Toole, E., 'Dublin residents had the right to turn a deaf ear to Garth Brooks' racket', *The Guardian*, 11 July 2014

Oldenburg, R., *The Great Good Place: Cafés, Coffee Shops, Bookstores, Bars, Hair Salons, and Other Hangouts at the Heart of a Community* (New York, Marlowe, 1999)

Power, V., *Send 'Em Home Sweatin'* (Dublin, Mercier Press, 2000)

Reynolds, A., *My Autobiography* (Dublin, Transworld International, 2010)

Reynolds, D., 'Country to Country: How Country and Western will take over Dublin next weekend', *Irish Independent*, 6 March 2016

Ryan, K., 'Nathan Carter offers gig tickets to fan who had windows smashed after he didn't stop playing Wagon Wheel', *Irish Mirror*, 18 May 2016

Sandburg, C., *The American Songbag* (New York, Harcourt, Brace & Company, 1927)

'Showband legend whose "Lovely Leitrim" made him 1960s star', *The Irish Times*, 6 October 2012

Smith, A., 'Keeping it all country', *Irish Independent*, 8 December 2014

Smyth, J., 'Dancing, Depravity and All That Jazz: The Public Dance Halls Act of 1935', *History Ireland*, Volume 1, Issue 2 (1993), pp. 51–55

Smyth, P., 'Garth Brooks says concerts cannot proceed', *The Irish Times*, 14 July 2014

'Spotlight: Nathan Carter – Making Country Music "cool" again', *The Harp*, 19 August 2015

Stewart, K., 'Country Music Gets Irish Welcome', *Billboard*, 22 April 1995

Stewart, K., 'International Global Country Pulse: Dublin', *Billboard*, 7 October 1995

Streissguth, M., *Like a Moth to a Flame: The Jim Reeves Story* (Nashville, Rutledge Hill Press, 1998), p. 190

Tosches, N., *Country: The Twisted Roots of Rock and Roll* (Boston, Da Capo Press, 2000)

'Tributes as country legend Gene Stewart passes away', *Ulster Herald*, 12 February 2016

Walker, G., 'Why it's time for the begrudgers to leave Daniel O'Donnell alone', *Belfast Telegraph*, 14 November 2012

Waters, J., *Jiving at the Crossroads* (Belfast, Blackstaff Press, 1991)

Williams, R. M., *Sing a Sad Song: The Life of Hank Williams* (Champaign, Illinois University Press, 1981)

Wolff, K., *Country Music: The Rough Guide* (London, Rough Guides, 2000)

Young, D., 'Country music in mourning for Gene Stuart', *Belfast Telegraph*, 12 February 2016

'You're not really much of a star', *Wicklow People*, 11 March 2004

Zimmerman, L., '*String Theory*: album review', *Elmore Magazine*, 23 August 2016

TV, FILM AND RADIO

A Little Bit Country, RTÉ Television, 29 October 2006

A Little Bit Country, TG4, 13 March 2013

A Man and His Music – A Tribute to Shay Hutchinson, filmed at Cappagh Parish Community Centre, Killyclogher, County Tyrone, 13 February 1994

Evening Extra, RTÉ Television, 13 April 1987

Ireland AM, TV3, 23 January 2015

Ireland's Ancient East, RTÉ Television, July 2016

Kimberley Jim, directed by Emil Nofal, Emil Nofal Productions, 1963

London Tonight, ITV, April 1994

Nationwide, RTÉ Television, 9 October 2017

On the Road with Lisa, Irish TV, 2 November 2015

Ros na Rún, TG4, 30 September 2013

RTÉ News, various dates

Secret Languages: Folk Art, RTÉ Television, 1982

Six One News, RTÉ Television, 10 July 2014

Talkback, BBC Radio Ulster, 17 May 2001

The Big Breakfast, Channel 4, April 1994

The Broken Circle Breakdown, directed by Felix Van Groeningen, 2012

The Frankie Kilbride Show, Shannonside Radio, 30 September 2012

The Late Late Show, RTÉ Television, various dates

The Late Late Show Country Music Special, RTÉ Television, 14 April 2017

The Marian Finucane Show, RTÉ Radio 1, various dates

The Nolan Show, BBC Radio Ulster, 5 June 2013

The Ryan Tubridy Show, RTÉ Radio 1, various dates

Today with Sean O'Rourke, RTÉ Radio 1, 14 February 2014

TV3 News, 10 July 2014

WEBSITES

http://bocktherobber.com

http://journalofmusic.com

http://ronancasey.ie

www.billmonroe.com

www.breakingnews.ie

www.eonline.com

www.galwaybayfm.ie

www.irish-showbands.com

www.irishtimes.com

www.jim-reeves.com

www.jordanmogeymusic.com

www.larrycunningham.ie

www.philmackcountry.com

www.quotes.net

www.rte.ie

www.thefreelibrary.com

www.thejournal.ie

www.wideopencountry.com

www.youtube.com

INDEX